D0221158

RUTH KINNA

The Government of No One
The Theory and Practice of Anarchism

A PELICAN BOOK

PELICAN
an imprint of
PENGUIN BOOKS

PELICAN BOOKS

UK | USA | Canada | Ireland | Australia
India | New Zealand | South Africa

Penguin Books is part of the Penguin Random
House group of companies whose addresses can
be found at global.penguinrandomhouse.com.

Penguin
Random House
UK

First published in 2019
001

Text copyright © Ruth Kinna, 2019
The moral right of the author has been asserted

Book design by Matthew Young
Set in 11/16.13 pt FreightText Pro
Typeset by Jouve (UK), Milton Keynes
Printed and bound in Great Britain by
Clays Ltd, Elcograf S.p.A.

A CIP catalogue record for this book is available
from the British Library

ISBN: 978–0–241–39655–1

Penguin Random House is committed to a
sustainable future for our business, our readers
and our planet. This book is made from Forest
Stewardship Council® certified paper.

www.greenpenguin.co.uk

Contents

Acknowledgements

A number of people have contributed to the writing of this book by commenting on drafts, helping locate information and providing examples of anarchist practice. First and foremost, thanks to Casiana Ionita for reading the text so closely and giving excellent advice about the presentation of the arguments; Robert Knight for comments on the first draft and suggestions for finessing the text and Claire Péligry for scrupulous, helpful editing. Peter Ryley shared his knowledge of Henry Seymour. Special thanks too to the independent researcher and visual artist Daniel Huckfield for his meticulous work on Seymour's life. Natasha King helped me think about power and privilege and Marina Maximova, Robert Graham and Andrew Cornell assisted with research on hard-to-find activists.

Anarchism – Myths and Realities

In 1999 activists in Seattle spectacularly sabotaged the meeting of the World Trade Organization. The event launched what became known as the alterglobalization or global justice campaign, a complex, anti-capitalist 'movement of movements' widely described as anarchist. The same year, James Bond went head-to-head with Victor Zokas aka Renard in the movie *The World Is Not Enough*. Renard, an ex-Soviet army and KGB officer, brutal even by the standards of Bond's antagonists, is also reportedly anarchist. His back story tells how he worked as a freelance assassin for anti-capitalists organizing before the alterglobalization movement fell under the media spotlight.

On one level, it is easy to distinguish the fact from the fiction. Renard is an invention of scriptwriters and moviemakers. The Seattle shutdown of the WTO is documented history. Yet on another level, the attribution of the anarchist label to both the killer and the street movement is confusing: the fiction appears to capture something about the reality. Film-goers may have to suspend their disbelief about the bullet permanently lodged in Renard's brain, but the emotional instability his injury explains and which underpins his anarchism hardly seems demanding. On the contrary, his ruthlessness and single-mindedness play to a deeply rooted view of anarchism which continues to influence public analysis of activist movements. Admittedly, the anarchism of the alterglobalizers was not automatically condemned as sadistic, aggressive or vengeful, but leading politicians of the time commented on the dangerous mix of vandals and carnival clowns it attracted: the movement was by turns dismissed as unbalanced and unthinking. And once street protests resulted in property damage, as in Gothenburg in 2001, it was possible for authorities to mobilize against 'the anarchists' in its ranks. Both before and since, the use of the 'A' word has provided a green light to aggressive policing. The global justice movement was no exception. The protesters who converged in Genoa in 2001 for the meeting of the G8 met with savage police violence.

The cultural stereotypes of the anarchist that furnish Renard's characterization are not only distorting, they are also disabling. They conceal a history of critique and resistance that is empowering and normalize practices that are discriminatory and oppressive, even in instances where unfairness and injustice are patently obvious and widely acknowledged. Being anarchist means challenging the status quo to realize egalitarian principles and foster co-operative, non-dominating behaviours. Anarchist actions can take multiple forms, many of which are easily absorbed into everyday life. As we will see in the following pages, Renard is far from being anarchism's default setting.

Thinking like an anarchist

In 1919 the sculptor and printmaker Eric Gill wrote to the *Burlington Magazine* to protest Sir Frederic Kenyon's proposals to the Imperial War Graves Commission. The Commission had been established in May 1917 to identify the graves of soldiers who had already been buried and to record the deaths of those who had no known grave. At the end of the war three notable architects, Sir Edwin Lutyens, Sir Herbert Baker and Sir Reginald Blomfeld, were invited to design the war cemeteries. Kenyon, Director of the British Museum, was appointed to give coherence to the architectural plans. In his November 1918 report he urged the War Graves Commission to adopt the principle of equality. As Kenyon put it, 'what was done for one should be done for all, and that all, whatever their military rank or position in civil life, should have equal treatment in their graves'. In practice, equality demanded that the Commission be given responsibility for the design of the individual memorials, as well as the layout of the cemeteries. Provision 'could not be left to individual initiative' because 'satisfactory' results were only likely to be obtained where 'money and good taste were not wanting'. In most cases there was a risk that 'no monument would be erected, or that it would be poor in quality'. The cemeteries would end up looking like English churchyards: 'jumbled' masses of monuments. The effect would be 'neither dignified nor inspiring' and the 'sense of comradeship and of common service would be lost'.[1]

Coupling equality with regularity, Kenyon recommended individual headstones record the name, rank, regiment and date of death of each soldier. Families would be able to include a form of words from a limited set of standard inscriptions but denied 'free scope for the effusion of the mortuary mason, the sentimental versifier, or the crank', for this too would compromise the military idea, which was to give 'the appearance of a battalion on parade' and suggest 'the spirit of discipline and order which is the soul of an army'.[2] Kenyon's major concession to 'variety in uniformity' was to suggest that the appropriate regimental badges be automatically incorporated on the headstones.

Gill objected to the totality of Kenyon's vision and linked his corrupted egalitarianism to the mass production processes that architectural integrity implied. The War Graves Commission was right to seek the advice of architects but should never have given them *'leadership'*. The 'designing of monuments is properly the business of those who *make* monuments' – sculptors and tombstone makers. As a stone mason himself, Gill clearly had a vested interest in securing some of the contracts the War Graves Commission might have awarded, but his argument was about the social relationships that craft work sustained. Had the War Graves Commission given sculptors the task of engraving the headstones, it would have realized Kenyon's egalitarian aims and been far better equipped to take account of the 'sentiment of the nation, poor as well as rich'. His complaint centred on power and ownership:

The commission's attitude in the matter is the more easily understood inasmuch as it is the whole trend of our time to impose the ideas of the few upon the many while being careful to hide the process under a guise of democratic sympathy and social reform. Thus the idea that half a million headstones should be made according to the ideas of a few architects (an idea worthy of the

Prussian or the Ptolemy at his best) instead of according to those of several thousand stone-masons and twenty million relatives is not surprising, and under the plea of commemorating 'the sense of comradeship and common service' and 'the spirit of discipline and order' *etc.* it is hoped that the very widespread desire of relatives to have some personal control of the monuments to their dead will be overcome.[3]

Gill thought Kenyon's appeal to equality disingenuous. His proposals amounted to a demand for regimentation, driven by thrift and conformity. And his vision of the cemetery as a battalion on parade was numbing, not inspiring. To illustrate the point Gill observed: 'A crowd in Trafalgar Square is very impressive; but if you were to replace it by an equal number of tailor's dummies it is not certain that the result, however architectural, would be equally impressive.'[4] If the War Graves Commission was serious about honouring the dead, it should ensure that the dead were commemorated as fathers, brothers, lovers and sons not as cogs in a bloodied fighting force. The net effect was to dispossess the families of their loved ones. Indeed, Gill wondered about the legal powers Kenyon's proposals assumed: Were the soldiers' bodies as well as the land in which they were buried the 'absolute property of the government'?[5] Whatever the truth of the matter, he concluded that soldiers had been asked to lay down their lives for the greater good of the nation and were now being compelled to sacrifice their deaths too.

Gill's objections were ignored but in pressing his complaint he expressed a profoundly if not explicitly anarchist sentiment, outlining in plain words anarchism's mainsprings, interests, horizons and spirit. Its mainsprings are individual. Gill highlighted this by his wish that sculptors and relatives decide how best to commemorate their dead. He believed in general that life was enriched when individuals were able to make their own judgements and impoverished when decisions were entrusted to remote bodies, whatever their qualifications or virtues. As he wrote in his letter, the War Graves Commission had no 'right to dictate to relatives as to what shall or shall not be inscribed upon the stone' or how the dead should be remembered. It had the power but '*not the right* . . . to enslave, intellectually, morally, aesthetically, or physically, even one man, and certainly not a very large number of men'.[6] Acknowledging that individual judgement entailed responsibility, Gill accepted that individuals could make mistakes. But so too could governments. And the consequences of their errors were usually far more costly.

Anarchism's interests are collaborative. Gill expressed this aspect of anarchism in his call to the War Graves Commission to employ 'small men and not big firms' and by his hostility to 'the commercial success of organized production'. The controversial view he expressed in his autobiography was that it was 'incomparably more horrible' that 'men of business should rule us and impose their foul point of view on the world' than 'the whole race of men and women should rot their bodies with lechery and drunkenness'.[7] Horrible 'men of business' were interested in amassing money. Small producers were not. As members of their communities they were not only less likely to exploit the bereaved but uniquely equipped to express their feelings. Behind this critique was the idea that social relationships should encourage association and amity and minimize exploitation and utility.

Anarchism's horizons are expansive. Gill's protest appeared to be narrowly focused on the production of headstones and the technicalities of their inscription, yet it was centrally concerned with the ideological biases of Kenyon's proposals and the government's readiness to push its own agendas on the citizens it claimed to honour. He wrote as an artist who believed that everyone could make and remake the world through their activity. Accordingly, instead of talking about abstractions like capitalism or modes of production, Gill explained the depersonalizing effects of mass production. Instead of decrying militarism, he showed how the values of discipline and command were being smuggled into public consciousness through the design of headstones. When he talked more abstractly about the rights of the citizen not to be enslaved, he brought the question of self-determination down to the raw ground of grief, loss and memory. Instead of attacking nationalism philosophically, he disputed Kenyon's conflation of death with patriotic duty. This made the offensiveness of the concept real and intelligible. Repeatedly drawing on his own practice, Gill showed how high-level decisions play out in everyday life and how complex and seemingly intractable problems affecting ordinary people can be disentangled at their roots. In this, too, he adopted a typically anarchist perspective.

The aim of this book is to explain anarchist thought and practice. The first chapter opens some thirty years after Pierre-Joseph Proudhon published *What is Property?*, the first constructive defence of anarchy. I take as my starting point the anarchists' restatement of the critique of government enslavement towards the end of the nineteenth century. Rather than presenting a chronological account of anarchism's development, I adopt a thematic approach. My aim is to show that while the emergence of anarchism in the nineteenth century resulted in the construction of an ideology, it also represented the crystallization of a fluid political tradition that extends beyond the historical and geographical boundaries that the ideology assumes. The second chapter focuses on the anarchist critique of domination and subsequent chapters explore anarchist practices, planning and prospects. Anarchist histories are thus included in each of the chapters, but to provide a narrative arc the focus gradually shifts from the nineteenth to the twenty-first century.

My approach is more impressionistic than ideological in the sense that I make no attempt to classify the constellation of concepts that anarchism describes or systematically analyse the ways that anarchists have understood ideas of liberty, equality and so forth.[8] While I am interested to show how anarchism was constructed in the late nineteenth century, I do not attempt to demarcate the boundaries of anarchism as some later historians have done.[9] I do not believe that anarchism is endlessly porous and inevitably there are some 'anarchisms' that I ignore (notably 'market anarchism',[10] 'anarcho-capitalism'[11] and 'national anarchism'[12]). However, my contention is that anarchism can be read historically both backwards and forwards from its origins and plotted from multiple geographical sites and at different angles. One of the attractions of anarchism is that it has no single moment of enlightenment, no before or after 'science'. Connected to this is my view that anarchism has strong affinities with a wide range of non-anarchist ideas and practices: Gill is just one example. To indicate these I place the work of non-anarchists alongside the writing of those who explicitly identified as anarchist.

The discussions present anarchism as a history of ideas in conversation rather than strictly in context, as has become the convention in histories of ideas. I try to show how anarchists have responded to their situations and the circumstances in which they have found themselves, but I juxtapose the work of authors who have explored questions about education, violence, class and so forth at different times and in different locations to emphasize their engagement with the tradition they have sought to develop. I have included accounts of well-known anarchists but, conscious of the concerns that many anarchists have about the dangers of constructing an anarchist 'canon', I have discussed the work of less well-known and some obscure figures, too. None of these should be understood as representative (a term that anarchists typically regard as anathema). Rather the selection is intended to build a multi-layered picture of anarchism and showcase its rich diversity. Similarly, I have focused selectively on the ideas of the writers I mention: I am providing a snapshot, not an exhaustive or even indicative account of any individual's work.

While I mention anarchist groups and movements, the analysis leans towards the individuals who comprise or have comprised them. I have been influenced here by Vladimiro Muñoz's *Biographical Encyclopedia*, a study of twenty notable figures.[13] Following his example, I have included short sketches of my cast of characters and their networks to give a flavour of their lives and indicate some of the important interconnections between activists. It should become plain that anarchists are not saints and that a few have been involved in some sharp and dubious practices. I hope that by the end of this book readers will appreciate the extraordinary courage and creativity generations of anarchist activists have shown in confronting injustice and understand how anarchist perspectives can animate our politics.

CHAPTER 1
Traditions

Some like to define anarchism etymologically by tracing the roots of the doctrine to the ancient Greek word *anarchia*. This translates roughly as 'the government of no one'. Self-identifying anarchists have done this too, usually to draw attention to the oppression they claim government entails and the equality anarchists advocate. While monarchists accept the government of one, anarchists call for the government of no one. It's a powerful strapline and easy to understand. The problem with it is that it situates anarchism in a framework of government that uses the rejection of anarchy for its justification. So anarchy immediately becomes a condition of disorder. In political thought, the same applies. The prevailing view is that human beings want to escape from the inconvenience or violence of anarchy and, because they have the wit to do so (uniquely, we are told), they submit to government. Anarchy is the order they run away from. It implies chaos, sometimes vigilantism, sometimes mob rule, and it cannot guarantee peace or security.

How then, should we start thinking about anarchism? Finding a starting point that fits the spirit of the subject is difficult because anarchists typically resist the categorization of their movements and principles. They are usually suspicious of attempts to fix anarchism's origins, either in time or space, and they reject selective accounts that lavish special attention on particular historical figures. Why? Because labelling looks like an attempt to determine boundaries that anarchists themselves have not fixed, because the identification of origins seems an unwelcome first step towards the ideological construction of a set of fixed traditions that anarchists prefer to see as permeable and fluid, and finally, because dating and locating the emergence of anarchism to the foundation of particular groups appears both arbitrary and exclusionary. This last move can also create a Eurocentric bias which is exaggerated and further distorted by the elevation of special individuals or identification of key texts. Overall the effect is to attribute the power of anarchist invention to a collection of individuals of particular genius – characteristically, white men – who cleverly articulated a great idea, parcelled it up and exported it across the world.

My entry point is that anarchism began to emerge as a distinctive movement in mid-nineteenth-century Europe – France, Germany, Italy and Spain – in a period of European state dominance. That is not to say that it appeared as ready-made or that this location fixes anarchism's ideology. What I would like to suggest is that anarchism emerged through critical engagement with other radical and progressive movements and in the face of concerted opposition from conservative and reactionary forces. This circumstance gave anarchism a particular political flavour. Anarchists came to be distinguished from non-anarchists by their responses to specific issues and events. They were frequently identified by their expulsion from other political groups and by the targeted repression of religious and government institutions.

My second proposition is that anarchism was elaborated by critics as well as figures like P.-J. Proudhon, Michael Bakunin, Louise Michel and John Most who proudly called themselves anarchists. For the first group, the writings and practices of these anarchists were critically important to its ideological construction. Some early commentators understood that there was a relationship between the principles that anarchists expounded and the movements they were associated with. But even though they realized that anarchism was not a conventional philosophy, they still focused their attention on a small number of key figures. So while the field of anarchist studies is extremely wide (there are no key statements, no primary modes or sites for action, just endless examples of resistance, reaction and re-recreation), it is still possible to talk about anarchist traditions. Anarchism has been shaped by multiple histories and experiences which are recognizably anarchist because the branding of anarchism in the nineteenth century by advocates and opponents alike makes it possible to identify family resemblances across time and space.

Anarchism and the International

The break-up of the International Workingmen's Association (IWMA or First International) in 1872 is sometimes said to be the watershed moment for the European anarchist movement. In histories of socialism the split tends to be seen as the point at which the movement divided into two separate wings, one Marxist and the other anarchist. This is a simplification. The significance of the First International's collapse grew only as hostilities between anarchists and Marxists deepened, and it is more obvious in retrospect than it was at the time. In itself, the split left the designation of socialists uncertain. However, the timing of the collapse was indeed important for the subsequent development of socialism. For those who adopted the label anarchist the collapse of the IWMA crystallized an understanding of the state that had been discussed until that time in largely abstract terms.

The First International had been founded in London in 1864 by British and French labour leaders to advance workers' struggles against exploitation. Members were committed to a number of principles, but two were particularly significant: the idea that the struggle for emancipation could only be achieved by workers themselves, and the belief that class equality transcended distinctions based on colour, creed or nationality. This was the commitment to internationalism. Beyond these general rules little else kept the IWMA together, and throughout its history the association was plagued by factional rivalries and disputes.

In 1872 an argument between Karl Marx and Michael Bakunin that had been rumbling on since the late 1860s came to a head. Marx was a leading light in the International and had been elected to its executive council in 1864. Like Marx, Bakunin also enjoyed enormous prestige, having cut his teeth on the barricades during the 1848 revolutions, dodged two death sentences in 1850 and 51 and escaped from Siberia ten years later. A one-time associate of Marx in the 1840s, Bakunin was no longer close to him. Indeed, he had joined the Geneva section of the IWMA in 1868 as the leader of a separate body, the Alliance of Socialist Democracy. When he did so, Bakunin accused Marx of attempting to undermine the autonomy of the IWMA's federated bodies by tightening the executive's control. He also argued that Marx was wrong to call for the organization of political parties as a means of realizing revolution. At the time there was little scope for the organization of socialist parties in Europe. However, Bakunin objected to Marx's policy in principle, believing that involvement with lawmaking institutions would likely dampen the revolutionary ardour of the oppressed and enmesh it in the very systems that regulated their exploitation and oppression.

Running alongside this disagreement about organization and strategy was a theoretical dispute which turned on a set of ideas about the dynamics of historical change, the state, private property and class. These concepts formed part of a shared vocabulary in socialist circles but they could mean different things to different people. This was the case for Marx and Bakunin, as Bakunin attempted to show.

Bakunin's critique of Marx followed an encounter that Marx had had in the 1840s with Pierre-Joseph Proudhon, the first writer to positively embrace the epithet 'anarchist' to describe his politics. Probably best known as the author of *What is Property?*, Proudhon was an ex-printer, journalist and author who came to prominence in France as an advocate of workers' self-organization during the French Second Republic (1848–51). While Bakunin's reprise of some of Proudhon's arguments seemed to cement a basic division between anarchists and Marxists in the International, the battle lines were muddier than this partition implies. Marx had earlier ridiculed Proudhon's economics and had drawn attention to their different understandings of historical change. Against Proudhon he had argued that history was driven primarily by economic changes. Marx's materialist view was that innovations in production upset existing power balances. The groups who benefited from the introduction of new technologies and who possessed economic power would seek to secure the benefits that accrued to them by taking charge of the machinery of the state. They would fight for political power and so confront the existing elites who had similarly used their money and wealth to fix laws to their own advantage. For Marx, the confrontation was revolutionary and it represented the progressive energy of class war. Proudhon was also a revolutionary, but he did not subscribe to the idea of class war and he rejected what he considered to be the economic determinism of Marx's view.

Proudhon argued that Marx had misdescribed the character of economic and political power. For him, the former was derived from the possibility of claiming an exclusive right to property ownership. This was enshrined in law and enforced by the violence vested in the state (police, military, justice systems). He thought Marx was right that there were different patterns of ownership and that these changed over time, but genuine revolutionary transformation depended on the abolition of the exclusive right of private ownership and on the dismantling of the systems of government that were organized to guarantee it. Like Marx, Proudhon was a materialist, but his conception of legal reform made him appear an idealist in Marx's eyes. For Marx, Proudhon was a utopian who mistakenly believed that it was possible to change the world by changing our legal conception of property.

Where did Bakunin stand in all this? Somewhat surprisingly, he endorsed Marx's description of Proudhon's idealism and declared himself a follower of Marx's materialist history. Yet he also argued that Marx construed materialism too narrowly and consequently failed to appreciate what revolutionary transformation involved. So siding with Proudhon against Marx, Bakunin advanced a critique of Marx's theory which focused on the twin institutions of private property and the state.

Marx, Bakunin argued, was primarily interested in studying changes in patterns of ownership and the dynamics of class struggle. This was important work: Marx had explained the rise of the new industrial bourgeoisie, he had shown how this class had swept away the old aristocracy whose power had been rooted in land ownership and how it had also created a proletarian class that would pursue its interests through revolutionary struggle against capitalists. Yet, while acknowledging Marx's genius in this regard, Bakunin accused him of being blinkered by his analysis. Above all, Marx had failed to pay proper attention to the state and here Proudhon was right. Marx defined the state too narrowly as an instrument of class rule. According to Marx, Bakunin argued, whoever controlled the economy also had control of the political apparatus. While this construction usefully highlighted the corrupting power of the bourgeoisie and the partiality of the law, it wrongly underplayed the independent, oppressive power of the state. Thus for Marx, Bakunin argued, revolution meant seizing control of the ownership of the means of production. Marx believed wrongly, in Bakunin's view, that this was possible if the proletariat seized control of the state's machinery. Marx was unable to see that for as long as the state remained intact, the revolution would be stunted. Control of the means of production would bring class equality, in the sense that it would wipe out the economic power of the bourgeoisie, but it would not remove hierarchy: workers would still be subject to the dictates of the law. They would work for the state rather than private owners of capital. From Bakunin's perspective, Marx had explained the processes of revolutionary change, but his notion of class struggle restricted his understanding of what socialist transformation involved.

At the 1872 Hague conference of the International, Marx engineered Bakunin's expulsion. In doing so, he established a primary division in the socialist movement that in fact was never clean or complete. Persistent disagreements about the policy implications of the political theory meant that the determination of ideological boundaries remained fluid and uncertain for years. Indeed, the theoretical disagreements between Bakunin and Marx were never fully resolved and debates about class, state and historical change have rumbled on in socialist movements ever since. Even as socialists took sides, a number of those who aligned with Marxist groups discovered that they supported positions that were outlawed as anarchist. By the same token, some of those who sided with Bakunin continued to think of themselves as Marxists. In 1881, when the call to organize an anarchist International was issued, some anarchists argued that the old one had never disappeared.[1] Yet as far as the emergence of anarchism is concerned, the organizational collapse of the IWMA was significant.

The immediate result of the IWMA's demise was the realignment of its local federations. The Jura Federation of the International rallied around Bakunin and inaugurated a new International. This met a few days after the Hague conference in St Imier in Switzerland. To distinguish it from the followers of Marx, Bakuninists called it 'the anti-authoritarian International' without relinquishing the relationship to the IWMA. The anarchist tag was adopted soon afterwards. The American academic Richard Ely, a keen observer of European socialism, explained that Bakunin had formed 'a new International ... based on anarchic principles'. This substituted a 'Federal Council' for the General Council, meaning that the 'central organ (not authority), changed from year to year' and, moreover, that 'each land was left free to conduct its agitation in its own way, and every individual atom, *i.e.*, local organization, was left free to come and go as it pleased'.[2]

By 1877 a distinctively anarchist programme began to take shape. The Geneva section of the Jura Federation had four main points: abolition of the state, political abstention, rejection of the workers' candidatures, various means of propaganda and, in particular, propaganda by the deed.[3] The last plank, later linked to individual acts of violence, was a commitment to transmit anarchist principles by example to largely uneducated workers. In 1881 two major anarchist conferences were convened, the first in London and the second in Chicago. In Europe anarchism had a strong presence in Belgium, France, Spain, Switzerland and Italy. Anarchists were also organized in Germany, Argentina, Cuba, Egypt and Mexico. A Uruguayan section of the Bakuninist International was set up in Montevideo in 1872.[4] In North America the concentration of European migrants in Chicago and New York made these the important centres.

In 1889 the founding of the Second International formalized this organizational division of the socialist movement. The first meeting included anarchists, but the invitation was grudging. A motion passed at the Second International's 1893 Congress was designed to exclude anarchists from future meetings and it committed socialists to enter into electoral competition as a revolutionary tactic. The resolution to expel those who refused to follow this line (and the commitment to fight for revolutionary change by strictly constitutional methods) was too blunt an instrument to sort anarchists from dissident Marxists. Even Lenin was caught in the Second International's anarchist trap. But it reinforced the doctrinal significance of the IWMA's disintegration and signalled the victory of Marx's policy in the international revolutionary socialist movement.

The organizational collapse of the IWMA was felt in movement literatures, too. In the years following Bakunin's death in 1876 a plethora of pamphlets appeared that lauded him as founder of genuine revolutionary socialism and decried Marx as its Machiavellian manipulator. A number of leading anarchists, notably Peter Kropotkin, were subsequently motivated to theorize their hostility to Marxism, establishing clear theoretical boundaries between anarchist and non-anarchist socialism. In the late nineteenth century it was common for anarchists to refer to Marxism as state socialism. Although this hardening of line still left considerable latitude for confusion, and the division of the IWMA clearly passed some groups by, there was a growing view in the anarchist sections that

Marx had betrayed the commitment to self-emancipation and that anarchists should therefore take it upon themselves to uphold and protect the International's goals and values by maintaining their own organizations.

The Paris Commune and the Haymarket Affair

As anti-authoritarian exponents of the IWMA's politics, anarchists fleshed out the implications of their position with reference to two key events: the Paris Commune of 1871 and the Haymarket Affair of 1886. These two episodes served as rallying points for anarchists in the early years of the European movement and they were habitually celebrated in anarchist journals and at annual meetings.

The Paris Commune is a shorthand term to describe a series of events in France at the end of the Franco-Prussian War of 1870–71 – the last of the three wars of German unification engineered by Otto von Bismarck, which led to the collapse of Napoleon III's Second Empire and the founding of the French Third Republic. The Commune was declared in March 1871, following the catastrophic defeat of French forces by Bismarck's Prussian army, on the back of a crippling siege of Paris in September 1870. It was sparked by the refusal of Parisians to accede to the demands of the Republic's provisional government, based in Versailles under the leadership of Aldophe Thiers, which was then negotiating terms with Bismarck. It ended with the brutal suppression by the French government of the armed resistance that this refusal spawned. Frustrating Thiers's plans to disarm the city, Parisian workers concentrated in the areas of Montmartre,

Belleville and Buttes-Chaumont prevented government troops from confiscating the cannon of the National Guard. Seizing the guns, they constructed barricades and brought together left republicans, Proudhonists and other revolutionary socialists in the city's defence. These were the Communards. As historian John Merriman has shown, the resistance resulted in the biggest massacre in nineteenth-century Europe: an estimated 20,000 Parisians were slaughtered in the Bloody Week of the Commune's collapse in late May 1871. Many thousands more were deported to New Caledonia. They were not amnestied for ten years.

The other key anarchist event, the Haymarket Affair, started at a protest meeting in Chicago's Haymarket Square on 4 May 1886 and concluded with the execution of four anarchists in November 1887. The Haymarket meeting had been called after the killing of workers by police at a locally organized strike held on 3 May at the McCormick reaper factory in support of a national campaign for the eight-hour day. As police attempted to disperse the crowd, a bomb exploded, killing one police officer and wounding several others. The police opened fire on the crowd and in the skirmishes that followed, seven officers were killed. A Chicago police round-up netted eight anarchists: George Engel, Samuel Fielden, Adolph Fischer, Louis Lingg, Oscar Neebe, Albert Parsons, Michael Schwab and August Spies. All were active in Chicago's socialist networks as prominent radicals and labour organizers. Tried for instigating the bombing but not for the bombing itself, they were found guilty as charged. The case against them was flimsy, to say the least. The rigging of the jury, the incompetence of the jurors, a wanton disregard for the evidential basis of the law and the partiality of the judge ensured the prosecution's victory. The case sparked international protests, so obvious were the procedural flaws, and eventually went to appeal. This failed and the miscarriage of justice was not recognized until 1893. John Altgeld, the Governor of Illinois who quashed the original verdicts, observed that the presiding judge, Judge Gary, had displayed a degree of 'ferocity' and 'subserviency . . . without parallel in all history'.[5] Judge Jeffries, England's notorious seventeenth-century hanging judge, was moderate by comparison. Altgeld's decision resulted in an absolute pardon for Fielden, Schwab and Neebe, ending their terms of imprisonment. It came too late for Parsons, Spies, Engel and Fischer. They were all dead. It was also too late for Lingg, who had committed suicide in his cell while awaiting execution.

What made these events so significant for the anarchists emerging from the disintegration of the IWMA? Proudhonists were a significant force in the Commune. It was Proudhon's friend, the artist Gustave Courbet, who famously instigated the toppling of the column in the Place Vendôme. A number of other prominent Communards, including Louise Michel and Élisée Reclus, later emerged as leading figures in the anarchist movement. That's not to say that the Commune was an exclusively anarchist affair. Those who fought on the barricades identified with a plethora of revolutionary traditions. To complicate matters, the publication of Marx's *Civil War in France*, the official statement of the IWMA's General Council, linked the Commune strongly to the Red Doctor, as the British press dubbed him. Marxists as well as anarchists were able to make credible claims to the Commune's mantle.

Haymarket, in contrast, was an obviously anarchist affair. The defendants were arrested and charged because they were anarchists. The state attorney, Julius Grinnell, devised a strategy designed to put anarchism on trial. The accused responded in kind. Albert Parsons, who emerged as the most charismatic of the so-called Chicago martyrs, argued in an eight-hour address to the court that the defendants were on the stand because of their beliefs, not because of anything they had done. His co-defendants likewise delivered powerful speeches to explain and advocate anarchism rather than concentrate on protesting their innocence. Dispelling any doubts about the grounds of the convictions, Engel shouted 'Long Live Anarchy' just before the trapdoor was tripped. His last words and the final statements of the other three were widely reproduced in anarchist journals.

The horrifying brutality and evident injustice of the government actions was one strong thread tying these events together. And in responding to the violence that the Commune and Haymarket unleashed, anarchists argued that the limits of European republicanism and liberalism had been revealed. For those within the nascent anarchist movement, these two events exposed the continuity between these regimes and the tyrannies and the systems of absolutism that the great seventeenth- and eighteenth-century revolutions in Britain, America and France were supposed to have swept away. It appeared that class war raged as violently in these apparently virtuous, enlightened states as in the autocratic regimes that republicans and liberals jointly held in contempt. Neither France nor America was Russia, almost universally regarded as the 'sick man of Europe'. Nevertheless, Paris and Haymarket demonstrated that the state's credentials for toleration were fake. The anarchist critique that the Commune and Haymarket buttressed was that these progressive republics legitimized systems of state oppression that were as unjust and partial as anything that had gone before. As Louise Michel put it on her return from New Caledonia, 'the Social Revolution had been strangled. It was a France whose rulers mendaciously called themselves republicans, and they betrayed our every dream through their "opportunism".'[6]

The Pittsburgh Manifesto, the charter of the American revolutionary movement drafted by John Most in 1883, used the language of the US Declaration of Independence to advance an anarchist cause against bourgeois tyranny, 'citing not only the right but also the duty to overthrow a despotic government'.[7] Haymarket amplified the cruelty of the legitimate authorities. On the first anniversary of the executions, the London anarchist paper *Freedom* compared the trial of the Haymarket anarchists to that of Algernon Sidney, the English republican politician accused of treason against Charles II in 1683. The charge of 'constructive conspiracy', the editorial argued, was a revival 'by the American democracy' of the 'dangerous instrument of despotism' and a return to 'the worst days of monarchical absolutism'.[8] There was no greater prospect that ordinary people would achieve liberty and equality in these phoney egalitarian regimes than in the monarchies they had replaced. 'No illusions as to Governments were possible any longer in France,' Kropotkin commented in his 1893 Commune address.[9]

The anarchist critique of the state

The Commune and Haymarket were significant for two key reasons. First, the Commune crystallized the critique of the state that Bakunin had rehearsed in the abstract in his debates with Marx. Second, the ferocity of the government response to anarchism helped convince anarchists that government was violence. Together, the Commune and Haymarket furnished anarchists with a distinctive perspective on the state and a model for non-state, anarchist alternatives.

Bakunin delivered his analysis in *The Paris Commune and the Idea of the State*, a no-holds-barred attack on Marxist socialism. His argument was that the Commune was an expression of anti-authoritarianism which the authoritarian sections of the IWMA under Marx's sway had opposed and which Bismarck's forces had determined to crush. In Paris, the antagonistic politics of the IWMA and the reactionary forces behind the Commune's defeat converged. Considering the implications for socialist activism, Bakunin wrote that the lasting effect of the civil war in France was the establishment of the boundary between 'scientific communism' developed by Marx and 'the German school', on the one hand, and the revolutionary socialism of 'the Latin countries' on the other.[10] For Bakunin, authoritarian socialism was a variation of revolutionary republicanism. *The Civil War in France*, Marx's commentary on the Commune and the official statement of the IWMA General Council, had argued that the 'working class cannot simply lay hold of the ready-made state machinery, and wield it for its own purposes'.[11] Doubting his sincerity, Bakunin argued that Marx still imagined that revolution required the representatives of the proletariat to exercise power on behalf of the exploited and to use state violence to uphold proletarian class interests. This model assumed an identification between the goals of the workers and those of their representatives, which was both implausible and troubling. In any case, it replicated existing forms of government, albeit reformulated to suit the preferences of a rising, currently exploited social group.

In an appreciation of Bakunin published in 1905 Peter Kropotkin subsequently pressed Bakunin's argument. Bakunin had rightly recognized that the triumph of 'Bismarck's military state' in 1871 was 'at the same time' the triumph of 'German State-socialism'.[12] Also linking the Paris Commune to the 'Latin' sections of the IWMA and its defeat to German statism, Kropotkin argued that Marx's policy of state conquest was congruent with Bismarck's unification strategy and concluded that authoritarian socialism was an expression of German imperialism.

This inflammatory critique of statist organization had already begun to percolate in anarchist movements when the politicization of the Haymarket trial gave the defendants a platform to flesh out another anarchist anti-state critique. The Chicago anarchists did this by turning conventional politics on its head, using popular misconceptions about anarchy to draw attention to the dysfunction of established norms. One after another, the co-defendants argued that the court's rejection of anarchy in the name of civilization depended on the unconditional embrace of rules that benefited the bourgeoisie. Louis Lingg explained: 'Anarchy means no domination or authority of one man over another, yet you call that "disorder". A system which advocates no such "order" as shall require the services of rogues and thieves to defend it you call "disorder".[13]

The benefits that accrued to the bourgeoisie were numerous: status, wealth and leisure were chief among them. Like many anarchists, Albert Parsons believed that the power to extract surplus value from workers helped explain this advantage. Owners of land and machinery were able to pay workers for time worked and pocket the additional value of the goods and services that labour actually produced. Parsons also argued that this power was underpinned by a system of ownership that was based on the right to private property. This was Proudhon's argument. Distinguishing the exclusive right to private ownership – property-in-dominion – from the temporary right to possession or property-in-use, Proudhon argued that the former necessarily restricted property to those who first claimed it and their beneficiaries. For everybody else, it was 'impossible'. In contrast, because possession denied exclusive claims, property was left open to all. The existing regime was wrong in principle and injurious in practice. Responding to the charge of incitement, Samuel Fielden gave his account of Proudhon's theory.

> I have said you must abolish the private property
> system. Mr. English[14] said that I said 'It had no mercy;
> so ought you.' Probably if I said 'it had no mercy', I
> did not say the latter part of the sentence in that way.
> I probably said, 'So you ought not to have any mercy.'
> Is it doubted by anybody that the system has no mercy?
> Does it not pursue its natural course irrespective of whom

it hurts or upon whom it confers benefits? The private property system then, in my opinion, being a system that only subserves the interests of a few, and can only subserve the interests of the few, has no mercy. It cannot stop for the consideration of such a sentiment. Naturally it cannot. So you ought not to have mercy on the private property system.[15]

Hurling the charge of incivility back at their critics, anarchists described the relationships that private ownership created as tyrannous and enslaving. In the context of the abolition of slavery in America in 1865–6 and the Emancipation of the Serfs which liberated approximately 20 million Russian 'souls' in 1861, this was a contentious claim. The anarchist view was that these formal acts of liberation left the master–slave relationship intact. Their invocation of slavery was not intended to suggest that chattel and wage slavery were moral equivalents, but to draw attention to the institutional frameworks that allowed both forms of mastership to flourish. When Harriet Jacobs, a freed Black woman living in the Free States that prohibited slavery, discovered that money was not the key that unlocked doors to first-class carriages on the Philadelphia to New York railroad, she compared the institutional segregation of the North to the freedom that prevailed in the South, namely the ability to 'ride in a filthy box, behind the white people' without having to pay for the privilege. Saddened to find that 'the north aped the customs of slavery',[16] she identified the continuity of racism in America. The abolition of the laws that once permitted masters to own slaves had modified the condition of slavery but not ended it. Slaves were emancipated but not free. They had rights but they remained oppressed and exploited.

Likewise anarchists argued that absolutism had been swept away but mastership and tyranny remained. Slavery and mastership thus described the civic culture of the 'new world' and to anarchists it looked remarkably like the culture that prevailed in the old one. Declaring that 'the abolition of the serfdom system was the establishment of the wage-labor system', Parsons turned to Shakespeare in his defence:

> Shakespeare makes Shylock say at the bar of the Venetian court, 'You do take my life when you take the means whereby I live.' Now, the means of life are monopolized; the necessary means for the existence of all has been appropriated and monopolized by a few. The land, the implements of production and communication, the resources of life are now held as private property, and its owners exact tribute from the propertyless.

The welcome that former slave-owners gave to the terms of abolition convinced Parsons of the truth of this analysis. He explained:

> Under the wage slavery system the wage slave selects his master. Formerly the master selected the slave; today the slave selects his master . . . He is compelled to find one . . . the change of the industrial system . . . upon the question of the chattel slave system of the South and that of the so-called 'free laborer', and their wages . . . was a decided benefit to the former chattel slave owners who would not exchange the new system of wage labor at all for chattel

labor, because now the dead had to bury themselves and the sick take care of themselves, and now they don't have to employ overseers to look after them. They give them a task to do – a certain amount to do. They say: 'Now, here, perform this piece of work in a certain length of time', and if you don't . . . why, when you come around for your pay next Saturday, you simply find in the envelope which gives you your money, a note which informs you of the fact that you have been discharged. Now . . . the leather thong dipped in salt brine, for the chattel slave, had been exchanged under the wage slave system for the lash of hunger, an empty stomach and the ragged back of the wage-slave of free-born American sovereign citizens . . .[17]

Parsons's analysis pointed to a second facet of bourgeois incivility: the force essential to maintain the unequal relations that private ownership created. Protecting the rights of property owners required regiments of police and the institution of elaborate court and prison systems. Workers were not only exploited as labourers, but also forced to relinquish a proportion of their wages in taxation to pay for the institutions that guaranteed bourgeois rights, thus forking out for the privilege of their own oppression or, in Parsons's case, killing. And if these protections were deemed inadequate, owners were free to hire private security firms to enforce their rights. 'This private army is at the command and control of those who grind the faces of the poor, who keep wages down to the starvation point,' Parsons argued, referring to the armed Pinkerton officers that McCormick employed to break the union pickets prior to the Haymarket meeting. Violence was integral to bourgeois rule, wherever it operated. Parsons again: 'Originally the earth and its contents were held in common by all men. Then came a change brought about by violence, robbery and wholesale murder, called war.'[18]

Returning to Lingg's theme, Parsons concluded his address to the jury by asking what kind of anarchy the bourgeoisie wanted to defend. Webster's dictionary contained two definitions. Anarchy meant 'Without rulers or governors' and also 'Disorder and confusion'. Parsons had wrongly believed that the constitution upheld the former. He discovered to his cost that it in fact advocated the latter. To distinguish the two, he labelled the uncivil anarchy evident 'in all portions of the world and especially in this court-room', 'capitalistic Anarchy'. This idea was incompatible with civil liberty 'which means without rulers', or 'communistic Anarchy'.

In aftermath of the Commune and the Haymarket trial anarchists and their critics argued about the use of these two conceptions of anarchy. One was defined by the anarchists and the other by their opponents.

Anarchist socialism

In the period between the Commune and Haymarket, anarchism emerged as a doctrine associated with a particular critique of the state and capitalism and a model for revolutionary change defined by a distinctive conception of anarchy. In Paris anarchists found a prototype for revolutionary organization, seeing the Commune as a spontaneous action by subjugated peoples to resist bourgeois exploitation and government oppression. The Commune expressed the anti-authoritarian impulse that anarchists linked to self-emancipation and the type of decentralized federation that Marx appeared to reject.

In the Haymarket trial, the thinking behind this anti-authoritarian impulse was explained. The Haymarket anarchists exposed the continuities between monarchical and republican regimes and, importantly, labelled their analysis anarchist, using the drama of the trial to amplify their message. Proudhon's 1840 masterpiece *What is Property?* opens with a description of slavery as murder and property as theft. The Haymarket critique brought this argument to a new audience, familiarizing a discourse that anarchists thereafter routinely adopted. In 1942, long after Parsons was dead, the antimilitarist activist Frederick Lohr declared poverty to be 'the result of exploitation', adding that 'there could be no exploitation in the first place if there were no enslavement'. And since slavery was 'an inseparable concomitant of government', Lohr concluded, on other side of the Atlantic, that 'Government is *organised slavery*.'[19]

In America in particular, anarchists also linked women's oppression to patriarchal property rights and marriage contracts, often learning from leading abolitionists like Ezra Heywood. In *Uncivil Liberty*, first published in 1870, Heywood had argued that 'the old claim of tyranny, "The king can do no wrong"' was reasserted by majorities of men who thought of women as mere appendages. Only women designated prostitutes had rights to their children; 'any married father . . . by will or deed may dispose of his child'.[20] Lucy Parsons, a leading anarchist campaigner in Chicago, Albert's partner and a vocal advocate for the executed anarchists, described women as 'slaves of slaves', not only 'exploited more ruthlessly than men' but in unique ways.[21]

The conception of state violence and war that Parsons developed was similarly absorbed. This referred both to the right to resist tyranny that workers in Chicago had been denied and also to the war that anarchists believed was being conducted within states and globally across the world. On this issue, the experience of Haymarket and the Commune converged. Violence was meted out against workers who resisted exploitation and used to discipline those colonized by Europeans. Indeed, the Europeans' 'civilizing mission' gave the bourgeoisie free rein to press their rights, as the Communards knew. Louise Michel, deported for the part she played in the Commune, took her lessons from the Melanesian Kanak people she met during her exile on New Caledonia. The 1878 Kanak rebellion against the French was motivated by the same desire for liberty that she had sought in the Commune. Reflecting on European supremacism, she asked herself which group could claim to be superior. Her conclusion was that it was not 'the well-armed white who annihilates those who are less well armed'.[22]

Considering the state of American politics at the 1891 Chicago Martyrs commemoration, Kropotkin fused the model of the Commune with the Haymarket anarchists' commitment to class struggle:

Every year in the history of the American Labour movement has confirmed the views of our brothers. Every strike became a labour war. Workers were massacred during each strike . . . Every year, the conflict between

THE GOVERNMENT OF NO ONE

labour and money became more acute in the great republic . . . during the last great railway strike, it was seriously discussed whether it would not be advisable to call out all the 200,000 strikers, and to repair – an army of rebel workers – to one of the Western states (Oregon for instance) where the nationalization of the land and railways would be proclaimed and an immense commune covering the territory of the whole state would be started. Not merely a single city as it was in Paris, but a whole territory, with all its agricultural and industrial resources.[23]

The anarchist politics that Paris and Haymarket helped to forge still remained plural. Anarchists understood the possibilities of commune organization and the implications of the anti-capitalist, anti-statist critique that the Haymarket anarchists expressed in multiple ways. Anarchism's ideological boundaries also remained quite fluid, even in respect of Marxism. Bakunin and Kropotkin's analysis of the revolutionary socialist movement in the wake of the Commune treated Marxism as a form of statism, but anarchists were not uniformly antagonistic towards Marxism and sometimes engaged creatively with it. If Marx and Bakunin stood at opposite ends of a revolutionary socialist spectrum, plenty of anarchists looked for spaces in between. Haymarket spawned a libertarian socialist movement – even today referred to as the Haymarket synthesis or Chicago idea. This was constructed around the local, direct action and solidarity and linked both to labour organizing and Indigenous peoples' rural resistance.[24] The priority that the synthesis accorded to organizational behaviours downplayed the significance of theoretical divergence between the socialist movement's leading personalities and provided an antidote to the poisonous arguments that wrecked the IWMA.

Yet the Commune and Haymarket introduced rituals into the nascent anarchist movement which helped establish a distinctive anarchist identity. For years after the events, annual commemorations were organized by anarchist groups. These extended across the globe. Vladimiro Muñoz reports that a 'beautiful colored illustration' appeared in the centre pages of the March issue of the Uruguayan paper *El Derecho a la Vida* on the Commune's thirtieth anniversary.[25] Haymarket reinforced the picture of the heroic anarchist type. The dramatic account of the executions published in Paris in 1892 emphasized the unwavering, fearless dedication of the condemned. Reporting that loved ones were refused permission to 'kiss their husbands one last time', the commentary described how

> Fischer intoned the Marseillaise and his brothers in misfortune responded from their neighboring cells, singing the anthem before leaving for death.
>
> At eleven fifty-five minutes they came to fetch them . . . it was impossible to prolong their sufferings. Ah! What pleasure it would have been for the citizens to hear any one of them appeal for mercy!
>
> But our brothers did not offer these wretches the desired spectacle; they remained quiet and walked to the scaffold . . .
>
> Parsons started a speech . . . but the hood and the knot put an end to his words.

Spies shouted: '*Our voices, comrades, will speak louder after our death than they have ever done in our lives.*'

'Long live Anarchy!' Engel shouted.

'It's the happiest moment of my life,' Fischer shouted . . .

A second later, the trapdoor opened, throwing the four friends into the void at the same time. Parsons had his neck broken and barely moved, Engel, Fischer and Spies, struggling in convulsions, were impossible to look at.[26]

Telegrams received at the meeting of anarchists at the memorial held at London's Holborn Town Hall the same year struck a familiar note: from Meadow Lane, Leeds, 'Yorkshire anarchists send greeting to comrades celebrating Chicago. Hurrah for anarchy.' The greeting from the Liverpool comrades was: '[m]en die but principals [*sic*] live. Hurrah for the social revolution long live anarchy.' With another 'hurrah' the Manchester anarchists intoned '[o]ur comrades died that Anarchy might live, their spirit shall lead us to victory.' Glasgow anarchists joined 'in commemorating the death of our martyrs though the enemy did apparently overcome them yet is their triumph now Long Live Anarchy!' From Inverness, the message was: 'the north is awakening. For Liberty they lived, for liberty they died. It is for us to conquer' and Edinburgh: 'let the voice of the people be heard.'[27]

The unconcealed alarm of the bourgeoisie: the anarchist as terrorist

While anarchists articulated their theoretical principles and advanced a revolutionary identity, a negative stereotype of the anarchist as the state's most determined enemy also emerged. Indeed, the legacy of the Commune and Haymarket, coming soon after the division of the socialist movement into two apparently discrete wings – one more open to participation in ordinary politics than the other – proved to be momentous for anarchists.

In Paris, loyalty to civilized republican values established the limits of acceptable politics and legitimized the swift eradication of adversaries. John Merriman describes how the demonization of the Communards as a lazy, dirty rabble helped quicken the killings during the Bloody Week. Simultaneously betraying the racism and virulent supremacism of the dominant civilization, troops who casually dispatched the Communards often compared them to colonial peoples: not really human at all. According to Merriman, one anti-Communard 'intoned that Paris had been "in the power of negroes"'. Gaston Galliffet, the colonel who earned the nickname 'the slayer of the Commune', 'contrasted the Communards with North African Arabs', using the reference both to benchmark the Communards' savagery and to highlight their appalling godlessness and cosmopolitanism: as part of the same barbaric subspecies, Arabs were at least believers and patriots.[28]

In Chicago, the demonization of the underclass dovetailed with the criminalizing of anarchism. References to the anarchist beast and the anarchist peril began to circulate widely in the press, in cheap popular literatures and political commentaries. Michael Schaack, the police chief who headed up the Haymarket case, profited from the expertise he acquired in Chicago by publishing an international history of 'red terror'. In London's East End, an area populated by some of the poorest in the city, he found a 'crowd of boozy, beery, pot-valiant, squalid, frowsy, sodden Whitechapel outcasts who shrieked and fought in a small hall in their district'. These were the anarchists. Amid 'the fumes of scores of dirty pipes and a thousand other causes that made the air almost unbearable' Schaack found another group of anarchists, 'a fourth of whom were lushed, soggy Whitechapel women'.[29]

Cesare Lombroso, one of the leading criminologists of the age, used the Chicago anarchists to develop a scientific model of the ignoble anarchist criminal type. Applying Darwinian insights about species fitness to social science, Lombroso pioneered physiognomy – the study of facial features – to analyse degenerative behaviours. Noting some noble and genial facets in the physiognomy of Parsons and Neebe, he nevertheless concluded that all the accused exhibited the same hereditary 'degenerative characters common to criminals and to the insane'. Writing from his prison cell, Michael Schwab challenged the robustness of Lombroso's methods. Schwab charged Lombroso with using drawings of the men reproduced in Schaack's book to make his diagnosis, not the photographs that he had to hand. So challenged, Lombroso admitted that the photographic evidence failed to display the tell-tale 'degenerative' traits and thus failed to support his conclusions.[30] And yet, however flaky his methods, Lombroso caught the public mood and Schwab's protest was ignored. The popular view was that anarchists were defective types who posed a threat to the health and well-being of the community. By extension, anarchism was a disorder that required urgent remedy: a political as well as a social disease. In 1886, when the verdict on the Haymarket anarchists was announced, the British consul in Chicago told the Foreign Secretary in London how relieved and happy local people were: 'The sentence of the Jury has given the greatest satisfaction in this city and district ... The question was one which was considered as gravely concerning the safety of the State and caused much uneasiness.'[31]

In the years leading up to the First World War the perceived threat of anarchism was felt most sharply in the European autocracies. As a rule of thumb, the intensity of anti-socialist repression correlated with the survival of feudal systems of land ownership and revolutionaries fared least well in Spain, Germany and Russia and best in Britain, France and Switzerland. Similarly, the international campaign to outlaw anarchism was pressed hardest by the imperial powers, Austria-Hungary, Germany and Russia. However, antipathy towards anarchism was really a matter of degree. The international tensions created by the willingness of British, French and Swiss regimes to tolerate anarchists as political refugees owed as much to European power-politicking as it did to liberal principle. This became clearer as the nineteenth century progressed. Liberal regimes became increasingly intolerant of anarchists over time, tightening asylum rules and becoming less inclined to grant political status to those fighting extradition. Liberal regimes felt far less vulnerable to revolutionary pressures than the autocracies but the reaction to the Commune and Haymarket illustrated how vehement the aggression to anarchists was. And it played out in similar ways wherever anarchists happened to organize. The torturing of activists imprisoned at the Monjuich fortress in Barcelona in 1892, the shooting of the educationalist Francisco Ferrer in 1909, the hanging in 1911 of twelve Japanese anarchists for merely contemplating injury to the Emperor, the executions of Joe Hill in 1915 and of Sacco and Vanzetti in 1927 on trumped-up murder charges were some of the more notorious instances of the use of repression to quell anarchist opposition.

The conjunction of the IWMA's collapse with the Commune and Haymarket placed anarchism beyond the realm of ordinary politics and civility. The barriers to membership agreed by the Second International further underlined the anarchists' refusal to contemplate participation in established politics. Anarchism quickly became – and remains – an ideal type for terrorism studies. Modern terrorism, one leading analyst writes, 'began in the latter part of the nineteenth century as a strategy adopted by anarchist groups . . . to be used in the place of propaganda to create terror'.[32] Social histories have told a similar story. Anarchists appear as utopian chiliasts impelled to violence by their commitments to freedom.[33] Anarchism symbolizes 'the kind of terrorism that seems to be violent for the sake of violence itself – the irrational striking out . . . that seems to have no tactical or strategic purpose beyond the pure expression of alienation, anger and hatred'.[34]

This hostile understanding of anarchism seeped into the early analysis of the ideology. As much as anarchists regarded the Commune and the Haymarket trial as moments of heroic resistance which illuminated state tyranny and crystallized their politics, their opponents believed these events exemplified the wanton destructiveness of the anarchist creed. And as the nineteenth century progressed, the anarchists' best efforts to highlight the disorder and violence of state systems were largely resisted.

Three anarchisms

It would be misleading to say that nineteenth-century analysts set out to construct a stereotype of the anarchist as
bomb-thrower, though this was evident in Michael Schaack's
post-Haymarket history. Yet the subtext of irrationality and
fanaticism importantly shaped early accounts of anarchism
and the attempt to explain the destructiveness of the doctrine almost inevitably reinforced anarchism's negativity and
unintelligibility. Whether analysts focused on the actions,
ideas or characters of individual anarchists or on the body of
ideas anarchists expounded, anarchism emerged as a devi-
ant ideology. Examined in the context of post-revolutionary
ideas, anarchism was sometimes located in a longer history
of utopianism and millenarianism. This rendering of anarchism's history helped explain the tendency towards physical
violence and it also suggested that it was a peculiarly European phenomenon.

In reply to the question, 'Who were the anarchists?', three
early commentators, Paul Eltzbacher, Michael Schaack and
E. V. Zenker all replied: Proudhon, Bakunin and Kropotkin.
However, this small set was not exclusive. Eltzbacher, a law
professor-turned-Bolshevik active at the turn of the twentieth century selected seven 'especially prominent' sages to
undertake his analysis of anarchism. Apart from Proudhon,
Bakunin and Kropotkin he chose the eighteenth-century
philosopher William Godwin, the mid nineteenth-century
egoist Max Stirner, the Proudhonian-cum-Stirnerite Benjamin Tucker and the novelist Leo Tolstoy to complete the set.
Schaack, the detective who led the Haymarket investigation,

called Proudhon the real 'father of French anarchy', but keen to alert his readers to the revolutionaries responsible for spreading the anarchist contagion he also included Louise Michel on his list of prominent revolutionaries. E. V. Zenker, another law student and journalist active in the 1890s, had a longer list: Proudhon, Stirner, Bakunin, Kropotkin and Michel; the ex-Communards Élisée Reclus and Jean Grave; and Charles Malato, the son of a Communard. He added Carlo Cafiero and Errico Malatesta, both of whom supported Bakunin against Marx in the IWMA, and Severino Merlino, who joined the anarchist movement shortly after the First International's collapse. He also identified Tucker and the novelist and poet John Henry Mackay. As will be seen, there has been some movement in the outer layers of the constellation that Eltzbacher, Schaack and Zenker collectively created, but the inner core has remained stable over time.

Zenker mapped these individuals to currents of ideas, notably distinguishing anarchist communists from individualists. On this reckoning, Proudhon was a precursor of anarchism. Stirner, whom he dubbed Proudhon's German follower, was the other significant forerunner of the movement. Kropotkin was nominated the leading voice in communist school and Tucker the most important exponent of individualist anarchism. The communists were the larger set. They included Michel, Reclus, Grave, Malato, Cafiero, Malatesta and Merlino. He placed Mackay alongside Tucker but identified the school as otherwise largely American. Zenker believed that Tucker's independent anarchist school had been nurtured by intellectuals and abolitionists including Stephen Pearl Andrews and Josiah Warren.

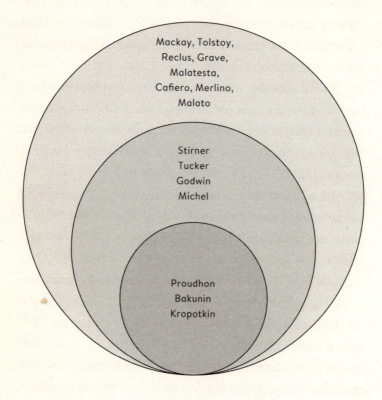

Figure 1.1
Early assessments of anarchism's leading figures contributed to the
construction of the anarchist canon

Zenker argued that the gap between Kropotkin and Tucker was quite wide, yet concluded that the libertarian impulse he traced to Proudhon and Stirner distinguished anarchism from what he called the 'Socialistic and the religious view of the world' and the 'religion of the absolute, infallible, all-mighty, and ever-present State'. Indeed, evoking the arguments that split the IWMA in anarchism's defence, Zenker concluded that the 'centralising tendency and the coercive character of the system of doing everything in common, without which Socialism cannot have the least success, will naturally and necessarily be replaced by Federalism and free association'.[35]

Although Zenker's analysis of anarchist individualism and communism interestingly pointed to the cultural and political pluralism of anarchism, the histories of socialist thought that he and Schaack presented were actually quite reductive. Schaack leaned heavily on the work of the New York academic Richard Ely, but displayed none of Ely's even-handedness. Ely had watched the disintegration of the First International and was an expert on European socialism. In his observations he articulated a widely felt tension between prospect of progressive change and the destructive power of movements determined to realize it. Keeping an open mind about anarchism, Ely identified it as a potentially civilizing force, capable of destroying 'old, antiquated institutions' and delivering 'the birth of a new civilization'.[36] Schaack, in contrast, used a distinction between physical and moral force popularized after the French Revolution to explore the development of socialism in western Europe and anarchism's relationship to it.

As a body of thought, Schaack understood socialism as

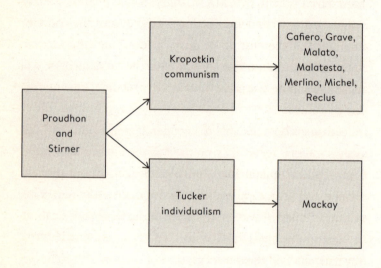

Figure 1.2
Ernst Zenker's analysis of anarchist schools, their instigators and leading exponents

an outgrowth of the early nineteenth-century utopianism of Étienne Cabet, Charles Fourier and Saint-Simon. This was a familiar analysis. Marx and Engels had used a variation of it in the 1848 *Communist Manifesto* to illustrate the distinctiveness of their own contribution. However, whereas Marx and Engels had identified the scientific turn as decisive for socialism's development, Schaack considered that modern socialism had matured under the influence of Russian nihilism, the anti-Tsarist 'dynamite' doctrine. Schaack acknowledged that socialism had a philosophical pedigree. He considered Marx and Engels to be the brains behind the modern movement. But he refused to accept that this extended to anarchism. Indeed, anarchism had produced no 'first-rates' or thinkers of their calibre. It had its roots in the homogeneous dogmatism of the utopians and was best thought of as a nihilist reflex rather than a philosophy. Having been adopted wholesale in Germany, it was exported to Chicago. The implication of this argument was that European anarchism overwhelmed American individualist traditions.

Zenker similarly drew out the naive utopianism, terrorism and millenarianism of anarchist doctrines, also plotting anarchism's historical trajectory in Europe. His pre-history extended back to Reformation heresies, forward to the French Revolution, and included the Jacobin communist and arch-conspirator 'Gracchus' Babeuf as well as Godwin and the utopian socialists Fourier and Saint-Simon. This narrative added a telltale childlike catastrophism to anarchism as well as a penchant for intrigue and secrecy. Like Schaack, Zenker associated these aspects of anarchism with Bakunin, the most unreliable and self-delusional anarchist. 'Bakunin

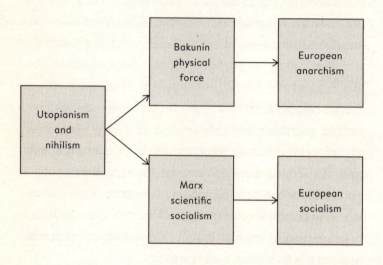

Figure 1.3
How Michael Schaack's and Ernst Zenker's histories model the
divergence of anarchism from Marxism

tried to deceive himself into thinking that he deplored the violence that was sometimes necessary, and wrapped himself in the protecting cloak of the believer in evolution'. He 'expressly excepted secret societies and plots from the means of bringing about this revolution. But this did not hinder him from becoming himself . . . the head of a secret society, formed according to all the rules of the conspirator's art'.[37] If Bakunin was not considered representative of anarchism, he nevertheless symbolized a pronounced anarchist tendency.

Canons

For all the suspicion that surrounds the attempt to describe anarchist politics, anarchists have produced a substantial body of literature to do just that. An eagerness to correct popular misconceptions and contest the accuracy of popular stereotypes has been an important motivator. As well as contesting critical accounts, anarchists also complicated the categories that commentators used to classify anarchism and corrected the Eurocentric biases of these histories.

When anarchists identified notables in their ranks, they usually referred to their extraordinary commitment and dedication. Biography played an important part in these estimations. Bakunin's early acolytes drew attention to his imprisonment by the Tsar, his dramatic escape from Siberia and his constant dedication to the cause of revolution. Bakunin was painted not so much as a man as a phenomenon. 'Such struggles as this man experienced, and the sufferings he endured,' Henry Seymour recorded, 'would have softened the activity of most men, but our hero was a *Bakounine*!' Having 'scarcely stepped foot in England,' Seymour gushed, 'he redoubled his enthusiasm for the cause of social revolution.'[38] Life stories exemplified anarchist values and virtues. Just as Bakunin was admired for his fortitude and energy, Louise Michel was celebrated by anarchists because of her defiant refusal to deny or excuse her actions in the Commune. Taking full responsibility for her part in the insurrection, she instead invited her accusers to execute her. Impressed by her courage, 10,000 people turned out to welcome her back to Paris 1881 when the Communards were amnestied. An article on Errico Malatesta written in 1912 when he faced deportation from the UK took special pains to describe his compassion, treating this as an embodiment of anarchist ethics. Those living in 'the poorer Italian quarters of Islington and Soho', the report read, 'know little and care less about his political beliefs. They know him as one who would give his last penny to help fellow-countrymen in distress, and who has saved hundreds of boys from drifting into hooliganism by teaching them useful trades in the little shop in Windmill Street where he carried on his business of engineer.'[39] Rudolf Rocker, a leading figure notably absent from Eltzbacher's list, was celebrated as a labour organizer who taught himself Yiddish in order to work with some of the most disadvantaged Jewish workers in London's East End. Emma Goldman, another absentee and one of the most prominent anarchists in America, established her reputation as a tireless and uncompromising campaigner for free speech and women's rights and against government repression. Her fearless defence of activists accused of violence was widely respected.

While these 'notables' were concentrated in Europe and

America, their practices were not geographically restricted. Collectively responsible for producing volumes of political tracts, essays, fiction and poetry, many also ran newspapers: *Arbeter Fraint* (Rocker), *Associazione* (Malatesta), *Freedom* (Kropotkin), *La Questione Sociale* (Malatesta), *Le Révolté/ La Révolte* (Kropotkin/Grave), *Liberty* (Tucker) and *Mother Earth* (Goldman). But this was just the tip of the iceberg: there were plenty more.[40] An expansive programme of publication supported by a global infrastructure for distribution and the facility to produce multiple translations of original work at speed ensured that authors were able to reach significant international audiences. As well as appearing in virtually all European languages Kropotkin's work was also translated into Japanese and Chinese. His writings were regularly serialized and reviewed in non-anarchist cultural journals and in anarchist and labour newspapers stretching from London to Christchurch, New Zealand.[41]

Following sometimes forced and sometimes voluntary migratory paths, groups of émigré anarchists set up clubs and societies which, even if they were often quite insular, became centres for a complex network of transit and smuggling routes. Books and pamphlets travelled with them. Individual meetings, chance encounters and personal friendships further facilitated the wide dissemination of ideas. By regularly embarking on extensive lecture tours anarchists systematically took their politics to new locations. To correct popular misperceptions of anarchism and mobilize support for anarchist initiatives they wrote in different registers, targeting workers and intellectuals: Malatesta's *Fra Contadini*, Kropotkin's *Appeal to the Young* and Tolstoy's *The Slavery of*

Our Time were classics in this vein. The historian of Chinese anarchism Arif Dirlik observes that Kropotkin's *Appeal* was 'responsible for converting . . . numbers of young [Chinese] radicals to anarchism' in the early decades of the twentieth century.[42] Ricardo Flores Magón regarded Kropotkin's *The Conquest of Bread* as 'a kind of anarchist bible'. The communes he helped establish in Mexicali and Tijuana during the revolution in Baja California in 1911 were inspired by it.[43]

The approach that anarchists took towards movement history similarly diluted anarchist Eurocentrism. Kropotkin's view was that anarchism was a politics of the people and that the movements that appeared in the nineteenth century were only the most modern manifestation of a kind of politics that could be found in all parts of the world and in every historical period. Anarchist thought, he argued, long predated the publication of Proudhon's *What is Property?* or the emergence of anarchist movements in 1870s Europe. Pressing his case, Kropotkin placed principles of individual sovereignty and resistance at the heart of anarchism. These, he claimed, were evident in ancient Greece and China. Their exponents had not been anarchists but advocates of a politics that anarchists also espoused. Treating anarchism as a resistance movement against top-down organization, Kropotkin found examples of anarchistic movements in early Christianity and Buddhism.

On Kropotkin's conception, anarchy involved challenging norms and experimenting with new forms of thought, expression and communication, where these undermined established hierarchies. It existed in every realm of activity, in cultural and well as social and political spheres. Anarchy thus encompassed individual and collective actions in the arts, literature and science, alongside the economy. But it was no single one of these things.

Rudolf Rocker borrowed Kropotkin's conception of timeless, universal resistance to produce an evolutionary history of post-French Revolutionary Europe and plot the development of anarchism in the industrial union or syndicalist movements of the late nineteenth and early twentieth centuries. Voltairine de Cleyre, a writer and educator active in Philadelphia, adopted a different tack and explored the relationship of anarchism to revolutionary republicanism, reviving some of the themes explored by the Haymarket anarchists. Thus while Rocker explored the ways that anarchist ideas were taken up by grass-roots movements over time, de Cleyre examined how cultural contexts shaped anarchism. Anarchism played out in different ways in different locations. In America anarchism was rooted in American traditions. It was a movement for liberty and independence against tyranny and militarism through resistance.

These variations in focus, different histories and competing judgements about anarchist principles helped keep the determination of anarchism open. The history of the IWMA welded anarchists to the advocacy of a decentralized federation as a means to support self-emancipation. But this commitment was fleshed out in a critique of prevailing religious, autocratic, liberal, republican and socialist doctrines. It took on a different hue in each geographical location and it was shaped by the special ways that anarchists responded to their predicaments. The recent recovery of neglected histories confirms that anarchism extended well beyond the activities of a handful of activists in western Europe and that it was transnational from the beginning.[44] Historians of non-European currents of ideas have similarly argued that it is possible to talk about indigenous anarchism in parts of the world that nineteenth-century European anarchists did not reach.[45] Anarchism attracted campaigners who had very clear, sometimes set notions of policy and principle. Charles Malato observed that the 'worker-philosopher' Jean Grave, editor the iconic French-language newspaper *La Révolte*, was 'capable of raising . . . storms by the extreme dogmatism of his reasoning'.[46] But it also drew activists who were not interested in formulating ideological positions. Together they produced a rich body of literature but no law. There was no party, no agreed policy, no philosophical canon. No gods, no masters – only an abundance of leaders, ideas, proposals and initiatives.

CHAPTER 2
Cultures

The anarchist critique of order as a form of disorder is not new. Towards the end of the play King Lear declares:

> Through tattered clothes great vices do appear;
> Robes and furred gowns hide all. Plate sin with gold,
> And the strong lance of justice hurtless breaks.
> Arm it in rags, a pigmy's straw does pierce it.
> None does offend – none, I say, none. I'll able 'em.
> Take that of me, my friend, who have the power
> To seal th' accuser's lips. Get thee glass eyes,
> And like a scurvy politician seem
> To see the things thou dost not.[1]

In the nineteenth century this kind of critique transformed anarchism into the revolutionary politics of outlaws. Like the protagonists of disorder, their critics, the anarchists reflected on questions of governance, institutional design and organizational efficiency. But because they set their face against private property and the institutions deemed necessary to preserve, regulate or appropriate it for the public good, anarchists adopted a stance to these questions that appeared negative, if not hostile. And because they believed that the new worlds that had emerged in the wake of the great eighteenth-century revolutions had failed to deliver liberty, equality and fraternity, they not only asked how existing social arrangements could be remodelled, but did so critically, in order to achieve further transformative change.

Defenders of the existing orders often asked questions about duty and obligation. How could citizens be induced to love their countries, serve their kings and presidents and respect the rights of others (especially property-owning minorities)? What could progressive governments do to ensure good governance across the globe? How could responsible governments protect citizens against outsiders, secure their economic well-being and ensure their access to resources? Anarchists also probed these questions and still do, but usually in an effort to expose the costs of obedience and the risks of self-aggrandisement. At the same time, they try to understand the mechanisms that maintain the stability of these regimes, notwithstanding their evident unfairness. In the language of nineteenth-century politics, they examine how mastership and wage slavery preserve systems of oppression.

In this chapter I will focus on the cultural critiques anarchists have advanced to explain the constancy of subjugation. I am using culture in the sense that Rudolf Rocker used the term, as an approach to living rather than as an aspect of social life associated with the rarefied enjoyments of intellectuals, or the special habits of elites.[2] Rocker's idea, which he advanced in his critique of twentieth-century dictatorships, both fascist and Stalinist, was that culture was about the study of human interventions in nature and the creation of social environments. This conception placed culture in relation to nature rather than in opposition to it, blurring the boundaries between human and non-human life and dissolving the 'artificial distinction' between 'nature peoples' and 'culture peoples'. For Rocker, there is never an absence of culture, only alternative cultures, more or less productive or destructive, more or less organic or plastic, more or less commodious or limited, more or less fulfilling or cheerless. 'Even slavery and despotism are manifestations of the general cultural movement,' he argued.[3]

Rocker's conception complicated histories that purported to reveal the foundations of national differences in order to assert the special character of particular groups of people. Discomfited by what he saw as the brutality and aggressiveness of European governments and the competitive, xenophobic sentiments they inspired, Rocker wondered how peoples captured by and integrated into these regimes could rise above their presumed national interests, set aside the privileges that inclusion in the nation bestowed and act in solidarity with others. The study of culture, encompassing the entire history of human interventions in nature and the 'crutches of concepts' used to explain it, gave him his answer. Setting out to isolate the factors that explained cultural turns, Rocker argued that culture was about mastery and perfection, but not necessarily about exploitation and stasis. On the contrary, it was a process through which individuals imparted their best selves in the world in order to improve their environments. The puzzle that culture posed, therefore, was to understand how cultures became degraded and how to repair them by fostering ways of living that enabled collaboration with others while also preserving nature.

Rocker linked the impoverishment of cultures to the

rise of the state, and in some 600 pages he explained what he meant by this term. Rather than attempt to replicate or summarize his analysis, I will outline three ideas of domination to explore the anarchist cultural critique, all of which emerged in the early period of the European movement. I will also look at some of the educational initiatives that anarchists have promoted to combat oppressive behaviours and promote alternative cultural practices. Some of the big questions that anarchists have asked about domination, pointedly with a view to promoting cultures of anarchy, are about learning – what, how and why we learn and acquire knowledge about the world. Working to undo the domination that secures co-operation in the state, anarchists have always been involved in education and they have set up free schools (often spelt 'skools' to distinguish them from state institutions) and experimented with curricula and pedagogy in both mainstream and alternative libertarian institutions. Their rejection of domination drives this interest, focusing attention on education as a process of unlearning and re-learning, empowering individuals to emancipate themselves to enable self-government.

Domination

The concept of domination is derived from the Latin 'dominus', which referred to the absolute power of a lord or master to rule a household, and the related term 'dominium' which designates ownership as well as rulership. In ordinary language domination is linked to the right to exercise power, the sovereignty and authority of the Church and State, as well as to the actual exercise of power, through the assertion of supremacy or in government. Because it has been defined in relation to the absolute power of the master, it is also applied to tyranny and arbitrary rule. In this sense, domination is associated with injustice, usurpation and the denial of liberty, especially through the cultivation of relations based on dependence.

Domination, then, ordinarily describes institutions in the broadest sense – organizational arrangements, norms and behaviours. To take an example from popular literature: in *Jane Eyre* Mr Rochester dominates as the master of his household. His customary habit is to adopt a tone of command. Even though he wants to avoid treating Jane as an inferior, their relationship is in fact based on domination because of the power advantages he enjoys. She tells him that for as long as he employs her, she is his dependant. She remains his 'paid subordinate' whether or not he growls at her. Non-domination describes countervailing practices which, in Charlotte Brontë's novel, are rooted in the cultivation of equality. This comes from resisting other people's certainties. Jane finds the strength to resist domination in sisterhood and voluntary agreement. She rises above the sense of victimhood fostered by Lowood School's tyrannous punishment regime when her rebellious schoolmate refuses to accede to Jane's public disgrace. Later, having found that she prefers a life 'free and honest' to one of material comfort and slavery,[4] she rejects the patriarchal authority asserted by St John, her would-be suitor, first by avowing her right to consent to his marriage proposal and then by firmly rejecting it.

All of these ideas resonate in anarchism. Domination is understood as a diffuse kind of power, embedded in hierarchy – pyramidal structures, pecking orders and chains of command – and in uneven access to economic or cultural resources. Domination also describes a type of unfreedom which can be exercised through habit, force or manipulation. Linked to privilege, domination is manifest as social power derived from status or unearned advantage, for example whiteness, maleness, physical ableness. This is felt as domination both in the marginalization of individuals who fail to fit the profile and in prejudice. However, the overlaps between these conceptions have given rise to multiple critiques. The rejection of domination unifies anarchists in shared struggles against the monopolization of resources and the centralization of power, representation, racism, imperialism and authority, while leaving the institutional and sociological mechanisms that explain it open to discussion. Here I will focus on three relationships of domination: domination and law, domination and hierarchy, and domination and conquest.

Domination and law

In anarchist critiques law often appears as a two-headed hydra. It has one life in abstract political and legal theory and another in practical policy implementation. From an anarchist perspective, legal theory grounds the implementation of law in necessity. It does this by buttressing two related ideas: that social groups are incapable of inventing their own regulatory systems and that social life in law's absence is unattractive. In theory, law is the instrument that brings security and freedom by constraining bad behaviours. John Locke, sometimes celebrated as one of the fathers of liberalism, said that where law ends, tyranny begins.[5]

The practical implementation of law removes the power of rule-making from the majority of people it manages. People know what law is, they know that it commands obedience and that transgression will result in punishment. However, most people have little knowledge of the content and scope of the law and lack the technical ability to participate meaningfully in making, interpreting or enforcing law. The mystery of the law reinforces the idea of its necessity. Whenever we call on the services of legal professionals – police, solicitors, barristers and judges – we implicitly recognize our reliance on law and our inability to conduct our affairs in its absence.

For anarchists like the 1848 revolutionary, political exile and journalist Sigmund Engländer, the abstraction of law from social life was a sign of political corruption. His conception of law and domination neatly paralleled the critique of wage slavery and mastership advanced by the Chicago anarchists, perhaps not surprisingly since he, like they, was heavily indebted to Proudhon. Emerging from the disarray of the IWMA he attacked law because it facilitated exploitation and dependency and because he thought lawmakers assumed they knew what was best for everyone. On both counts, law was inherently dominating.

The mismatch between the ideal and reality of law was at the heart of Engländer's analysis of domination. Reviewing a period of French revolutionary change between 1789 and 1848, Engländer used law as a kind of shorthand to refer both to an aspiration for perfection, based on a commitment to individual rights, 'the revolutionary idea of our century',[6] and a messy, protracted process of constitution-writing that assumed inequality. The ideal of law was that it would bring order through harmony. The reality was that it instituted division through competition and oppression.

The rule of law was supposed to guarantee justice in the republics that emerged after 1789, but in Engländer's view it was actually applied to regulate constitutional settlements that were underpinned by an exclusive right to private property. Depicted as 'the expression of universal reason, the public conscience, the justice, the mighty bulwark of mankind against barbarism',[7] law was in fact the expression of a 'social antagonism'. It was never neutral or 'blind'. In law, the revolutionary principle of individual right had seamlessly morphed into a very bourgeois right to private ownership. Law could only arbitrate disputes partially and in order to maintain the inequalities that the commitment to exclusive property rights created. Following Proudhon, Engländer argued that '[a]bolition of the economical exhaustion of man by man, and the abolition of the government of man by man', were just two aspects of the same problem. His summary view was that law dominated as 'a weapon wherewith to frighten, to enslave, and to torture the oppressed'.[8] It was 'the child of injustice and ambition' and 'the last lurking-place of faith in authority'.[9]

Engländer turned to philosophy to explain the transformation of law from a principle of right to an instrument of wrong. The key figures he identified were the eighteenth-century philosopher Jean-Jacques Rousseau and the Jacobins who had been enthused by his writings, Robespierre and Saint-Just. These three were the law's most forceful advocates. Casting his eye over their work, Engländer observed a fatal flaw in the theory and practice of lawmaking. As sworn opponents of absolutism, these revolutionaries appreciated the tyrannous power that kings enjoyed as a result of the exclusive right they claimed to make laws. Yet rather than challenging the principle of lawmaking – the source of tyranny – they simply relocated the power of lawmaking – sovereignty – from the monarch to the people.

Engländer did not explain the details of the philosophical arguments but these were discussed by other anarchists, notably by Proudhon, Bakunin and Kropotkin. Particularly critical of Rousseau, the anarchists argued that he had wrongly used the device of the state of nature – an imagined pre-political condition – to examine the formation of government. Rousseau had argued that individuals enter into a compact with each other and that this marked the start of a process which leads individuals from a state of nature into a system of law and government. The terms of Rousseau's compact were very generous: individual liberty and equality were guaranteed and law was rooted in the people's sovereign power. Nevertheless, the anarchists rejected Rousseau's story about government. They accused him of wrongly inventing an artificial distinction between primitive pre-political and civilized political orders and of misrepresenting social organization as a special achievement when, in fact, it was a characteristic feature of human existence. Theorized in this manner, the anarchists argued that government was wrongly depicted as the outcome of a conscious action undertaken to perfect social life. The same account miscast law as an instrument of social excellence.

Rousseau's theory of government was powerfully deployed

by revolutionaries struggling against royal absolutists, but from the anarchist perspective it was far from transformative. Evaluating its impact, Engländer argued that the radicals had wrested the power of lawmaking from monarchical control with the expectation that law would realize a general good, 'abolish all the vices of humanity' and make people free, happy and good. The abolition of monarchy tricked the philosophers into thinking that the removal of arbitrary power was sufficient to eradicate tyranny. This mixture of naivety and vanity had proved deeply conservative. After the revolution the lawmaker-philosophers were in charge, not the king. But '[o]therwise there was no difference between Louis XIV, who made his uncontrolled will equivalent to law' and 'Rousseau, Robespierre, St Just &c.'[10] The character of leadership altered dramatically, yet the principle of command was reinforced. Worse still, having empowered the people in theory, the revolutionaries then discovered that government was just too big and too complex to allow the people to actually make the rules. There were simply too many to exercise sovereignty directly. Faced with this reality, the well-meaning but deluded utopians were compelled to restore the feudal principle of representation, once used to constrain the monarch, to make the system operable.

When it came to writing the constitution, Engländer argued that the lawmakers compounded their errors by deliberately placing themselves 'outside society'. Desperate to ensure that constitutional law was unsullied by factional bargaining, the philosophers created special conventions and charged the people's representatives with devising universal rules that would benefit all. Since philosophy had already elicited the principles of right on which law would be based – life, liberty and property – the lawmakers automatically assumed that there was a natural correspondence between their ideals and the interests of the millions of individuals the law would supposedly empower. Confidently constituting themselves as 'the will and soul of the nation', they thus ended up introducing a set of rules that simultaneously recognized the people as sovereign and systematically disempowered the citizenry.

By enshrining the idea of justness against arbitrary monarchical whim, law commanded respect even while it tramped the rights and liberties of individuals into the dirt. On this view, the revolutionary idea of rights had been betrayed. Law dominated by securing obedience to oppression. 'Every arbitrary act of tyranny is tolerated, if . . . it is done by some twist of a law,' Engländer commented sourly.[11] Similarly, by channelling widely shared aspirations for freedom into institutions sanctified by the constitution, law dominated by detaching constitutional questions from arguments about power and policy. Every 'prophet sets up the twelve tables of the law; the French Socialists write no more theories, but issue formulated decrees even as charlatans juggle off receipts for wonderful cures'. In the unending struggle for control of law, '[e]very class hopes that when the war is over the law will remain with it. The law is to every party leader the mould into which the raw material is poured and society modelled'.[12] These partisan debates about the remit and proper application of legislation simultaneously rendered the social antagonisms that underpinned law invisible and opened up limitless possibilities for the regulation of social life. Trade, schools, healthcare could all be managed through legislation, in an effort to mitigate the effects of structural inequality, without ever threatening law's institutionalization.

Why was law dominating, if the people was able to voice its opinion and the laws that were enacted in its name made it happy? Engländer offered four reasons. His first response was that the normalization of law turned the real individuals who constituted the people into subjects and slaves. The people could only exercise decision-making power within a framework of law that was not of any individual's own making. Second, submitting to law involved the suspension of individual judgement. Individuals adhered to law and either neglected or were forced to ignore the 'inner voice' of their 'own reason'.[13] Albert Parsons had advanced the same view at his trial in Chicago:

> The natural and the imprescriptible [*sic*] right of all is the right of each to control oneself . . . Law is the enslaving power of man . . . Blackstone describes the law to be a rule of action, prescribing what is right and prohibiting what is wrong. Now, very true. Anarchists hold that it is wrong for one person to prescribe what is the right action for another person, and then compel that person to obey that rule. Therefore, right action consists in each person attending to his business and allowing everybody else to do likewise. Whoever prescribes a rule of action for another to obey is a tyrant, a usurper, and an enemy of liberty. This is precisely what every statute does.[14]

Third, the deferential effects of power exacerbated the regulatory impact of law-governed systems. Observing that the 'people conceives for those whom it has elected an absolute adoration',[15] Engländer acknowledged that only a mere 'knot of free ungovernable men desires that in the universal struggle for the post of lawgiver, the law itself may be broken up'.[16] His explanation of the unpopularity of the anarchist cause led him to uncover the final dominating effects of law. This was the homogenization of interests. Bundled together as the people, he argued, 'separate subjects or citizens are immovable or silent'.[17] Law was a far cry from the principle of individual right that the revolution had proclaimed and the idea of self-emancipation that the IWMA drew from it. It bestowed 'so-called sovereignty of the people' in a manner that killed 'individual liberty as much as does divine right' and which was 'as mystical and soul-deadening'.[18]

Engländer coupled his critique of law and domination with a proposal for institutional redesign. His suggestion was to divert the 'blood' that rushed to head of the 'State body' into 'separate veins'. Breaking down the body politic would overcome the need for representation and enable individuals and social groups to govern themselves directly, by their own rules: reconstitutionalizing on the basis of individual right. Linking domination to the alienating, stultifying effects of law on individuals, Engländer found the antidote to tyranny and mastership in the genius of rebellion and, borrowing Max Stirner's vocabulary, in egoism. In Engländer's anarchism, egoism – living without domination, 'for himself and by himself'[19] – required recognizing both the permanence of 'factions' and neighbourliness. While factions pointed to social pluralism, neighbourliness was another term for interdependence. Engländer's ambition was to substitute what he called 'social palpitations' for bourgeois 'harmony'.[20] On this view, non-domination became a process of human interaction driven by individuals struggling to be ruled in certain ways while always standing firm against the temptation to govern through the imposition of law.

Domination and hierarchy: Bakunin and Tolstoy

While Engländer was interested in institutional design, other anarchists examined the micropolitics of domination. In this perspective, domination refers to the formal and informal customs and practices that order everyday relationships, particularly by conferring status. A significant disagreement between Bakunin and Tolstoy about the mainsprings of obedience and authority highlights a division within anarchism about the ways in which hierarchy is perpetuated. However, there is general agreement about the privilege that domination establishes and the disparagement it normalizes. Domination establishes social hierarchies by distinguishing masters from subalterns.

The disagreement between Bakunin and Tolstoy was about God and authority. These terms described the idea of absolute truth and the right of command. For Bakunin, hierarchy was sustained by the unquestioning acceptance of authority backed by the knowledge of the divine being. Tolstoy agreed that hierarchy stemmed from the failure to challenge authority but argued that the prerequisite for non-domination was the recognition of God. Bakunin's professed atheism and Tolstoy's unorthodox Christianity appear to make the gap between their positions unbridgeable. As if to emphasize this, anarchists have often invoked Bakunin and Tolstoy to variously reject and embrace religion in the name of anarchism. Had Bakunin and Tolstoy rehearsed their ideas with each other directly, the commonalities of their critiques might have become more apparent: neither version of the thesis endorses religious institutionalism and both require individuals to consider what pronouncements they will accept as authoritative. Both distinguish consent from obedience and wilfulness from duty. Moreover, both call on individuals to exercise judgement, which often requires courage and it is an essential step towards non-domination.

Famously reversing Voltaire's dictum, 'if God did not exist, it would be necessary to invent him', Bakunin declared, *'if God really existed it would be necessary to abolish him'*.[21] His objection to the divine was philosophical and sociological. He used the term political theology to explain it.[22] The critique of philosophy turned on his belief that the idea of original sin structured orthodox western thought. Philosophers had absorbed the Christian idea of godly perfection and the story of human corruption and exile from Eden. Consequently, the problem that philosophy wrestled with was how to transcend the dirty, imperfect material world and how to improve corrupted humanity. Even modern philosophy – Bakunin had Hegel's Idealism in mind – adopted this starting point. Hegel placed reason with a capital 'R' rather than God at the heart of his metaphysics, but his complex, transformative, evolutionary history was only another mechanism designed to show how humanity would raise itself up from baseness and achieve perfection over time. Marxism, too, was a form of political theology, even though Marx advanced what he called a materialist theory. Bakunin argued that Marx's materialism had only succeeded in regrounding Hegel's Idealist philosophy in economics. This changed the motive force of history but did not succeed in turning Hegel on his head as Marx claimed. For whether history was linked to the release of reason in the world or to changes in patterns of ownership and production, the idea of progressive transformation towards perfection was common to both. Bakunin argued that a more thoroughgoing materialism was required to upend Hegel. Real materialism meant rejecting notions of eternal truth and the divine and rooting philosophy directly in human experience.

In this context, the idea of God was inevitably enslaving. 'God being master,' Bakunin argued, 'made man the slave.' God was 'truth, justice, goodness, beauty, power, and life, man is falsehood, iniquity, evil, ugliness, impotence, and death'.[23] Individuals could attain goodness but only through revelation and this was predicated on obedience to authority: subjection.

Bakunin examined the instrumentalization of philosophy in order to press his sociological critique. His argument was that faith functioned as an opiate which bred acceptance of the obvious injustices of social life. When this idea was hardwired into social life it enabled a whole class of functionaries to use the 'semblance of believing' to torment, oppress and exploit. Bakunin's list of exploiters was long: 'priests, monarchs, statesmen, soldiers, public and private financiers, officials of all sorts, policemen, gendarmes, jailers and executioners, monopolists, capitalists, tax-leeches, contractors and proprietors, lawyers, economists, politicians of all shades, down to the smallest vendors of sweetmeats'.[24] The most disadvantaged were inured to the hardships they experienced because of the comfort they took from their faith in God's benevolence and care.

The anarchist twist Bakunin added to this familiar argument was that the power structures that sanctioned authority were a manifestation of religious belief. Distinguishing atheism-as-faithlessness from anarchist atheism, Bakunin echoed some of Engländer's themes to critique radicals, freethinkers and Masons who assailed Church authorities but only sought to reform existing structures to profess a new political theology. These atheists attacked religious institutions and represented themselves as non-believers, but they remained wedded to hierarchy and mastership. For Bakunin, this was shallow atheism. While Bakunin often condemned the corruptions of religious institutions and the hypocrisies of the pious, his atheism struck at the characterization of humanity as vile, the notion of the perfection of the world-to-come and the beauty of the eternal. As a freethinker, Bakunin rejected this truth and the subordination it sanctioned, whether or not this was directly referenced to the divine.

Whereas Bakunin dismissed revelation as an enslaving fiction, Tolstoy argued that non-domination was the essential truth that the acceptance of God revealed. This is the central message of his short story 'Master and Man', written and published in 1895.[25] It describes the relationship between Vasilii Andreich Brekhunov, a man of status in his community – innkeeper, merchant and churchwarden – and Nikita, a peasant prone to bouts of drinking but industrious, skilful and strong. Nikita has all the virtues that Vasilii Andreich lacks. He is honest and good-natured, 'fond of animals', and attaches little value to monetary reward. Vasilii Andreich is dishonest and obsessed with material enrichment. He purloins the church money in his care to advance his business interests and exploits Nikita's goodwill to underpay him at irregular intervals of his choosing. Together they embark on a journey: Vasilii Andreich must get to another village in order to close a deal. Even though the weather is atrociously cold and the snow is falling as thick and fast as the night, Nikita harnesses his own favourite horse and they both set out on the sledge. Vasilii Andreich is well covered in fur. Nikita is barely equipped, having sold his good boots for vodka and anyway lacking the wherewithal to afford warm clothing.

Two bad choices encapsulate the nature of Vasilii Andreich's mastership of Nikita. The first is Vasilii Andreich's decision to take the faster but less secure route to their destination, against Nikita's instinct. The second is to push on to the village after getting hopelessly lost in the dark and arriving by chance at the home of a wealthy, welcoming farmer. Vasilii Andreich turns down the invitation of an overnight stay, fearful that time lost will cost money. Nikita, frozen, wet-through and exhausted, is desperate for him to accept but does not contest the decision. His general subservience is signalled by his carefully ordered genuflections at the farm, first to the icons and subsequently to the master of the house, the company seated at the table and finally the women waiting on them. The particular duty he feels is summed up in his comment, '[i]f you say we go, we go'.[26] What Vasilii Andreich dictates Nikita accepts, even when he strongly disagrees.

Tolstoy tells us that Nikita leaves the farm because he 'was long accustomed to having no will of his own and doing as others bid'.[27]

The mastership Tolstoy embraces and which Bakunin disputes is the unmediated duty to God. While Nikita's naive faith makes him vulnerable to his earthly master's cruelty and meanness, Tolstoy treats his acceptance of God's will approvingly. Marooned in the snow with no hope of survival, Nikita faces death, but he is calm. One reason is that he has found life pretty unbearable, but the deeper explanation is that he perceives dying as a new stage in his relationship with God, 'the greatest of all masters'.[28] Vasilii Andreich's unexpected epiphany reinforces Tolstoy's message, exposing the possibility of a different social ordering. Also realizing that they are stuck, Vasilii Andreich initially attempts to save himself by taking the horse and leaving Nikita to his fate. When the horse brings him back to Nikita, he revises his initial judgement. He was wrong to think Nikita's life worthless and that his own was made meaningful by his wealth and status. Now appreciating that his obsession with material well-being has caused him to lead an impoverished life, Vasilii Andreich acts selflessly, covering Nikita with his furs and lying over him to keep him warm. Nikita survives the night as a result. Tolstoy describes this last act as Vasilii Andreich's discovery of God, but there is no rite or ritual. Vasilii Andreich comprehends his calling through the joy and bliss he feels, knowing that Nikita lives.

While Bakunin and Tolstoy explained domination in very different ways, they advanced similar critiques. Both railed against the iniquity of hierarchy, but whereas Bakunin called on the oppressed to rise against masters, Tolstoy implored masters to accept their equal subordination to God and relinquish their unearned privilege. Bakunin would have likely encouraged Nikita to defy God as a first step to his emancipation, following the example of Adam and Eve – Bakunin's novel reading of Genesis.[29] But the subordination that Bakunin resisted as dominating is not equivalent to the obedience to God that Tolstoy believed essential for non-domination. Although Tolstoy treated non-resistance as godly, he shared Bakunin's worries about the imposition of belief. Nikita adopts the rituals of the Church and the hierarchies that go with it. Yet he intuits God from his relationship to the natural world and his faith comes from within. Although Nikita does not challenge Vasilii Andreich, he does not accept his orders as authoritative either. And in the end, divine truth reveals the slavishness of Vasilii Andreich's behaviour. It does not sanction hierarchy.

The overlaps between Bakunin and Tolstoy are also evident in their accounts of domination and authority. Bakunin equated authority with the hierarchical principles that underpinned and structured government. Tolstoy showed that authority is embedded in norms and habituated behaviours. Tolstoy's masters, like Bakunin's oppressors, are by no means distinguished individuals. They are unexceptional, relatively privileged people – functionaries of all sorts – who make the most of the power advantages that hierarchy affords them. Their self-advancement through hierarchy is the essence of domination. Bakunin wanted judgement and consent to replace command and obedience. Fixed, universal and constant authority should give way to the 'continual exchange of mutual, temporary, and, above all, voluntary authority and subordination'.[30] For Tolstoy the rejection of hierarchy meant tapping into truth to resist ways of living that sustain mastership: refusing to serve mammon, refusing to exploit privilege. In both instances, non-domination flows from disobedience and it empowers individuals to do only what they think is right and resist what they know to be wrong.

Domination and conquest: Élisée Reclus and Voltairine de Cleyre

In conventional politics, conquest refers to the subjugation of one group of people in war. In just-war theory it legitimizes the exercise of what John Locke termed the most 'despotical power' over warmongers. So when Africans were deemed to have placed themselves in a state of war with the Royal Africa Company in the seventeenth century, it seemed right to Locke that their captors were permitted to sell their captives to American plantation owners.[31] In anarchist politics, by contrast, conquest describes the institutional and social processes that cement domination and it always involves enslavement and usually killing, too. Violence is integral to conquest, but other processes – homogenization, monopolization, centralization, nationalization and internationalization – also play a role. Domination can proceed seemingly without violence, though not without the power advantages that the capability to exercise it involves.

In thinking about conquest, anarchists often collapse the distinction between government by consent and government by usurpation. That is not to say that anarchists are insensitive to the relative harms and benefits of different types of regime. As Kropotkin noted, Parisian authorities did not enjoy the same power that governors in Odessa had to publically flog men and women. In France the Revolution had established citizenship rights and rulers were forced to respect them.[32] The anarchist argument about conquest turns instead on the processes of state formation, not the limitations that extend from the legitimating stories – such as Rousseau's – that governors spin. In this respect, Bakunin's recommendation that philosophers give up theorizing experience and start using experience to theorize was an important spur for anarchists to examine the factors explaining the rise of modern states.

Scepticism about the explanatory gap between history and political theory is not distinctively anarchist. The twentieth-century philosopher Simone Weil did not express any anarchist sympathies when she observed that the 'single and separate . . . territorial aggregate[s] whose various parts recognize the authority of the same State' have come into being in the course of protracted, often bloody histories.[33] Her brief history of France showed how national identity was also constructed through the process of conquest. The French had been made by force, Weil argued, and integration had been achieved by atrocity, not consent. '[T]he kings of France are praised for having assimilated the countries they conquered',[34] but the truth was that they uprooted their inhabitants – exposing them to the most 'dangerous malady' human societies could suffer.[35]

In anarchist politics, doubt about the robustness of the theoretical distinction between consent and usurpation supports a general critique of state-building. The gruesome history of state formation does not reinforce the integrity of the nation (as it does for Weil), but instead emphasizes the contingency of states and the commonality of the factors explaining both the initial consolidation of territorial power and its subsequent deployment to exploit peoples and resources beyond the state's borders. In other words, the gap between consent and usurpation is filled by a concept of colonization. Colonization is experienced by different peoples in very different ways but is integral both to the territorialization of European states and their subsequent appropriation of non-European lands. This argument was made in the nineteenth and early twentieth centuries by the ex-Communard and geographer Élisée Reclus and the feminist writer and educator Voltairine de Cleyre, among others. While Reclus explored the reasons for Europe's hegemony and the destructive power of European civilization, de Cleyre described the impact of colonization on the indigenous peoples living in Mexico.

The hypothesis informing Reclus's spatial history was that global change was driven by movements of ideas and peoples, brought together principally by trade and in war and mediated by the existence of environmental barriers and passageways – mountain ranges, deserts, plains, rivers and natural harbours. Benefiting from a temperate climate and a largely navigable landscape, Europe was an obvious point of convergence. Yet for Reclus Europe had only acquired its hegemonic position relatively recently and the linear stories Europeans told to glorify it were partial and unpersuasive.

The roots of European civilization could, of course, be traced to ancient Greece and Rome, but Reclus observed that the Greeks had not been originators. They had taken their knowledge from Asia Minor, Egypt, Syria and the Chaldeans. Babylon, Memphis, regions of India, Persia and Indonesia all pre-dated Athens as 'world centres' of learning. Europeans had absorbed the wisdom of the East – metallurgy, the domestication of animals, written language, industry, arts, science, metaphysics, religion and mythology – to establish pre-eminence. Historical and geographical luck explained the westward flow of ideas. The communities that thrived in Central Asia, India and Iran, for example, were drawn from populations that remained widely dispersed and relatively isolated; consequently their practices and ideas were also generally localized.

Processes of internationalization – akin to what we now call globalization – and Europeanization, hastened by technological change, in part explained the domination that Europeans exerted. For example, advances in marine engineering and navigational science facilitated global interconnections and enabled the British to settle in Ireland, America, Australia and New Zealand. Critical mass and flexibility also played a part in securing Europe's hegemony. Apart from the fact that English was introduced in all the lands Britain conquered, the plasticity of the language boosted its widespread adoption in Europe and across the world. The replication of European institutions, costumes and manners, apparently 'pushed to absurdity'[36] in Japan, further explained cultural homogenization.

The philosopher and art historian Ananda Coomaraswamy observed similar trends in India. Europeanization not only promoted the worst aspects of European culture, its 'Teutonic and Imperial' civilizing mission and the 'novel and fascinating theory of *laissez-faire*', but in doing so it also smothered the best in Indian traditions, its 'religious philosophy' and 'faith in the application of philosophy to social problems'. And because the modern world 'is not the ancient world of slow communications' the net loss was felt instantly; 'what is done in India or Japan to-day has immediate spiritual and economic results in Europe and America'.[37] Reclus concurred. He too associated the hegemony of Europe with its materialist, acquisitive culture. Europe was the smallest land mass and Europeans constituted about a quarter of the world's population. Nevertheless, Europe possessed more than half the world's wealth.[38] These statistics were telling.

Europeans colonized by extending regimes of private property ownership through war. Reclus admitted that this regime was not total, not even in Europe. At the start of the twentieth century, he observed, there 'is not a single European country in which the traditions of the old communal property have entirely disappeared'.[39] He also believed that resistance had challenged oppression. But the Europeans' drive for private acquisition was still totalizing. There were three reasons. First, the colonizers' thirst for enrichment was unquenchable. Second, the structural inequalities that private ownership cemented fuelled resentments that were easily projected through racism and supremacism. A three-year stay in Louisiana in the early 1850s taught him that chattel slavery was habitually described as a 'cause of progress' willed by 'the doctrines of our holy religion, and the most sacred laws of family and property'.[40] Third, the instability of the social antagonisms that private property instituted necessitated the permanent deployment of armed force. It was for this reason that Reclus described colonization as a generalized condition of war, exemplified by sporadic, increasingly industrialized conflicts. Writing during the 1898 Spanish-American War he argued:

> War is upon us; terrible war with its atrocities and unspeakable stupidity draws near. We hear its distant echo. Each one of us has friends or relations calling themselves heroes because they massacre Matabeles or Malagasys, Dervishes or Dacoits, inhabitants of the Philippine Isles or Cuba, coloured men, whites or blacks.
>
> But danger breaks forth around us, it already presses on us. The Spaniards, our neighbours, and civilised English-speaking men – North Americans rush on one another with cries of hatred, coarse words and deadly weapons. An explosion of hatred and fury precedes the cannon's roar and the bombardment of cities. The American government appeals to Edison's genius, to the science of all inventors in order that they discover new wonders in the art of exterminating their fellow creatures.[41]

Nearly forty years Reclus's junior and radicalized by the injustice of the Haymarket trial, Voltairine de Cleyre presented a critique of colonization that chimed closely with his. Her 1911 analysis was framed by a reflection on the Mexican Revolution. Like Reclus, she identified land ownership as the primary issue at stake in the conflict and she associated different regimes of ownership with alternative cultures. Thus the customs of the indigenous peoples were communistic.

'By them', she explained, 'the woods, the waters, and the lands' are held in common. All were free to take what they needed to build cabins and irrigate crops. 'Tillable lands were allotted by mutual agreement before sowing, and reverted to the tribe after harvesting, for re-allotment. Pasturage, the right to collect fuel, were for all.' These were mutual aid societies: 'Neighbor assisted neighbor to build his cabin, plough his ground, to gather and store his crop.'[42]

Colonization was the imposition of a 'ready-made system of exploitation, imported and foisted upon' the indigenous population 'by which they have been dispossessed of their homes' and 'compelled to become slave-tenants of those who robbed them'.[43] In Mexico, under the Díaz regime (1876–1911), colonization was characterized by a programme of land acquisition that created *haciendas* so vast that they rivalled the acreage of US states. De Cleyre compared the effects of colonization to the Norman Conquest:

> Historians relate with horror the iron deeds of William the Conqueror, who in the eleventh century created the New Forest by laying waste the farms of England, destroying the homes of the people to make room for the deer. But his edicts were mercy compared with the action of the Mexican government toward the Indians. In order to introduce 'progressive civilization' the Díaz régime granted away immense concessions of land, to native and foreign capitalists – chiefly foreign indeed . . . Mostly these concessions were granted to capitalistic combinations, which were to build railroads . . . 'develop' mineral resources, or establish 'modern industries'.[44]

Yet insofar as colonization appealed to the magic of law, it was also reminiscent of the English enclosures or Highland clearances:

> Mankind invents a written sign to aid its intercommunication; and forthwith all manner of miracles are wrought with the sign. Even such a miracle as that of a part of the solid earth passes under the mastery of an impotent sheet of paper; and a distant bit of animated flesh which never even saw the ground, acquires the power to expel hundreds, thousands, of like bits of flesh, though they grew upon that ground as the trees grow, labored it with their hands, and fertilized it with their bones for a thousand years.[45]

A Land Act passed in 1894 was one of the potent instruments used in Mexico to privatize enormous tracts of common land and even occupied lands *to which the occupants could not show a legal title*. The 'hocus-pocus of legality' which completely disregarded 'ancient tribal rights and customs' thus permitted 'the educated and the powerful' to go 'to the courts . . . and put in a claim', ejecting those who had lived there for generations.[46]

The dehumanizing effects of cultural imperialism and the casual racism it produced completed de Cleyre's account of colonization. The lack of 'book-knowledge' shown by the indigenous peoples was reason enough to 'conclude that people are necessarily unintelligent because they are illiterate'.[47] Colonizer logic dictated that there was no advantage in 'putting the weapon of learning in the people's hands'. And having once assumed that the local people were stupid, it was a short step to cast them as resources, to be managed by those who knew best how to maximize productivity. Displacement followed. Just as a park might today be fracked to feed an energy need, the Yaquis of Sonora in the north of Mexico were casually ordered to go en masse to Yucatan, some two and a half thousand miles south as the crow flies, to labour as slaves on disease-ridden hemp plantations. The resistance which colonization provoked finally rendered the colonized obstacles to progress and civilization, justifying their pacification by routine imprisonment and frequent troop deployments. The horror of the violence meted out to local people in the name of development is memorably depicted in B. Traven's 1930s 'Jungle Novels'. De Cleyre's tone is more measured, but she exposes the same flaws in colonizer reasoning: 'Economists . . . will say that these ignorant people, with their primitive institutions and methods, will not develop the agricultural resources of Mexico, and that they must give way before those who will so develop its resources; that such is the law of human development'.[48]

Education

The anarchists' colossal ambition is to combat domination. Anarchism requires individuals to be self-reliant and co-operative, ready to make judgements and listen to others, take initiatives, share the benefits and support others in times of need. Opponents sometimes accuse anarchists of harbouring unrealistic ideas of human goodness because of the critique of domination they advance. Their argument runs like this: anarchy is all very well in principle, but people are actually acquisitive, selfish and uncooperative. Reduced to a belief in human goodness and evaluated against select-ive cultural practices, anarchy is easily made to appear un-realistically utopian.

In fact, anarchists have rarely denied the complexity of human behaviours; Bakunin's rejection of the thesis of human wickedness does not assume that people are 'natural-ly' good. Kropotkin once said that humans divined the most important insights about ethics – that human well-being de-pends on co-operation – from observing the behaviours of non-human species. He did not suggest what non-humans learned in return, except perhaps to steer clear of humans, but the implication was that the quality of human social re-lations depended on the development of co-operative prac-tices. In promoting the principle of mutual aid, Kropotkin sought to counter the conventional view that co-operation required discipline and obedience. Accepting Rousseau's in-sight that individuals are products of their environments, he called for continuing programmes of non-dominating cul-tural change to promote life-enhancing ways of living. This is revolution as de Cleyre understood the term, 'some great and subversive change in the social institutions of a people, whether sexual, religious, political, or economic'.[49] Education is a favourite recipe in this anarchist cookbook.

Anarchists typically understand education as an approach to life, tapping into long-established conventions that em-phasize processes of socialization and moral development as well as learning or knowledge acquisition.[50] Expressing a widely held anarchist view, Lucy Parsons defined education as creation of 'self-thinking individuals'.[51] Working on the other side of the Pacific in late Qing dynasty China, the foremost anarchist organizer Shifu likewise distinguished 'formal education' from 'education in the transformation of quotidian life'.[52] Distancing himself from campaigns his comrades promoted to instruct people about the basics of anarchism, he pushed for an education that demanded understanding of the 'causes of the vileness of society', the abandonment of 'false morality and corrupt systems'. This kind of deep learning required the eradication of 'the clever people' and the disregard of 'the teachings of so-called sages'. Shifu's was a programme of disobedience and anti-government activism intended to restore 'the essential beauty' of 'human morality'.[53] 'We must learn to think differently,' said, in a similar vein, Alexander Berkman, editor of the *Blast*, 'before the revolution can come'. His language was strongly gendered, but the nature of his conception was clear:

We must learn to think differently about government and authority, for as long as we act as we do today, there will be intolerance, persecution, and oppression, even when organised government is abolished. We must learn to respect the humanity of our fellow man, not to invade him or coerce him, to consider his liberty as sacred as our own; to respect his freedom and his personality, to foreswear compulsion in any form: to understand that the cure for the evils of liberty is more liberty, that liberty is the mother of order.

And furthermore we must learn that equality means equal opportunity, that monopoly is the denial of it, and that only brotherhood secures equality. We can learn this only by freeing ourselves from the false idea of capitalism and property, of mine and thine, of the narrow conception of ownership.[54]

For all these anarchists, education meant demystifying power and authority and fostering autonomy. However, it did not mean schooling. Indeed, nineteenth- and early twentieth-century anarchists believed that schools served a crude ideological function. The Chicago anarchist Oscar Neebe remembered that his schooling had been designed to reinforce Church authority. He wrote: 'I was educated in the protestant religion and was taught to hate those who believed in another form or way concerning a God; my religion I was told was the only, the best.'[55] His comrade Adolph Fischer wrote at greater length about the politics of schooling:

It happened during the last year of my school days that our tutor of historical science one day chanced to refer to socialism, which movement was at that time beginning to flourish in Germany, and which he told us meant 'division of property'. I am inclined to believe now that it was a general instruction given by the government to the patriotic pedagogues to periodically describe to their elder pupils socialism as a most horrible thing. It is, as is well known, a customary policy on the part of the respective monarchial governments of the old world to prejudice the undeveloped minds of the youth against everything which is disagreeable to the despots through the medium of the school teachers. For instance, I remember quite distinctly that before the outbreak and during the Franco-German war we were made to believe by our teachers that every Frenchman was at least a scoundrel, if not a criminal. On the other hand, the kings were praised as the representative of God, and obedience and loyalty to them was described as the highest virtues.[56]

Since the nineteenth century anarchists have consistently argued that the possibilities for education have been severely constrained by the institutions and practices that have been adopted ostensibly to advance learning. Anarchists have offered various explanations for this divergence. They have also responded differently to the challenges that schooling and education pose for anarchist cultural change. Yet while some anarchists have argued that socialization sits as uneasily as schooling with principles of self-mastery, these discussions and debates point to a critical anarchist model of education.

Scholasticism, schooling and socialization

There is a long history of anarchist opposition to the hierarchy of knowledge and to compulsory schooling. Writing in the 1840s when the influential Prussian school system was still in its infancy, Max Stirner summarized the problem of elitism and mass education by highlighting a historical shift from humanism to realism. Humanism was associated with Reformation thought and realism was a term Stirner adopted to describe the spirit of the post-revolutionary period. In humanism education was animated by 'subjection': the mastery of adults over children, the rulers over the ruled and the powerful over the powerless. It was a *'means to power'*. It 'raised him who possessed it over the weak, who lacked it, and the educated man counted in his circle . . . as the mighty, the powerful, the imposing one, for he was an *authority*'.

Stirner summed up the idea wrought by realism as 'everyone is *his own master*'. The Revolution 'broke through the master-servant economy' and destroyed the principles of power and exclusivity in humanism. It was as a consequence of this shift that 'the task of finding true universal education now presented itself'.[57] Stirner argued that the state had played the lead role in this process of change and that it had reached a hiatus such that humanist and realist systems worked in tandem and neither prevailed. With the impetus of the state, education had been realized universally, but the influence of the old principles was undiminished.

The general critique of education that Stirner's argument supports is that the conflict between the elitist advancement of learning and the egalitarian impulse for universal education results in the ruin of education and the maintenance of knowledge hierarchies. The effort to inculcate excellence universally on the scholastic model results in the spread of mere instruction to support social conservatism. Learners are induced to learn what is regarded to be valuable or useful and denied the latitude that elites traditionally enjoyed to engage creatively with the full range of social and cultural influences they encounter. This move towards instruction is exacerbated by government control of schools. This was the complaint that the Haymarket anarchists had made of their own education and it was echoed by Kropotkin and Tolstoy in the 1880s when a series of school reforms paved the way to aggressive Russification: the promotion of Russian Orthodoxy and the Russian language. Mass education was used to counter the spread of revolutionary doctrines and in the process it became a colonizing, repressive instrument.

Since the nineteenth century, anarchists have argued that state regulation of education enables governments to mould or set curricula, select and enforce languages of instruction, reinforce patriarchy through gendered training programmes and build allegiance to manufactured national cultures. Equality of access to schools and the crumbling of education into instruction reconstruct the master-servant relationship and cultures of domination. Moreover, elitism is maintained even though scholasticism has been replaced by meritocracy. Indeed, the normalization of elitist values can be gauged by the embrace of meritocracy as a principle of national education in the era of mass instruction.[58]

Tracing the rejection of compulsory schooling to Godwin, Colin Ward, one of the most influential anarchists of the twentieth century, modelled his concept of anarchist education on three principles: the rejection of state education, the ditching of classroom learning and the rebalancing of education towards practical skills and away from book-learning.[59] Inspired by the private schools which working people had established in parts of the UK to educate their children before they were forced to send them to state institutions, Ward disputed the necessity and value of state education. The existence of these schools gave the lie to the claim that state provision met a need that could not otherwise be satisfied. Moreover, in stark contrast to their elite counterparts, these private schools were flexible to children's needs, typically less disciplinarian than state schools and run locally under the control of the parents. Ward's argument was that the state spoiled these grass-roots institutions when it soaked them up.

Ward disputed the value of classroom learning because

he believed that it prioritized instruction over flourishing. Children were institutionalized through the experience of schooling but not stimulated by the instruction it provided. His view was that children should not be removed from society (placed in what Kropotkin called 'small prisons for little ones'),[60] but that they should instead be encouraged to engage with and learn about the world around them. Factories, farms, urban environments were all potential places for learning, he argued.

The third pillar of Ward's educational programme, the rebalancing of education away from book-learning, reflected his view that schooling was geared too narrowly to the cultivation of academic success. As a self-taught social theorist, Ward did not set his face against academic learning, but he was highly critical of the concept of the school as a filtering system. His view of state education was that it was designed to identify those children best able to master particular sets of skills. All children were expected to follow the same programmes of instruction, irrespective of their proclivities and those who failed to demonstrate the acquisition of the skills state education prized were also devalued. Taking his lead from the eighteenth-century socialist Charles Fourier and a host of anarchist educators, Ward recommended the adoption of a practice-based approach that enabled children to follow their creative bents *by doing*. Why learn about music when you can listen to musicians or even play? Why study nutrition when you can cook and eat?

Herbert Read and Paul Goodman, both Ward's contemporaries, sharpened this critique by revisiting the sociological changes that Stirner had contemplated in the 1840s. A lot had changed in the intervening period and neither Read nor Goodman believed that the revolutionary changes promised by Stirner's realist revolution had been achieved. Writing in the late 1940s, Read argued that modern schooling had been turned into 'an acquisitive process, directed to *vocation*'. In the seventy-year period following the introduction of elementary schooling in Britain, education had been entirely disconnected from the idea of individual flourishing. Humanism had all but disappeared. Leonard Ayres, the American educator and educationalist, promoted the kind of institutional approach that caused Read to despair. Contemplating the wisdom of introducing military drill into US high schools in 1917, Ayres observed:

> There are three questions that are always in order when it is proposed to establish a new course in the public schools to train workers for a definite trade or vocation. The first is: 'What knowledge and skill required in the trade can the school give?' The second is: 'What will the new course cost in time and money?' The third question is: 'What can we learn about such courses from the experience of localities where they have been in operation?' These three questions are always relevant, whether the new course is for boys or for girls and whether it is designed to reach all of the pupils or only those who choose to enter it.[61]

Like Ward, Read was worried about the management of schools and the adequacy of the means adopted to educate learners – how far education had become geared to instruction and book-learning, for example. But in his view, these arguments were symptomatic of a broader failure, which he called the 'failure to specify clearly enough' the aims of education. Returning to the moral and behavioural aspects of education, Read considered that the discussion of aims had been obscured by arguments about delivery of teaching. His comments were not directed at Ward specifically, but they had some relevance to his position. Ward believed that removing children from the 'ghetto of childhood' and 'sharing interests and activities with those of the adult world' was a 'step toward a more habitable environment for our fellow citizens, young or old'.[62] Read's worry was that the adoption of innovative teaching methods would not prevent children being socialized into worlds that were structured by values inimical to non-dominating cultures, even if they attended schools that were not run by the state.

For Read, schooling was fundamentally rigged to the 'competitive system' and designed to deliver 'efficiency, progress, success'. As an art historian who associated education with creativity, growth and self-fulfilment, Read judged these impoverished goals. He noted, too, that unpacking their meaning was 'necessarily excluded' from education debates.[63] Not only, then, was government able to determine the cultural values that education met, it was also empowered to remove debates about cultural purpose from public agendas. This form of agenda setting explained why subsequent generations of children were variously required to recite articles of faith, learn military discipline and meet the needs of business to advance national power globally.

Goodman further pressed Read's arguments. Noted for mixing self with sociological analysis, Goodman wrote about his sense of anomie from the vacuity of American consumerism and suburban living and the effects of corporate advancement, rationalization, affluence and bureaucratic welfare systems in post-war America. These were almost entirely detrimental and he used the term 'the empty society' to describe the prevailing culture. Some of the most obvious symptoms of the 'empty society' were middle-class withdrawal into the suburbs, the urban ghettoization of poor and Black American populations, the growth of public media and the concomitant depletion of intelligent news reporting, social breakdown and delinquency. America, he argued in 1966, was 'on a course' heading towards 'empty and immoral empire or to exhaustion and fascism'.[64]

These seismic sociological shifts were played out in education. Like Read, Goodman argued that modern education was designed to meet government agendas. But insofar as these were shaped by competitive advantage and global market success, he also argued that the usefulness of educating the general population had been comprehensively outstripped by economic realities. Only a 'few percent with elaborate academic training' were required to sustain bureaucratic systems, yet 'all the young are subjected to twelve years of schooling and over 40% go to college'.[65] Most of this time was wasted for reasons that Ward elaborated; American schooling was compulsory miseducation.[66] Goodman further linked the pointlessness of classroom activity to the smooth operation of 'the profit system', whose continued health pointedly exposed the miscalculations of Marxist imaginings. Indeed the rudeness of capitalism's health was inversely related to the physical and psychological sickness of the individuals captured within it. The profit system locked people into mindless, paralysing relationships of dependency: the poorest earned just enough money to buy the endless streams of throwaway goods that better-off technicians, trained to 'execute a detail of a program handed down', were tasked with producing.[67] Everyone submitted to this 'inhuman routine' from 'fear and helplessness' and because powerlessness afforded a sufficient, albeit thin veneer of security. Considerations of 'special vocation, profession, functional independence, way of life, way of being in the community, or corporate responsibility for the public good' could be set aside for as long as individual activity 'pays off in the common coin'.[68] Schooling, like work, was essentially designed to prepare learners to become cogs in this cultural machine. Teachers had become 'personnel in a school system, rather than contributing to the growing up of the young'.[69] And education served to hold the young 'on ice': keep them busy before they entered the world of work and give them the illusion of belonging.

Goodman diverged from Read when he suggested that the cultural values of the Prussianized American school system – efficiency, progress and success – were not faulty in themselves. The problem was in their conceptual bias. Efficiency could be tied to human scale as easily as it could be fastened to economies of scale; progress attached to environmental care and community interaction and detached from individual advancement. Likewise, it was possible to measure success by psychological well-being, not wealth or income.

Goodman explained the tendency to default to the least good alternatives and the concealment of the most desirable with reference to the orthodoxy of science. Bizarrely and wrongly presented as a neutral, pure discipline that could be applied to solve any problem, 'science' had been turned into an ideological tool in order to charge appointed experts with the determination of social goods and values. In bureaucratic systems the magical, irrefutable expertise of 'science' was invoked to champion ideas of progress, technological advancement and economic strength. It promoted and sustained a culture that was the very antithesis of anarchy.[70] For anarchy, Goodman argued, 'is grounded in a rather definite social-psychological hypothesis':

> that forceful, graceful, and intelligent behaviour occurs only when there is an uncoerced and direct response to the environment; that in most human affairs, more harm than good results from compulsion, top-down direction, bureaucratic planning, pre-ordained curricula, jails, conscription, States. Sometimes it is necessary to limit freedom, as we keep a child from running across a highway, but this is usually at the expense of force, grace, and learning: and in the long run it is usually wiser to remove the danger and simplify the rules than to hamper the activity.[71]

There are some significant differences between Stirner, Ward, Read and Goodman and these continue to play out in anarchist politics. For example, hitching education to a set of moral norms, as Goodman proposed, has alarmed anarchists wedded to Stirner's egoist position that individuals must always find and define their own. For Stirner, inviting individuals to master practices whose value has already been determined frustrated creative self-development and was a form of social control.[72] Even though a lot of anarchists have leaned towards Goodman and distinguished the norms, practices and ways of living that emerged from co-operative social interactions from the manufactured, imposed norms that sprang from the needs of government, Stirner's critique has also had a strong purchase. Not untypically, the London-based post-war antimilitarist Frederick Lohr adopted a view that owed something to 'social' and 'egoist' ideas. On the one hand, his coupling of 'bourgeois materialism' with the artificial 'conception of economic man' essential to Soviet communism spoke to a vision of technology and social emptiness that chimed with Goodman's view. On the other hand, his critique of socialization had a Stirnerite flavour. 'Man cannot be socialised,' he declared. 'To socialise man is to dehumanise him, to make him a robot, to give him a collective conscience instead of allowing him to develop a personal consciousness.'[73] To resolve the tension Lohr argued that individuals were social beings. Anarchism did not socialize, Lohr argued, because it recognized that 'nature is social'.

Goodman was less equivocal. Anarchism educated and moralized and it did so in order to counter domination. Like Read, he believed that education necessarily moralized because it was part of a social process. The anarchist goal was not to set education against creativity or individual will, as Stirner appeared to do, but to release creativity through education. The question, for them, was how to specify moral values in ways that enable self-mastery through socialization and always remain alert to the possibility of domination.

Anarchists have made a number of practical proposals to tackle knowledge hierarchies. In order to overcome divisions between intellectual and manual workers, nineteenth-century

	Anarchist Education	State Education
Concept	Education as self-mastery and socialization	Education as service and socialization
Management	Community-based education	State-run education
Methods	Practice-based learning	Vocational training
Aims	Learning to be a critical member of the community	Learning to be a productive member of society

Figure 2.1
Anarchist conceptions of socialization shape the framing, delivery and design of education

anarchists promoted what Bakunin called integrated education. The thinking behind this idea was that 'no *class* can rule over the working masses, exploiting them, superior to them because it knows more'.[74] Bakunin's proposal was to ensure all children received an integrated or all-round training which developed manual alongside mental skills to enhance both capabilities. Another anarchist response has been to set up alternative institutions – free skools. Louise Michel was an early advocate and practitioner, but Francisco Ferrer's Modern School, founded in 1901, is probably the best-known historical initiative. The experiment in Barcelona sparked the rise of a movement and in the early twentieth century Ferrer schools sprang up across Europe and in America. Describing himself as a positivist and idealist, Ferrer promoted the teaching of advanced arts and science – from Ibsen to Darwin – in an effort to offset the influence of conservative Catholicism. Replacing 'dogma' with a rational method aimed to stimulate pupils so that they could flourish as individuals while also learning how to contribute 'to the uplifting of the whole community'. Education, Ferrer argued, was not just about 'the training of . . . intelligence', it was also about 'the heart and the will'.[75]

The critical pedagogy advanced by the twentieth-century educator and philosopher Paulo Freire is probably the most powerful influence active on contemporary anarchist thinking about education.[76] While Freire used Marxist humanism as a touchstone for his thinking, anarchists have been inspired by his exploration of the ways that classroom relations replicate and reinforce wider forms of social oppression. For Freire, the teacher-pupil relationship is essentially one of the oppressor and the oppressed. The possibility of delivering transformative programmes of education (such as those that Ferrer imagined) depends both on the abandonment of neutrality and the development of non-oppressive practices. Once learners acknowledge that education moralizes and that it serves a political function they are able, too, to blur the boundaries between instructors and learners. All instructors are learners and all learners possess valuable knowledge and experience. While anarchists have combined the ideas that Freire articulated in various measures, versions of both are typically found in the two major approaches to knowledge acquisition they have experimented with: propaganda and skill-sharing.

Propaganda may seem an odd term for anarchists to adopt to describe a strategy intended to support the development of non-dominating cultures. Indeed, such is the pervasiveness of corporate advertising and the strength of the association of propaganda with the idea of systemic and 'conscious manipulation', that some anarchists avoid the term altogether.[77] However, before the experience of inter-war dictatorship and the explosion of media newspeak, propaganda was readily associated with open debate and political persuasion. Webster's 1913 dictionary defines 'propagandism' as the 'art or practice of propagating tenets or principles; zeal in propagating one's opinion'.[78] This was how anarchists understood propaganda in the early years of the movement. And when contemporary anarchists use the term, this is often how they still understand it.

Propaganda by the deed is by far the most notorious form

of anarchist propagandism but is not an accurate guide to it. Wrongly conflated with assassination and individual acts of terror, propaganda by the deed developed as part of a wider educational strategy that involved writing, leafleting, publishing and visual art as well as symbolic performance and disobedience. In these multiple forms, anarchist propaganda is designed to explain and advance anarchist ideas. It is replete with guidance, proposals and recommendations but is intended to close the gap between the 'enlightened' and the 'unenlightened' and avoid the need for vanguard movements charged with leading the exploited to revolution. The earliest advocates of propaganda by the deed, Errico Malatesta and Carlo Cafiero, exhorted anarchists to adopt the policy precisely because they thought that the demonstration of anarchism through action – 'insurrectional deeds' – would disrupt existing class relations more effectively than written propaganda and therefore bring the public to anarchism under its own steam.[79]

Propagandistic deeds can take multiple forms. For writers like Lawrence Ferlinghetti, expressive writing might be considered in this bracket because it educates both by communicating anarchist ideas and by making forms of cultural expression like poetry, which have traditionally been reserved for elites, available to all. Unlike more traditional forms of written propaganda – manifestos, constitutions, newspapers, flyers and information sheets – creative writing does not function to deliver ideas to passive consumers but to engage people in ways that are themselves transformative. Visual and performance art works in a similar manner, communicating both through content and in form to build and sustain activism. Talking about his art practice, Gord Hill argues that 'propaganda is a vital part of resistance movements'. As propaganda, music, visual art and literary work can inspire, educate and motivate, help build cultures of resistance and maintain their histories.[80]

Malatesta and Cafiero appreciated that propaganda could be used to bamboozle or mislead. They were consequently wary of propagandists who assumed they knew better than their audiences or who sought to extend knowledge without inviting discussion or offering explanation – instruction without understanding. A telltale sign was the use of obscure language, abstract ideas or scholastic methods to impress, befuddle and belittle. A perennial anarchist complaint about party-approved forms of Marxism is that it presents socialism as scientific, encouraging abstruse theory that is difficult to understand and a technical approach to political argument; Marxism politicized science to use it as a tool to beat the bourgeoisie, but in Goodman's terms, it promoted a concept of scientific objectivity or neutrality. The beauty of propaganda by the deed was that it did not rely on the mastery of complex theory. Burning land registry documents or refusing to respect a prohibition on a meeting in order to provoke an aggressive police response effectively taught hard lessons about the flimsiness of private property rights and legal bias and intolerance. Even if these lessons were inspired by heaps of written propaganda and a good amount of anarchist theory, the actions were hands-on, vivid and intelligible. Deeds educated to the extent that they transformed compliance into rebellion, fostering the critical, non-dominating cultures that anarchists championed.

Sensitive to the pitfalls of propaganda that Malatesta and Cafiero identified, anarchists have used a variety of techniques to avoid coaching or coercing opinion through written materials. Godwin used open-ended questions in his writing to invite readers to formulate their own responses to the questions he posed. Some anarchists write anonymously to discourage intellectualism. Others sign to show that they are only speaking for themselves and that all opinions carry equal weight. When it came to written propaganda, Malatesta liked to write dialogues using colloquialisms that the most disadvantaged could readily understand. Tolstoy wrote about mundane incidents and events in ways that made them seem strange. The technique, called defamiliarization, allowed him to draw attention to hierarchy, the normalization of violence in everyday relationships and conformity without telling readers what to think. Anarchists who joined Nestor Makhno's anti-Tsarist, anti-Bolshevik revolutionary insurgent army to fight for anarchism between 1917 and 1922 posted declarations in the areas they occupied permitting all socialists 'to propagate their ideas, theories, views and opinions freely, both orally and in writing'.[81] The thinking behind this right of free speech was that 'no party, political or ideological group, placed above or outside the labouring masses to "govern" or "guide" them ever succeeds in emancipating them'.[82] Activists who subvert media messages – subvertizers – use similar techniques to illuminate systemic, normalized oppression. Posters published under the banner of London's Metropolitan Police which advertise disproportionate stop-and-search and arrest statistics play with authoritative public information messaging. The appropriation of the official stamp is used to provide succinct, instantly comprehensible data of institutionalized racism. Pasted on the sides of bus shelters, the propaganda reaches large numbers of people, leaving them free to ponder the message.

Skill-sharing is about supporting or enabling others either by transferring knowledge or through practice-based learning. Though rarely cited as a model, Kropotkin's 1880 pamphlet *An Appeal to the Young* is an exemplary description of the first type of skill-sharing. It invites newly trained lawyers, doctors, engineers, poets, artists and teachers – professionals of all stripes – to set aside personal career ambitions to benefit the least well off and for the sake of social transformation. In modern activism, the idea is more likely to be referred to as accompaniment, but it similarly refers to the practice of using specialist skills or status to support disadvantaged people. Accompaniment is sometimes linked to protection work, that is, standing with vulnerable groups or un-newsworthy people to prevent state attacks against them. More broadly, it extends to many other types of skill-sharing: disseminating research findings to expose repressive practices, providing translation, contesting phoney science, helping to prevent deportations and advancing or protecting land claims against settler governments and corporate exploitation.

Practice-based learning differs from knowledge-transfer in that the skills are developed principally through reciprocity. Simple online searches will quickly locate accessible and often richly illustrated toolkits explaining consensus decision-making, subvertizing techniques, offering advice about squatting, hands-on training for street medics, bike repair, assisting prisoner support, women's health and conflict resolution; providing information about running co-operatives, consent and the prevention of interpersonal violence. The list is almost endless.

Another difference between these types of skill-sharing is the social division each assumes. Knowledge-transfer is predicated on the existence of privilege, practice-based learning is not, at least not in the same way. Emma Goldman once commented that 'all those who work for their living, whether with hand or brain, all those who must sell their skill, knowledge, experience and ability, are proletarians'.[83] Yet she recognized that intellectual workers had more latitude to decide whether to perpetuate bourgeois traditions or break with them and that, in this regard, they were advantaged. Specialists in practice also possess intellectual skills often derived from relative advantage, but their practical skills are usually derived from experience, not directly from access to elite institutions.

How far the privilege associated with skill-sharing disqualifies it as a tool of anarchist education is a moot point. Disagreement on this issue turns on philosophical questions about the degree to which knowledge generated under conditions of domination can or should be applied or set aside. The view that it could be extended was often advanced by nineteenth-century European anarchists. Bakunin's conception of 'integral' education and Ferrer's Modern School curriculum assumed that it was possible to rescue knowledge from bourgeois culture and put it to good use. Their primary concern was to provide equal access to 'advanced' learning. One of Shifu's aims as an organizer was to ensure that '"the people" would gain control of scientific knowledge and its uses'.[84] Similarly acknowledging the value of high art, Tolstoy devoted considerable time to devising methods of teaching that would enable children to appreciate classical and baroque music and poetry – two of his particular passions – driven by their own curiosity. Adopting particular standards for learning and guiding children towards their appreciation did not diminish the importance of local 'folk' art. There was no trade-off in cultural appreciation. Rather, there were different spheres in which knowledge circulated and anarchist cultures emerged from their interpenetration.

Significant figures in late twentieth-century anarchism have taken a different view. John Zerzan, the anti-civilization activist (sometimes labelled primitivist), argues that bourgeois culture is compromised by its symbolic systems of learning. Knowledge is underpinned by linear, instrumental reasoning and this is manipulative and alienating. Some anarchist feminists active in the 1970s advanced similar critiques to explain patriarchy and experimented with mosaic patterning to generate new ways of thinking. Zerzan's critique reprises Goodman's theme of the empty society, connecting the vacuity of modernity with an approach to knowledge that presents the world as an object of study. Yet he draws different conclusions. Zerzan's view is that what passes as knowledge mistakenly detaches humans from nature and results in domination. The view that humans – or at least some humans – can 'know' the world results not only in the construction of human hierarchies of knowledge but also in the uniform domination of non-human life.

The argument has two prongs. First, Zerzan presents an

analysis of colonization that suggests that the spread of western doctrines has repressed the innovative, sensual and non-symbolic practices that root knowledge in ecology. In contrast to Reclus, who argued that Europeanization threatened to wipe out the philosophical and religious traditions that had nurtured it, Zerzan argues that that colonization works hand-in-hand with domestication and it acculturates. In his view, the risk of colonization is not that 'the daughter' – Europe – will return to negate the 'mother' – Asia Minor. Instead, culture is itself is a 'false notion'. It entails the promotion of an aggressive human taming of the human and non-human worlds. Zerzan accordingly links privilege to the denial and destruction of approaches to knowledge that, once practised globally, are now preserved by Indigenous peoples. Uniquely, and in the face of genocidal repression, these peoples have managed to avoid or minimize the effects of domestication.

The second strand of Zerzan's critique comes from a rejection of Goodman's qualified defence of 'science'. Distinguishing between the bureaucratic ideology of science and the Aristotelian conception of science 'as an act of wonder', Goodman advanced the view promoted by earlier generations of nineteenth- and early twentieth-century anarchists who not only 'advocated the cause of "science" against tradition, religion and superstition',[85] as Bakunin had done, but also adopted it as a principle on which an anarchist society should operate. Similarly Goodman's conception of science was linked to broad vision of social transformation. Accordingly, he designated 'human ecology' as 'one area of science' that citizens had a duty to learn about. To prevent governments making judgements for individuals, Goodman called on them to mug up on 'physical science, physical and mental hygiene, sociology and political economy, to analyze problems of urbanism, transportation, pollution, degenerative disease, mental disease, pesticides, indiscriminate use of antibiotics and other powerful drugs, and so forth'.[86] For Zerzan, this is a faulty approach. Education cannot come from within hierarchical symbolic systems. It comes, instead, through re-wilding: reconnecting to undomesticated, genuinely ecological and gentler systems of knowing.[87]

Skill-sharing and the cultures of anarchy

While knowledge-transfer and practice-based learning often shade into one another, the philosophies that underpin these two types of skill-sharing point to distinctive cultures of anarchy. Giving one of the fullest accounts of knowledge-transfer as a non-dominating practice, Kropotkin believed not only that the generation and sharing of knowledge could facilitate transnational education but also that the extension of anarchy as a grass-roots practice depended on it. Drawing on the work of the geographer Alexander von Humboldt, he distinguished between local knowledge, or *Heimatkunde*, and global knowledge, or *Erdkunde*, to imagine the construction of transnational knowledge communities. These would function from childhood and throughout adulthood to provide a platform for the development of learning from below. Everyone would find out about their own localities and about the world outside through knowledge exchange. Learning would be advanced through dialogue and the free flow of ideas, the abandonment of copyright, travel and inter-cultural exchanges. Local peoples would be able to shape their own environments by applying knowledge they gained about other localities to their own and sharing insights about practice. The cultural historian Nadine Willems talks about the 'intellectual zones of congruence' and 'fluidity of ideas' that characterized Reclus's interactions with the philosopher Ishikawa Sanshirō, one of the Japanese activists executed in 1911.[88] This is how Kropotkin imagined the generation of global knowledge.

Whereas statist cultures charged intellectuals with the task of deciding what was best for social advancement, anarchist cultures would empower locals to determine how they wanted to live. Indeed, given that Kropotkin believed that language was linked to different ways of knowing, he also thought it possible to develop global knowledge from multiple perspectives, not merely western or European. Tolstoy approached translation in a similar vein – as a dialogue or conversation. As the most translated author in Japan at the turn of the twentieth century, he pushed an approach that challenged 'unequal power relations' and supported 'a transnational exchange conducted on equal grounds'. His view 'implied a non-hierarchical world order beyond the epistemological limits of East-West relations'. Specifically, the 'production of knowledge relied on mutual translations and retranslations as action and reaction, utterance and response, definition and redefinition'. Moral vocabularies 'were negotiated between languages to produce new languages. Translation was thus multidirectional and dialectical, blurring the distinction between "original" and "translated".'[89] For

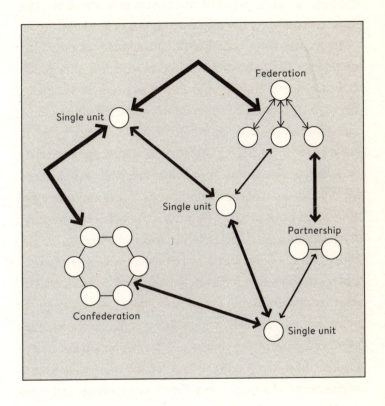

Figure 2.2
The generation of global knowledge (erdkunde, grey surround)
through the exchange and flow of local knowledge (heimatkunde,
white units).

Kropotkin, this quality of exchange constituted 'science'. The 'savants of Western Europe will object,' Kropotkin argued, but authentic scientists recognized that learning involved 'bringing all works of importance, written in any language, to the knowledge of the whole of the scientific world'.[90]

Anarchists less enamoured of knowledge-transfer also imagine the development of anarchist cultures on a global scale. Yet where priority is given to practice-based learning anarchist cultures tend to be linked to the construction of transnational solidarities rather than the development of global knowledge. Non-dominating anarchist culture is fostered through networks, physical and virtual, and through participation in local resistance actions. These are connected by a shared opposition to domination: neoliberal economics and authoritarian government. The geographer and social theorist Simon Springer describes recent waves of emancipatory struggles that locals have organized 'from below' in order to challenge elite rule and capitalist exploitation as profoundly educative. By taking action in public spaces, participants discover 'both *power* and *demos*'. This kind of emancipation 'must accordingly be understood as an awakening, a (re)discovery of power that is deeply rooted in processes of mobilization and transformation'.[91]

The anticipated impact of these two types of skill-sharing is comparable. In both cases the transformative power of education is realized. Kropotkin talked about dissolving class boundaries. The solidarity that knowledge-transfer builds brings hope to the poor, strengthens workers' resistance movements and transforms intellectuals and workers. Dispelling the prejudices that intellectuals harbour about the social inferiority of the workers and the suspicions workers have of socially privileged elites, knowledge-transfer melts the boundaries between 'us' and 'them' and creates a sense of 'we'.[92] Realized on a global scale, it softens the religious and nationalist antagonisms that Churches and states encourage. In a more recent discussion of accompaniment, Staughton Lynd explains that privileged activists 'unselfconsciously offer a service of unquestioned usefulness' to exploited groups and that this involves mutual exchange and learning. The 'journalist, minister, doctor, lawyer, teacher' must 'feel a profound respect for the insights and perspectives of his or her collaborator'. Their relationship is based on the pursuit of a common cause, neither customer service nor uncritical endorsement.[93]

Leaning towards practice-based learning, migrant solidarity activists argue that skill-sharing is about mutuality, not instruction. It is a process of intercultural exchange which fosters an anarchist ethic of mutual aid. The ethics of practice-based learning, like the generation of anarchist science, contributes to the construction of local and global networks through affinity and to movement-building. Anti-Poverty activists in Ontario conduct their work on the basis that 'organisers are a part of the communities in which we organize – primarily as poor people, but also as neighbours and workers'.

We aren't outsiders and we know we are no better than the people we are organising with. We do not think we know best what someone needs but we do acknowledge that we have particular kinds of skills and knowledge that

are an asset. Most of our organisers and members are or
have been on social assistance or low wage workers and we
have an intimate understanding of how the system works
and the impact it has on people. The people who we are
organising with are not our 'clients,' they are people with
whom we are united in struggle.[94]

In both formats, skill-sharing is part of a virtuous circle,
something like [Bakunin's 'continual exchange of mutual,
temporary, and, above all, voluntary authority'. It facilitates
perpetual education to combat domination and advance
anarchist social change over time.

Non-domination: culture and anarchy

In the conclusion to *Nationalism and Culture,* Rudolf Rocker
counterposed anarchy to the state, as if there was a binary
choice between them. Yet his conception of culture as the
study of human interventions in nature and the creation
of social environments presents anarchy as a perpetual response to domination not its negation or alternative. On this
view, social life can be more or less anarchist; social orders
can be more or less law-governed, more or less hierarchical
and more or less colonizing.

Anarchists reject the power advantages that law protects,
the kind of compliance that hierarchy secures and the brutal
exploitation that colonization facilitates, because they contend that the choice between anarchy and domination is
one that dominators insist upon in order to justify the status
quo. The importance attached to education reflects the anarchist view that anarchy and domination are oppositional

THE GOVERNMENT OF NO ONE

forces which operate in relation to each other. Even while anarchists argue that schooling socializes individuals to prevailing social norms, tailoring learning through instruction, they hold on to the idea that education is always potentially transformative. Disentangling social order from the orders into which we are acculturated is a step towards anarchy.

113

CHAPTER 3
Practices

How have anarchists devised their educational projects? How have they tried to spread cultures of non-domination and how does anarchist action relate to anarchy? To respond to these questions, I will look at two big debates – one about organization and violence and the other about class and intersectionality – and then explore the possibilities of anarchy in action.

In the late 2000s, despondency about the emergence of 'protest tourism' in seemingly ill-defined mass actions sparked a call to 'give up activism': anarchists should focus less on the aesthetics of militancy and redirect their attention to effective, targeted actions.[1] While this critique of anti-capitalist social justice campaigning struck a chord with some anarchists, the pejorative use of 'activism' was highly unusual. For activism is rarely linked to specific types of action. Indeed, in a general sense it captures the moral drive that runs through anarchist politics. Anarchists see inaction as compliance. In Lucy Parsons's words: 'Passivity while slavery is stealing over us is a crime.' Describing her own journey to anarchism, she dismissed the idea that 'material barriers' to anarchist changes would 'melt away, or be voted or prayed into nothingness': 'Crumbling they may be with their own weight and the decay of time' but 'to quietly stand under until they fall is to be buried in the crash'.[2] As will become clear, her oblique reference to the 'rocks' that had to be removed coupled with her refusal to say precisely how this should be done has given anarchists plenty to discuss. But the commitment to act – activism – is not one of the topics. As *Reality Now*, a zine that came out of the 1980s Ottawa punk scene put it: 'There are many ways to struggle against fascist control . . . and there is not only one way in which we will overcome fascism.' But 'if we don't struggle for change, for balance (each in our own ways), then the choices we are left with are personal betrayal or death'.[3]

Two dramatic moments in nineteenth- and twentieth-century history deeply influenced anarchist ideas about activism and violence. The first was the wave of killings and high-profile assassinations perpetrated in Europe between the assassination of Tsar Alexander II in 1881 and that of Archduke Franz Ferdinand in 1914. These events have become milestones for the period of 'propaganda by the deed'. The second was the outbreak of the First World War and the Bolshevik takeover during the Russian Revolution. State reactions to propaganda by the deed prompted anarchists to reflect on the effectiveness of their activism, while the war and revolution led them to reassess the legitimacy of violence.

A short history of anarchist activism and violence

Critics on both left and right of the political spectrum, as distant from each other as Lenin as was from Michael Schaack, shared the view that propaganda by the deed described a strategic commitment to terrorism. In fact, the presumed meaning of the initiative that Malatesta and Cafiero articulated in the 1870s emerged from a series of unrelated acts, none of them committed by anarchists. Attempts on the life of the German Kaiser in 1878 and the kings of Spain and Italy shortly after the term was coined established the flimsy, preliminary link to political violence.

The 1881 International London Anarchist Congress solidified the association between propaganda by the deed and political violence. Activists from across Europe and the Americas gathered to discuss revolutionary action. There were nuanced arguments about tailoring activism to local contexts, adopting mixed methods and rooting revolutionary action in ethical principles. But these were smothered by mainstream press reports of a resolution to advance anarchy through the study of chemistry and the embrace of modern technologies. The reports fostered a dark, conspiratorial image of anarchy conveniently ignoring the reasons anarchists gave for advocating physical force in some contexts.

For some, including Albert Parsons, the justification was straightforward: anarchists were at war with a tyrannous state and must organize to protect themselves. Another defence of physical force came from those eager to capitalize on the outrage that the early spate of assassination attempts had provoked. John Most, author of the cult classic *The Science of Revolutionary Warfare* and principal author of the 1883 Pittsburgh Manifesto, perfectly embodied this stance. As well as providing some not-so-reliable advice on bomb-making, poisons and other paraphernalia, Most invoked the idea of propagandistic deeds to issue chilling calls for anti-bourgeois violence. In 1881 he paid the price when he was imprisoned for publishing an article applauding the Tsar's assassination. Commenting on the moral panic anarchism stirred and the resulting anti-anarchist repression, David Nicoll gave his version of this thesis. There was a hint of vengeance in his defence. Referring to the garrotting of four anarchists in Jerez in 1892 and the police shooting of nine workers at an eight-hour day demonstration in 1891 he wrote:

> The Anarchists are 'criminals', 'vermin', 'gallows carrion'. Well, shower hard names upon us. Hunt us down like mad dogs. Strangle us, as you have done our comrades at Xeres! Shoot us down, as you did the strikers at Fourmiers, and then be surprised if your houses are shattered with dynamite, and if people shrink from officials of the law as dangerous company. 'Justice' has been done! Has it, gentlemen of the middle-classes? Justice?[4]

The able assistance anarchists received from agent provocateurs, the scandal-mongering press and, in France and Germany, the police themselves, helped establish a distinctively anarchist 'propaganda by the deed'. By the time anarchist assassinations reached a peak in France in the early 1890s and in Spain in 1904–5, propaganda by the deed was a synonym for anarchism and terrorism. High-profile killings included the assassinations of the French President Carnot (1894), Empress Elizabeth of Austria (1898) and US President McKinley (1901). Some anarchists also targeted civilians. Émile Henry, one of the most notorious anarchist propagandists and the son of the Communard Fortuné Henry, reasoned that inaction in the face of obvious injustice made everyone complicit in it. His claim, 'there are no innocents' could be seen as a foretaste of Martin Luther King's 'there comes a time when silence is betrayal', even though his actions were of course entirely contrary: Henry bombed public spaces, notoriously the Parisian Café Terminus near Gare Saint-Lazare.

Some anarchists considered assassination as an integral part of revolutionary struggle, particularly where rulers cultivated godly status and brooked no opposition. Uchiyama Gudō, one of the activists involved in the 1910 plot to kill Emperor Meiji, thought that the Emperor's dispatch would expose the myth of imperial power. The Emperor was a divine symbol of state. As part of a wider revolutionary action, his killing was a 'symbolic act of blood-letting', and a perfect act of propaganda in this sense.[5] Louise Michel argued similarly that tyrannicide was *practical* when tyranny 'has a single head, or at most a small number' and that it was better to 'risk only one person' than send a 'beloved crowd to another slaughter'.[6] However, the predominant European nineteenth-century anarchist view was that the assassinations and bombings of the 1890s were part of a state-led cycle of violence and usually an expression of frustration and despair.

In answer to her question 'Is homicidal outrage the local outcome of anarchist convictions?' Charlotte Wilson gave a firm 'No'.[7] She explained anarchist violence as the result of the brutalizing effects of capitalism and the state and a predictable response to anti-anarchist clamp-downs. Wilson avoided Nicoll's dark mutterings. Yet she agreed that widely circulated reports of the treatment meted out to anarchists held at the fortress of Monjuich in Barcelona in 1892 rivalled the Commune as a touchstone for violence. Testimony detailing the use of sleep deprivation, beatings, denailing and testicle-compression 'by means of a guitar string' were singled out as drivers for revenge attacks.[8] Anarchists did not have to search long to find other examples. The Japanese activists mis-tried for plotting against Emperor Meiji were sentenced to death merely for contemplating his injury. Their espousal of 'alien' anarchist ideas was enough to convict them. There was no hard evidence against Kotoko Shusui, the leading exponent of anarchist communism in Japan at the time, but he, too, was hanged and his execution was widely reported in Europe. Faced with these examples, some anarchists presented belligerent defences of anarchist propagandists. Charles Malato's discussion of President Carnot's assassin, Sante Geronimo Caserio, threw republican arguments back at the bourgeoisie who condemned his murderous act as inexcusable. 'Learned proffessors [sic], you teach your pupils to admire the grand classical tyrannicides, Harmodius, Aristogiton [sic], Brutus. Why do you not teach them to admire Caserio?'[9]

Anarchists disagreed privately about assassination. Yet in contrast to Lenin or Schaack, they did not see violence as an ideological response to domination. Indeed, the irony of the anti-anarchist critiques by Lenin, Schaack and others was that the killings which gave propaganda by the deed its meaning actually initiated a debate about activism. The incidence of violence and the negative public reactions it generated towards anarchists focused anarchist attention on their principles: how well was anarchist education advanced through violence? To what degree did any form of activism render anarchists vulnerable to state repression? In the course of the late nineteenth and early twentieth centuries, anarchist responses resulted in two major splits in the movement. The first separated organizationalists from anti-organizationalists and the second evolutionists from revolutionists.

The organizational debate

How far should anarchists seek to press their activism by forging links with mass movements – particularly labour movements? This question raised two concerns. Some worried that it wedded anarchism to forms of self-defeating action. Others thought that anarchists would be unable to sustain organizations which could withstand domination. The ensuing debate divided anarchists into organizationalists and individualists. Later, in response to changes in movement politics, organizationalists further subdivided into anarchist-syndicalist and platformist groups.

The primary distinction between organizationalists and individualists came to the fore in French and Italian movements, but it went far beyond them to the exiled communities in Britain, North America and Egypt. It was centrally concerned with the question of how violence and illegalism could be justified. Errico Malatesta, a vocal organizationalist, mapped anti-organizationalism on to a type of philosophical individualism which constructed individuals as free abstract beings. This was a bourgeois idea and Malatesta's worry was that it kindled a desire to show a disdain for social norms by the flouting of all moral rules. Thus it was devoid of the idea of 'neighbourliness' that Engländer coupled with egoism to promote the exercise of individual judgement in community. Supporting Malatesta's view, Kropotkin described individualism as the brainwave of the 'poets of the upper classes like Stirner and Nietzsche'; although it was given fine 'refined literary' expression, this kind of individualism centred on brute self-assertion and the refusal to acknowledge any prohibitions on action.

For Kropotkin and other organizationalists, Nietzschean and Stirnerite individualism led to degraded, unethical forms of activism: it encouraged amoralism which might appear to be creative to artistic types but in reality was unoriginal; it made actions predictable in a way that individually judged, ethical acts of revolt were not. An act of '*revolt* against a hated force', Kropotkin noted, was necessarily shaped by the convictions of each activist. Turning to the Gospel account of Christ's arrest to illustrate the point, he noted that revolt had led 'Peter to cut off the ear of a Roman (so the popular legend says) and . . . another to stand by and weep'.[10] But individualism, he argued, always resulted in the most spectacular illegality. It was gestural rather than genuinely revolutionary.

In 1912 the distinction between the organizationalist and individualist position became crucial to Malatesta's fight against deportation from the UK. Kropotkin wrote to the press to clarify it. He explained that unlike the 'men in the Labour revolt who repeat in another form the conclusions about the right to the individual to revolt against society', Malatesta had 'persistently directed his efforts towards showing to such rebels that society could never be reorganized in the interests of justice and equity if the negative principles they profess took the upper hand'.[11]

Anti-organizationalists like Luigi Parmeggiani had two responses. The first was a practical rejoinder: illegalism, in the form of expropriation, helped sustain anarchist activism; bank raids provided much needed funds to underwrite publishing and so forth. The second was the argument that any effort to legislate on permissible actions was inherently dominating. Even if some of the booty captured in the course of anarchist raids ended up in the hands of individual anarchists and never found its way into propaganda activities, anti-organizationalists still held that organizationalists were wrong to try to constrain individual will or control the impulse to revolt: bourgeois moral codes had to be destroyed, not just reshaped. From this perspective, Kropotkin's conflation of anti-organizationalist individualism with amoralism was wide of the mark. While some anti-organizationalists did indeed understand illegalism as an expression of liberation, not all individualists equated illegalism with violence. For example, Émile Armand, a noted advocate of free love and Stirnerite individualist was an amoralist in Malatesta and Kropotkin's terms. Yet he renounced violence. Indeed, some anti-organizationalist individualists differed little from Kropotkin and struggled to distinguish their expressions of freedom from Kropotkin's idea of revolt.

With the emergence of new labour unions in the late 1880s, the organizational debate took a new turn. As mass anarchist movements mushroomed across Europe, Central and Latin America and the Far East, a well-defined anarchist-syndicalist group emerged. Rudolf Rocker, a long-time labour organizer, helped spearhead the new movement. He took some of his inspiration from Bakunin, who, he rightly noted, had called on anarchists to build federations capable of teaching theory through practice and realizing workers' emancipation through practical action in the 1870s.[12] Syndicalism, Rocker argued, was an evolution of anarchism. Not only did it advance First Internationalist principles, it was a perfect vehicle to extend anarchist education through labour activism: it would build solidarity and could combat domination through the construction of federated unions equipped to run the economy independently of the bosses.

Some organizationalists were less enthusiastic about the syndicalist turn. Malatesta and Kropotkin believed that the independence of the unions should be respected and preserved; anarchists should work with labour organizations without compromising anarchist or worker autonomy. This meant that while anarchists should continue to undertake insurrectionary actions and encourage workers to organize mass resistance through sabotage and strike, they should not seek to take a direct role in establishing mass anarchist organizations.

The final twist in the organizational debate came in the Ukraine during the Russian Civil War where Nestor Makhno's insurgent militia army waged an anarchist campaign against white and red counter-revolutionary forces until 1922. In the course of the fighting Makhno argued that success depended on the adoption of strong organizational structures. Critics argued that the changes he introduced compromised principles of voluntary enlistment, freely accepted discipline and the egalitarianism of the militia's command structures. Yet when the militia was eventually overwhelmed by the Red Army, Makhno went into exile and the Makhnovists formalized his ideas in the Organizational Platform. The Platform, as it became known, wedded anarchism to class struggle, revolution, unity of theory and tactics and federalism. It oriented activism to rural and urban movement-building and libertarian education. Strongly anti-individualist in tone, it demanded collective responsibility and condemned the 'practice of operating on one's individual responsibility'.[13]

Evolutionists and revolutionists

In parallel to the divide between organizationalists and anti-organizationalists there was another division which complicated discussion – between evolutionists and revolutionists. To clarify the often turbulent debate we need to remember that there was no strict dichotomy between evolution and revolution. The argument was really about how or where violence should fit in processes of change.

The evolutionists considered their ideas revolutionary but followed Proudhon in advocating gradual, non-violent transformation. They rejected violence, particularly armed struggle, in favour of incremental change. They equated revolution with the violent overthrow of existing authority and they feared that this would result in the transfer of power to new elites. This was unacceptable. Instead, evolutionists argued, anarchist action should be driven by the constant activism of autonomous groups and individuals.

Revolutionists also understood anarchist transformation as a gradual, incremental process, but, unlike the evolutionists, they added that evolution involved periods of sudden, rapid transformation and that these might well be violent or cataclysmic. This model of punctuated evolution was articulated by Kropotkin and Élisée Reclus. Like the evolutionists, they rejected the French-Jacobin model of revolution but at the same time they anticipated that capitalists would use every means at their disposal to defend their advantages. Similarly, the twentieth-century syndicalist Tom Brown argued it was simply naive to imagine that revolutionary goals could be accomplished 'without arousing the fiercest opposition and the most bitter hatred of the employing class'.[14] Anarchist revolution was not therefore directed at the conquest of political power, but it necessarily involved preparing for state violence: anarchists would need to find ways of withstanding intense reactionary aggression and of sustaining their revolutionary forces during periods of fighting. The killing-spree that had followed the Commune was understood as a grim warning.

The overall effect of the evolutionist-revolutionist debate was to harden the sectarian divide between communists and individualists which had started to form with the organizationalist/anti-organizationalist debate. It also reinforced the centrality of the question of violence. Many anarchists who identified as individualists (for example, Benjamin Tucker, Henry Seymour and John Henry Mackay) were leading evolutionists. Highly suspicious of anarchist communism, Mackay called for social disaggregation and increasing individual independence in order to advance anarchy. The solution to the 'social question' was to 'no longer keep one's self in mutual dependence', but to 'open up for one's self and thereby for others the way to independence; no longer to make the ridiculous claim of the strong "Become weak!"; no longer to trust in the help "from above", but at last to rely on one's own exertions'.[15] Activism was individual, not organizational on this view.

Yet to the extent that the revolution-evolution debate pinpointed a gulf between communists committed to violent revolution and individualists wedded to non-violent change, it was misleading. For example, James Guillaume, a leading anti-authoritarian in the First International who advocated the construction of decentralized federations, also called for the adoption of non-violent evolutionary strategies. This involved building mass anarchist movements from the local to the international. The individualist-communist division also concealed flaws involved in the mapping of organizationalism to revolutionism. Firstly, it blurred the boundaries between organizationalists like Malatesta and Kropotkin, on the one hand, who encouraged insurrectionary acts for as long as they were tailored to collective emancipation, and, on the other, syndicalists and platformists who were not keen on insurrectionary activism. Secondly, it downplayed the revolutionary aspirations of individualists like Parmeggiani, who believed that individual acts of revolt were inherently anarchist, whether or not they were tailored to collective emancipation. The opposition was thus simplistic because it obscured at least four alternative activist positions and a range of possible subdivisions within anarchist movements.

These debates about organization and violence were renewed after 1914 in the wake of the division of the anarchist movement; they entered a new phase after 1917 after the Bolshevik seizure of power when anarchism became marginal as an intellectual currency in the international socialist movement. The 1914 split was triggered when Kropotkin called on comrades to back the French and British mobilization against Germany and the Austro-Hungarian Empire.

Figure 3.1

Commitments to revolutionary and evolutionary principles complicate anarchist organizationalist and anti-organizationalist distinctions

It ripped the anarchist movement apart: a majority, which was fiercely opposed to war, returned to first principles – the idea of workers' self-emancipation – and in the new context of militarism and war reaffirmed its revolutionary commitment to destroy capitalism. The success of the Bolshevik coup prompted further reflections on anarchist activism, focusing particular attention on its relationship to violence. Two broad positions emerged from the war and revolution debates. The first detached emancipatory struggle and educational change from violence, the second found the link between activism and violence in the rejection of class dictatorship, whether bourgeois or proletarian (as represented by the Bolsheviks), rather than in non-violence or pacifism.

Non-violent activism was spurred on by the growth of syndicalism at the end of the nineteenth century. Ferdinand Domela Nieuwenhuis was one of several who linked militarism to nationalism and antimilitarism to internationalism and espoused anarchist-syndicalist methods to combat militarism. A one-time comrade of Kropotkin, he thought Kropotkin's response to the war had been chauvinistic. Nieuwenhuis's rejection of violence, informed by an analysis of capitalist state competition, led him to call for the refusal of military service and a general strike: only this could prevent the descent into mass slaughter. Though Nieuwenhuis's efforts failed, anarchist non-violence continued to be aligned with anti-war activism and antimilitarism after his death in 1919. Picking up Nieuwenhuis's baton, Bart de Ligt gave antimilitarism a stricter Tolstoyan commitment to non-violence. He recommended mass activism and the use of confrontational, non-violent methods to fight militarism. De Ligt's highly influential book *The Conquest of Violence* helped change the tenor of evolutionary anarchism by forging it into collective, militant resistance politics.

The alternative position to De Ligt was a restatement of the anarchists' long-held rejection of all government as a form of violence. Both the Bolshevik takeover and rise of fascism were seen as making the linkage between the state and dictatorship clearer than ever. As Rocker argued, dictatorship is 'a definite form of state power; the state in a state of siege'. Like all advocates of the state idea, 'advocates of dictatorship proceed from the assumption that any alleged advance and every temporal necessity must be forced upon the people from above'.[16] Lenin's idea of the vanguard party strengthened the critique. Two key figures, Emma Goldman and Alexander Berkman, had first been 'dazzled' by the 'glitter of Bolshevism' when they arrived in Russia in 1919, as Goldman later recalled.[17] But one year later they left Lenin's Russia convinced that little separated Bolshevism from the monopolistic, elite forms of representation championed by the bourgeoisie; the anarchist 'social revolution' should be the antithesis of these forms of organizational violence. It was based, Berkman wrote, 'on entirely different principles, on a new conception and attitude'.[18]

A decade later, in Spain, Goldman clarified the difference between the anarchist and Bolshevik position; the character of the social revolution did not turn, as some antimilitarists argued, on the question of armed resistance. 'Passive resistance is all right for some people,' she wrote, 'but I cannot see for the life of me how it would work in the face of armed resistance.[19] Instead anarchists should organize for social revolution through propaganda and education. The anarchist defeat in Russia was thus explained as an organizational failure. The 'unorganized' Russian anarchists had been just a 'handful of refugees from other lands and exiles from prisons'. The Spanish, by contrast, 'had perfected a remarkable organization'. Overcoming 'all persecution, prison, torture', they had persisted in their propaganda and, for a quarter of a century, persistently talked 'about the importance of . . . Libertarian Communism'. Even though the international powers – France, Britain, Germany, Italy and Soviet Russia – connived to defeat the Spanish Revolution, these educational efforts had paid off for the anarchist political ideal had become the 'flesh of the Spanish militant workers and blood of their blood'.[20]

Since 1945 non-violent antimilitarism and anti-dictatorial violence have converged to form the backdrop for activism. The arrival of the nuclear age, the onset of the Cold War, the grip of the consumer cultures that Goodman and others abhorred and the appearance of communitarian countercultural movements in the 1960s, together with a wave of urban guerrilla groups in the 1970s, are some of the factors behind this. The arms race advertised the nature of the monopoly of nuclear violence concentrated in the superpowers' hands and provided a fillip to non-violent antimilitarist activism. At the same time what Herbert Marcuse called the one-dimensionality of late capitalism raised questions about the effects of domination – repression, alienation, isolation, obedience and restraint – and the quality of personal relationships fostered by hierarchy and exploitation. Armed struggle seemed irrelevant in this analysis.

The emergence of urban guerrilla movements prompted a new debate about political violence. One of the central arguments of the widely circulated pamphlet *You Can't Blow Up a Social Relationship* was that urban guerrillaism replicates the relationships of domination in the state. It was 'vanguardist and authoritarian'.[21] This critique was applied equally to the London-based Angry Brigade and the Vancouver Squamish Five, both of which were squarely located within anarchist milieu, as well as the Red Army Faction, notorious in West Germany, which was not. Echoing some of Goldman's themes, but tying illegality to armed struggle in a manner she would not have recognized, the pamphlet's authors argued:

> It is fractured thinking to identify the essence of revolution as illegality or as armed confrontation with the repressive instruments of the state. This totally obscures the essence of our objection to this society which is not simply a disgust with state violence . . . The essence of revolution is not armed confrontation with the state but the nature of the movements which back it up, and this will depend on the kinds of relationships and ideas amongst people in the groups, community councils, workers councils, etc. that emerge in the social conflict.[22]

Anarchists still argue about violence. Indeed a number of leading anarchist academics have argued that the turn to non-violence has tended to reinforce the tendency to evaluate activist actions through the lens of violence. As the political scientist Francis Dupuis-Déri notes, the 'violence versus non-violence debate is a perennial source of tension in progressive and radical circles, where the ethics of using force are of greater concern than they apparently are for the political elites, including liberals'.[23] One example of this is the debate about the 'black bloc' – the protest tactic associated with police confrontation. Another is tactical diversity. The researcher Anna Feigenbaum talks against the grain of the 'need for resistant tactics to be specific, situational and flexible enough to adapt to different people's realities and capabilities'. Tactical diversity, resonant with the fluidity of historical anarchist activism, encourages activists to ask whether a proposed action is 'effective at generating power' rather than ask whether it is 'peaceful or violent'.[24] In 1971 George Jackson argued that it was a mistake to believe that violence is driven by 'romanticism or precipitous idealistic fervor'.[25] Advocates of tactical diversity agree and also argue that it can educate. A recent statement of the 'incomprehensible' Black anarchist position, reminiscent of Black Panther Assata Shakur's 1973 statement 'To My People', is framed as a call to arms against 'current plantation trends'. It proposes the construction of programmes 'that meet the essential needs of the people' and demonstrate the bankruptcy of state-run or sanctioned support systems.[26] Liberation 'by any means necessary' involves every means. Feigenbaum observes that tactical diversity has been articulated most forcefully in recent years by Black Americans and Indigenous peoples as a refusal of 'pathological displays of pacifism'. This comment indicates how far the violence/nonviolence binary has been hardwired into anarchist conceptions of activism that are rooted in a history that is essentially west European.[27]

Contemporary anarchist activism

The history of past struggles continues to weigh heavily on anarchist thinking about activism. Here I will focus on how present projects, movements and currents of ideas map and re-map ideas from the past. Naturally, this is a selection and like all selections it has some gaps. Moreover, it is commutable. As Francis Dupuis-Déri notes: '[t]alk to another anarchist and you'll get a different history of anarchism'.[28] Like him, I pick six currents in anarchist thought: insurrectionism, class-struggle anarchism, post-left anarchy, social anarchism, postanarchism and small 'a' anarchism. Overlaps between these positions reflect the interplay of movements and ideas in anarchist circles and the messiness of anarchist political culture.[29] The distinctions may appear arbitrary from some perspectives, but they should help highlight the theoretical and practice-based principles that shape current activism.

INSURRECTIONARY ANARCHISM

Insurrectionary anarchism is a 'refusal to negotiate or compromise with enemies'.[30] It is not an ideological position but a diverse current which assumes multiple forms.[31] It is often described as a politics of attack and its presence is seen in militant, clandestine acts of sabotage directed against corporate and state organizations and in political communiqués. Nineteenth-century French and Italian illegalism are part of the pre-history but anti-capitalist tract *The Coming Insurrection* is sometimes regarded as the modern insurrectionists' 'foundational insurrectionary work'.[32] This text, first published in 2007, by the Invisible Committee, was linked to the activities of nine activists in Tarnac, France, who meddled with electric rail cables in 2008 and were arrested on charges of terrorism, conspiracy and sabotage.

Alfredo Bonanno is another important influence. Eager to counter what he saw as the reification of nineteenth-century anarchist ideas – the tendency to treat historical anarchist writings as philosophy and to extract abstract, general principles from de-contextualized readings of them,[33] Bonanno developed his idea of insurrection both as a critique of Italian comrades who remained wedded to an outdated idea of revolution and of English anarchists like Ward and Read, whom he accused of neutralizing anarchist politics. Returning to history, he pitted their 'Kropotkinite' anarchism against the elastic revolutionary politics he derived from Malatesta. Taking up Malatesta's critique of Kropotkin's rigid determinism, Bonanno argued that the militant non-violence of postwar 'Kropotkinism' was as inflexible as Kropotkin's pro-war stance had been. He wanted to revive activist traditions that prioritized flexibility.

Like Bonanno, modern insurrectionists typically eschew mass activism and reject programmatic proposals which promote locally determined revolts and insurrections. Their emphasis is 'on free, temporary, and informal association'.[34] For the philosopher and translator Wolfi Landstreicher, the 'significant question' is 'how each individual will act, and that, for anarchists, is determined by each individual in terms of their desires, dreams, capabilities and circumstances, in terms of the life they are trying to create'.[35] Rejecting 'organizations that seek members – unions, parties, federations and the like – and equate the revolution with the power of their organization subsuming the individual into the group',[36] insurrectionists favour autonomous organization. They need to be based on an affinity model: 'a small group, volitionally organized and maintained, which must work toward defining the oppression of its members and what form their struggle for liberation must take'.[37]

CLASS-STRUGGLE ANARCHISM

Class struggle is also an umbrella term. The origins of the term are difficult to pin down. In the 1960s the social ecologist Murray Bookchin urged anarchists to reclaim the language of class struggle from Marxists in order to build resilient and powerful revolutionary movements. Since then, class-struggle anarchists have used it as part of a strategic effort to distinguish anarchist organizing from looser forms of social movement activism. In this context, class struggle anarchism has emerged as a critical response to the rise of feminist, ecological and other movements perceived to sideline class in their analysis of oppression. Class-struggle anarchists are usually feminist, anti-racist and green, but they are first and foremost anti-capitalist egalitarians who struggle against bourgeois privilege and state power.

Class-struggle anarchists commonly trace their intellectual roots to the anarchist communism of Kropotkin, Bakunin, Rocker and Malatesta. Some of their most important groups are the prisoner support network, Anarchist Black Cross, the International of Anarchist Federations (IAF-IFA) and the Platformist Anarkismo.net project.[38] Revolutionary unionism also falls within the family, though it is not explicitly anarchist.

The IAF traces its roots back to the IWMA and adopts principles of decentralized federation and autonomy to facilitate local struggles: their aim is the 'abolition of all forms of authority, whether economical, political, social, religious, cultural or sexual, the construction of a free society, without classes or States or frontiers, founded on anarchist federalism and mutual aid'.[39] With local bodies in Europe and South America and links to associations across the world, the IAF affiliates mobilize against repressive laws, electoral campaigning and for prisoner release and workers' rights.

Anarkismo traces its lineage to the Makhnovist Platform, advocating organizational practices designed to build anarchist cultures through direct action in urban and rural working-class communities. It includes the Johannesburg-based Zabalaza Anarchist Communist Front,[40] a tight-knit group of individuals who adopt collective responsibility to advance their propaganda. Founded in 2003, Zabalaza seeks to co-ordinate activism within and between labour organizations and social movements, rather than build anarchist mass movements. By capitalizing on popular disaffection with the ANC, it advocates the abolition of private ownership and the division of labour, workers' self-management and the realization of distribution according to need.

Revolutionary unions continue the traditions of the syndicalist organizations of the early twentieth century. Their priorities are to build worker solidarity and re-organize production for the benefit of the producer classes. Like most of their predecessors, they are formally detached or semi-detached from anarchist activism. The iconic Industrial Workers of the World (IWW or Wobblies), for example, is completely independent. The union's only explicit reference to anarchism notes its rejection of 'all alliances, direct or indirect, with any political parties or anti-political sects'.[41] In contrast to the Wobblies, the International Workers' Association (IWA) treads a softer line, not only committing itself to the realization of 'libertarian communism' but also allowing 'provisional alliances' with other non-party, non-vanguard 'proletarian, union and revolutionary organizations'.[42] Nevertheless, overall revolutionary unions are part of an anti-capitalist, antimilitarist, anti-parliamentary class-struggle movement, which dovetails with anarchism, or at least some of its currents. And many anarchists are active members of them.

Like other anarchists, class-struggle anarchists invoke internationalism and anti-colonialism, but they often engage more readily with left, dissenting Marxist traditions – notably autonomism and workers' council movements – than with other non-class-struggle anarchists. Philosophically, class-struggle anarchists are usually profoundly unsympathetic to individualist anarchisms. Some also condemn the idea of insurrection as deeply flawed – a latter-day expression of propaganda by the deed. They see the attempt of some insurrectionists to restrict the 'activist' label to insurrectionary anarchism and disqualify non-violent protest as a symptom of this failing.[43]

POST-LEFT ANARCHY

Post-left anarchy is a subversive, transgressive current of anarchism. Bob Black and Hakim Bey (aka Peter Lamborn Wilson) are among its most celebrated advocates but, as Black explains, it gives voice to a number of 'revolutionary themes' and steers clear of developing anarchist programmes. Post-left anarchy seeks to be 'unambiguously anti-political', 'hedonistic' and proudly individualist: 'the freedom and happiness of the individual' are benchmarks of 'the good society'. Black once sponsored Groucho Marxism and 'communist egoism' – a politics that blended Stirner and Marx – but is probably best known for advocating the abolition of work and its utopian transformation into play. He also rejects the emancipatory promise of technology (echoing some of the ideas Zerzan develops in his critique of the empty society). He positions post-left anarchy against 'anarcho-leftist fundamentalisms'.[44] These include class-struggle anarchism and anarcho-syndicalism –which for him are organizational forms that promise social transformation but negate its possibility: 'Anarchism would turn a mental hospital into a mental ward; anarchy makes of it a phalanstery. Anarchism legalizes drugs; anarchy takes them. Anarchy is chaos, and *Chaos* is anarchy.'[45]

Hakim Bey (described as the 'goofy Sufi' by an appreciative Black) intensifies the surrealist and mystical elements of post-left anarchy (Black says that he turns chaos into a 'shout for joy, demanding marvels without cease').[46] Like the nineteenth-century evolutionist John Henry Mackay, Bey abandons what he calls big-R revolution: that is a transformative, cataclysmic event or project of total emancipation. But where Mackay advocated evolutionism, Bey calls for a more expansive kind of revolutionary change through the discovery or creation of temporary autonomous zones (TAZ). He sees these as spaces that facilitate surreal, fantastic utopian projects and the transformation of everyday living.

Bey is hostile, too, to conventional propagandistic deeds. He wants to reconfigure activism through poetic terrorism: 'Art as crime; crime as art'.[47] CrimethInc.'s four-point anti-programme is an exemplary statement of this brand of post-left anarchic activism:

1. Make politics relevant to our everyday experience of life again. The farther away the object of our political concern, the less it will mean to us, the less real and pressing it will seem to us, and the more wearisome politics will be.

2. All political activity must be joyous and exciting in itself. You cannot escape from dreariness with more dreariness.

3. To accomplish those first two steps, entirely new political approaches and methods must be created. The old ones are outdated, outmoded. Perhaps they were NEVER any good, and that's why our world is the way it is now.

4. Enjoy yourselves! There is never any excuse for being bored . . . or boring! Join us in making the 'revolution' a game; a game played for the highest stakes of all, but a joyous, carefree game nonetheless![48]

The Escapologists' Manifesto is a variation of the same idea (see table below):

SOCIAL ANARCHISM

In a general sense social anarchism refers to the idea that anarchism enables the expression and development of mutual aid. This is the term Kropotkin and others coined to describe

Escape from	Escape to
Protestant work ethic	Idleness
Convention	Rebellion
Boredom	Excitement
Consumption	Creativity
Celebrity	Equality
Cars	Public transport
Noise	Sound
Greed	Humanism
Stagnation	Exercise of mind and body
The corporation	Self-sufficiency
Supermarkets	Cottage industries
Television	Books
Anxiety	Rationalism
Government	Anarchy
Solitude	Community
Vanity	Altruism
Objects	Information
Fear of otherness	Enrichment by others

Figure 3.2
The remedies for dull convention found in the Escapologists'
Manifesto[49]

interdependence in human and non-human communities and the ethical commitment to solidarity and voluntary co-operation. It was deployed against those who constructed human beings abstractly as a-social, self-interested beings and who concluded that social order demanded the imposition of law in order to provide security. The term was also used by socialist anarchists to critique anarchist individualists. Although the latter did not assume that people were incapable of voluntary co-operation, social anarchists argued that that these individualists wrongly believed that it was necessary to uphold their rights against communities. In doing so, they allowed forms of property that were likely to produce inequalities.

In contemporary anarchism, social anarchism is used to describe both the practice of alternative ways of living and an anarchist ethic of care; building anarchist cultures of non-domination. For the anarchist organizer and writer Cindy Milstein mutual aid 'is one of the most beautiful of anarchism's ethics'.

> It implies a lavish, boundless sense of generosity, in which people support each other and each other's projects. It expresses an openhanded spirit of abundance, in which kindness is never in short supply. It points to new relations of sharing and helping, mentoring and giving back, as the very basis for social organization.[50]

In a narrower sense, social anarchism describes a particular idea of freedom and programmatic strategy. Murray Bookchin pioneered this usage in a now infamous assault on what he called 'lifestyle' anarchism. This spelt the abandonment of society for the promotion of pleasure seeking by 'free-booting, self-seeking, egoistic monads'.[51] With writers like Bey and Black clearly in his sights, Bookchin attacked individualist conceptions of freedom as autonomy and an array of movements that adopted practices that betrayed individualist tendencies. Dismissing lifestyle practices as bourgeois, he argued that social anarchism was about the construction of decentralized, democratic federations and the abandonment of capitalism and he defined social-anarchist freedom as the collective rejection of oppression with the aim of individual self-realization. Structural change was a prerequisite for voluntary agreement, egalitarian association and ecological community. Bookchin's programme had an ethical dimension, too. Mobilizing change at local levels required rekindling the ideals of the 'Left that Was' to rediscover a 'rich generosity of spirit, a commitment to a humane world, a rare degree of political independence, a vibrant revolutionary spirit, and an unwavering opposition to capitalism'.[52] Described like this, social anarchism dovetails with revolutionary unionism and class-struggle anarchism, but it tailors activism to the 'waning of the working class as a revolutionary subject'.[53]

Social anarchism sorts activists into different camps and not always with the clarity that Bookchin wanted. Understood as a commitment to mutual aid, social anarchism encompasses a plethora of local actions and everyday utopian experiments designed to put social relationships on a new footing by 'creating new logics, habits, spaces, opportunities and physical realities' within existing systems.[54] Punk movements, projects like Food Not Bombs and animal liberation activism have been vital to these initiatives. Indeed, in parts of East Asia – the Philippines, Indonesia, Malaysia, the Wuhan region of China and Japan – these kinds of experiments are said to have breathed new life into moribund anarchist traditions.[55] This type of social anarchism can be easily dismissed as lifestyle, yet it is often inspired by a 'comprehensive approach to social change'. To borrow Matthew Wilson's neat formulation: 'it is not about *style*, it is about *life*'.[56] In contrast, Bookchin's social anarchist programme tends to restrict activism by directing it into particular organizational channels; it disparages forms of activity that depart from it. It consequently risks labelling social anarchist experiments as 'lifestyle', whether or not activists identify with the major tenets of post-left anarchy that Bookchin despised.

POSTANARCHISM

Postanarchism seeks to give expression to critiques of domination by re-articulating anarchist ideas about freedom and change. It has an affinity with post-left anarchy. It too critiques the historical traditions that class-struggle anarchists identify with and reinforces the critique of 'leftism'. However, postanarchists are more interested in poststructuralist political theory than movement practices. Their attention is trained on Enlightenment thinking: Bookchin is one of the writers identified with this tradition, but Bakunin and Kropotkin emerge as the architects of the outmoded political theory that Bookchin and others seek to keep alive.

Seeing power as a relation of force that operates at micro levels, affecting everyday social relations, postanarchists question the conventional anarchist commitment to the abolition of the state. Their argument is not so far removed from the anti-anarchist critique advanced in the 1870s: the view that power can be abolished is rooted in a conception of human nature and a thesis of liberation as perfection; anarchism thus adopts an idea of revolution as a moment of liberating transformation which eradicates the corrupting power of the state, enabling individuals to realize their natural goodness and sociability.

The implications for activism come from the postanarchist re-theorization of anarchist politics. There are two related moves. Both are linked to the rediscovery of post-structuralist currents in the history of anarchist thought. First, Stirner's egoism rescues anarchy from anarch*ism* to invoke a constantly creative, transgressive resistance politics. Second, Malatesta's critique of Kropotkin's determinism corrects the idea of anarchy as the end-state utopia realized through the progressive march of history and re-roots it in the performance of insurrectionary practices.

SMALL 'A' ANARCHISM

Small 'a' anarchism focuses on movements rather than theory but it also describes a change from big 'A' anarchism – the anarchism of the founding fathers, Proudhon, Bakunin and Kropotkin. The small 'a' is understood in a variety of ways, sometimes to show the evolution of anarchist principles and aspirations over time, sometimes with greater emphasis on the obsolescence of revolution in a post-materialist, post-industrial era. It is sometimes used to expose the limitations of nineteenth-century anarchist theory, sometimes to emphasize anarchism's ethical core. However, running through all this is the idea that historical anarchism is an ideology-to-rival-Marxism and that anarchist activism should be understood as protean and plural.[57]

One explanation for this shift is that big 'A' anarchism was feminized during the 1960s, marking the moment when Bakunin-Kropotkin-type class struggle gave way to a less muscular form of activism. By virtue of her relative neglect, Emma Goldman emerges as a symbol of anarchism re-born and the phrase that promoted her work to a generation of seventies activists – 'if you can't dance, it's not my revolution' – encapsulates the gap between the two varieties of anarchism.[58] Historicized in this manner, the Spanish revolution represents the last gasp of proletarian anarchist catastrophism. And Goldman's rhythmic revolution inaugurates a form of fluid activism that not only animated post-war feminism, civil rights and anti-colonial movements but also later ecological and social justice campaigns.

Small 'a' anarchism promotes 'horizontalism', that is organizational practices that counter hierarchy and domination. It rejects big 'A' anarchist leftism and programmatic change but brings Wobbly-inspired ideas of leaderfulness into connection with social anarchist ethics and post-left principles of autonomy. Similarly, small 'a' anarchism mobilizes networked groups and associations in mass demonstrations, using self-organization, direct action, revolutionary union strike tactics and consensual participatory democracy as tools to contest capitalism. In many respects, small 'a' anarchism dovetails with social anarchism. Yet small 'a' anarchists tend to identify as social movement activists and tend to theorize from experience rather than refer to the history

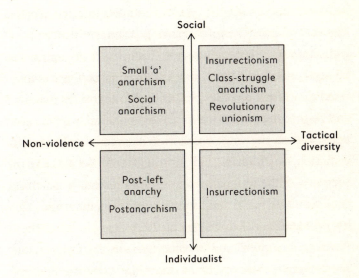

Figure 3.3
Subdivisions created by the commitment to non-violence in social anarchist and individualist groups

of ideas and the work of leading historical figures. The tendency of small 'a' anarchists to link historical anarchism to class-struggle politics further widens the gap between these two currents.

The sometimes confusing overlaps and tensions within the activist landscape are the result of complex internal debates. The central questions of revolution and transformation, organization and freedom have deep historical roots and cannot be neatly resolved. Contemporary anarchist activism is theorized as a result of practice, but it also theorizes practices and re-theorizes historical practice in altered political contexts. Just as the stark opposition between revolution and evolution, organization and anti-organization exaggerate the sharpness of the boundaries that separate historical anarchists, disputes about social and lifestyle anarchism, mass and affinity organization risk downplaying the overlaps between them. Research into global and transnational anarchist movements shows that anti-authoritarians have always fought on multiple fronts. Historian Kirwin Shaffer notes that the 'men, women, and sometimes even children' who entered into anarchist struggles in early twentieth-century Cuba did not choose between labour and countercultural community activism. They 'took part in all facets of Cuban anarchism both inside and outside the workplace'.[59] Likewise, the distinctive feature of contemporary anarchist activism is that its dividing lines have changed. Insofar as activism has been largely moulded by debates conducted by those operating in conditions defined by consumer capitalism and liberal democracy of one sort or another, it is predicated on resistance rather than revolutionary

THE GOVERNMENT OF NO ONE

advance. While movement subdivisions are real enough, when anarchists enter into campaigns and associations they show that distinctions are easily muddied.

Reflecting on class struggle and lifestyle divisions in Canada, Allan Antliff argues:

> People are interested in building a movement with foundations in the everyday lives of communities they are part of – I am thinking of things like establishing affordable housing, sustaining info-shops, artistic pursuits, alternative education projects, social justice struggles, stuff that matters in their everyday lives. When you are engaged in that sort of work you tend to look outward and focus on the challenges of bringing people into the movement or working in solidarity with allies. That doesn't leave much time for infighting.[60]

Activism and oppression

Which groups have anarchists tried to appeal to in their propaganda? In the nineteenth century, anarchists often referred to the mass, but since the idea of the mass was appropriated by illiberal, anti-democratic crowd psychologists and European classical elitists like Robert Michels, it has come to be associated with irrationality: the mass is seen as a herd to be feared and despised. Anarchists by contrast see it as both the numerical majority and the most disadvantaged. Anarchist debates about class and intersectionality bring out some of the tensions in this conception and help show how anarchists have addressed the issue of inequalities between groups of oppressed peoples.

CLASS

The critique of domination gives anarchists a wide lens to identify instances of oppression. Their integral analysis of state oppression and capitalist exploitation has also provided a fertile
ground for building alliances with non-anarchist socialists.
Anarchists have often been energetic union organizers and
have pursued sometimes aggressive anti-bourgeois agendas to
mobilize class actions: it is not difficult to find the language
of class struggle in anarchist writing. In that sense, Ricardo
Flores Magón's 1911 *Manifesto of the Mexican Liberal Party* often
sounds virtually indistinguishable from Marx and Engels's
1848 *Communist Manifesto*:

> [H]umanity remains divided into two classes whose
> interests are diametrically opposed – the capitalist class
> and the working class; the class that has possession of
> the land, the machinery of production and the means of
> transporting wealth, and the class that must rely on its
> muscle and intelligence to support itself.
>
> Between these two social classes there cannot exist any
> bond of friendship or fraternity, for the possessing class
> always seeks to perpetuate the existing economic, political
> and social system which guarantees it tranquil enjoyment
> of the fruits of its robberies, while the working class exerts
> itself to destroy the iniquitous system and institute one in
> which the land, the houses, the machinery of production and
> the means of transportation shall be for the common use.[61]

Yet Magón's analysis was also typically anarchist in the way it
drew on a critique of private property ownership and government. In talking about class, anarchists often devote as much

attention to issues of social exclusion and dependency as to prevailing Marxist concerns like the ownership of the means of production or the extraction of surplus value. Anarchists have also rejected aspects of Marx's theory and have rarely adopted it uncritically.

The anarchist objection to Marxist class analysis is that it is underpinned by a thesis of progress. Marxists tend to see revolution as the outcome of a process of change led by transformations in the economy which then lead to the emergence of worker solidarity and awareness of the collective power of workers as a revolutionary force. Without mentioning Marx, Alexander Berkman put the case against Marxists. The idea that workers had a 'mission' was a 'false and misleading conception, essentially a religious, metaphysical sentiment'. It erroneously 'suggests a duty or task imposed from the outside, by some external power'. Correcting this view, Berkman added: 'There is no power outside of man with can free him . . . Neither heaven nor history can do it.' History could 'teach a lesson', but it could 'not impose a task'.

The second objection, which follows from the first, turns on the historical determination of the proletariat as the 'universal liberating class' and the special status that Marxism attaches to urban, industrial workers as the agents of revolutionary change. Anarchists see Marx's reliance on the proletariat as misguided and socially divisive.

Those anarchists who dismissed Marx's notion of a universal revolutionary class but still agreed that it was possible to identify potential agents of revolution within the oppressed, argued that Marx had misunderstood the nature of oppression in capitalism. Marx was wrong to expect the proletariat, the most advantaged workers, to fight for revolutionary change: instead it was the lumpenproletariat, the precarious groups he dismissed as 'social scum',[62] who were the most revolutionary. Miss M. P. LeCompte, delegate of the Boston revolutionists at the 1881 London meeting, focused on tramps:

> It is the most intelligent of all the revolutionary elements among the people for it is of no class. Students, actors, clerks, workingmen have all been swept into the highways of America as tramps by failures of firms, banks and business houses in the great crashes that every now and then disorganises American life, but the larger part come from the mills and factories where there is a 'lockout' or where they have been blacklisted for taking part in strikes – As tramps they learned to take everything they could lay hands on – to slay the bloodhounds the farmers set on them, to burn down his barns and hamstring his horses, and to keep up such a reign of terror that the farmer gladly paid him the food as tribute that he denied him as charity. These tramps returned to industry. Keep up in the shops the same spirit they had on the land . . . It is said among employers that one returned tramp will black sheep a fold of a hundred steady-going workingmen.[63]

The argument that Marx's class theory was socially divisive initially focused on the subordination of the aspirations of rural workers to the interests of the industrial proletariat. For anarchists across Europe and in Central and South America, where vast estates controlled by landed elites were the norm, Marxism not only ignored the plight of the rural poor but bypassed the pressing issue of land ownership as a distraction from real revolutionary politics. As the delegate representing the Mexican confederation of labour at the London conference told the gathering, the 'social question in Mexico' was 'an agrarian question as in Ireland and Russia'.[64] Worried that the sidelining of rural workers' demands would foster arrogance in the urban proletariat, European anarchists like Reclus stressed that both sets of workers were engaged in the same revolutionary projects. Rural workers were not bumpkins, reactionaries or lackeys, part of the 'idiocy of rural life' as Marx believed.[65]

Admittedly, Berkman gave more ground than Reclus to the Marxist view that urban workers were more likely than their rural counterparts to lead the struggle against capitalism. He described proletarian struggle as 'the concern of everyone'. Yet he too believed that the 'toilers' needed the 'the aid of other social groups' to bring about emancipation. 'If the industrial proletariat is the advance-guard of revolution,' he continued, 'the farm labourer is its backbone.' Berkman concluded that the 'work of the social revolution lies in the hands of both the industrial worker and the farm labourer'.[66]

Both arguments were elaborated by the writer and literary critic Gustav Landauer. Like Berkman, Landauer attacked Marx's class theory as wrong-headed. Marx's efforts to show scientifically how and why the proletariat was destined to bring about socialist revolution were 'absurd and peculiar'.[67] But Landauer's innovative objections to Marx were that his idea of class was sociologically faulty and socially repressive.

On the first point, Landauer argued that the oppressed encompassed a much wider group than Marx's conception included. Looking at the urban landscape and at the changes that capitalism had wrought in the late nineteenth century, he noted that whole new categories of workers had emerged: retail store workers, draftsmen, technicians, regiments of petty bureaucrats, union and party workers. Members of these groups were not proletarians, but they were nevertheless dependent on purchasers of their goods and services and, 'from a psychological point of view', rightly designated slaves.[68] For Landauer, the oppressed were the vast body of workers who had no stake in capitalism: those who lived under constant threat of unemployment, those who faced destitution as a result of old age, workplace injury or illness, those without disposable income and access to means of spiritual or cultural life. It included 'poor writers and artists, doctors, military officers' as well as industrial workers. And because capitalism resulted in constant insecurity and fluid movement between social groups, it also included 'bums, vagabonds, pimps, swindlers, or habitual criminals' – the lumpen that Miss LeCompte had talked about.[69]

To highlight the dangerously totalizing character of Marxist class analysis, Landauer compared Marx's invocation of class to the nationalists' appeal to the nation: it was designed to impose a single, uniform pattern of life on diverse communities. This construction was wrong because it ignored the complexity of human society. This was always, in fact, a '*society of societies; a league of leagues of leagues; a commonwealth of commonwealths of commonwealths; a republic of republics of republics*'.[70] Marxist class struggle left no place for diversity within the proletariat, let alone across the mass of the oppressed. Dragooned into adjunct unions of political parties, workers would be exhorted to sacrifice self-interest to the proletarian good, taking up revolution but breeding conformity. For regardless of the revolutionary status that Marxism bestowed upon them, in official unions workers had more reason to maintain and manipulate the system for their own ends than they had in destroying it. It followed that the Marxist focus on class struggle would bankrupt the socialist vision. In his obsession to wrest control of the ownership of the means of production, Marx skirted over the deadening, polluting effects of industrial production, the mindless boredom of labour and the structural impacts of capitalist-driven technology. Anarchists wanted to inherit the earth not the drab, dirty world that Marxist communism seemed to promise on the back of the capitalist transition.

The different social typologies of class and systems of classification anarchists have developed to distinguish mass from elites point to varying understandings of social uniformity and cohesion in social struggles. Malatesta used work as a criterion to sort the oppressed from the exploiters. Broadly, workers were typically (but not exclusively) those who laboured manually. The exploiters were the idle who either exploited workers directly as owners or who used their mental skills to prey on the workers indirectly. Priests and lawyers were both 'gangrene', and necessarily part of the exploiter class. So were journalists. The status of 'engineers, doctors, artists, and teachers' depended on their employment; cobblers, general practitioners, primary teachers, artisans, builders and nurses were all part of the oppressed.[71]

A hundred years later, the UK group Class War published an account of class that used social status and preciousness as primary determinants of exclusion. Like Malatesta's scheme, this left open the possibility of jumping class barriers but rooted class advantage in social outlook as much as occupation. Unlike the middle class, the working class relies exclusively on its own labour power to secure its wellbeing. The middle class has advantages derived from education which give it a stake in the system. Because the middle class is better educated, it is also better fed, healthier and more assertive. All this means that it can be 'bribed' in ways that workers cannot. The middle class is not inured to injustice but it remains the workers' class enemy. Various 'lily-livered' members of the alternative middle class – 'hippies', 'inner city posers' and other 'rebels without a cause' – attack capitalist injustice. But their opposition comes from security and it sustains capitalism rather than threatens it. The promotion of all sorts of single-issue campaigns – for peace, ecology, feminism and animal rights – is a tell-tale sign of class advantage. These are not causes that the working class care about. For it is necessarily 'pre-occupied with . . . pressing problems like getting or keeping hold of a job, low pay, finding a place to live and generally trying to make the best of life within a pretty unpleasant society not of their making'.[72]

The conceptualization of class difference and antagonism thus has significant repercussions for activism. It affects judgements not only about who the oppressed are but also about how the mass can – or should – be mobilized.

INTERSECTIONALITY

The concept of class is used most frequently by anarchists keen to assert their links to dominant European historical traditions. It features less prominently in literature produced by advocates of post-left anarchy, small 'a' anarchists and postanarchists – currents that tend to keep this past at arm's length. Yet if 'class' sorts anarchists into two broad blocs, the question of intersectionality adds another dimension to the debate about the direction of anarchist activism.

Intersectionality is the view that 'racial, sexual, heterosexual, and class oppression' are 'interlocking'; that 'integrated analysis and practice' is required to combat the 'major systems of oppression' responsible for creating 'the conditions of our lives'.[73] Intersectional approaches to activism not only flatly reject the Class War dismissal of single-issue politics but also the label itself. Audre Lorde's words provide the counter: 'There is no such thing as a single-issue struggle because we do not live single-issue lives.'[74]

A large body of anarchists have readily adopted the language of intersectionality from the Black feminists who first articulated it. However, anarchists disagree about the ways that non-class and class oppressions should be theorized and about what follows from intersectionality in terms of action.

One view, presented by Wayne Price, is that 'all oppressions are intertwined and overlapping, leaning on and supporting each other'. Price rejects any 'strict pluralism' that treats oppressions as if they were 'in parallel to each other' but at the same time takes issue with Class War's dismissal of non-class oppressions as 'single-issue' bourgeois distractions. He also criticizes the view, associated with rigid forms of Marxism, that all forms of oppression are rooted in economic exploitation. Accordingly, Price argues that white supremacism is not just 'a matter of economics'; racism 'affects not only the economy but also the politics and culture of society'. Likewise, 'the oppression of women goes way back in prehistory and is very deep in the structures of our society'. Yet if these are not stand-alone oppressions, they are connected to each other through economic exploitation: chattel slavery was motivated by 'clearly economic reasons'; women's oppression 'directly affects, and is affected by, the class structure'; ecological destruction 'is related to the drive of capitalism to constantly accumulate capital'. Multiple oppressions are not functions of changes in modes of production; because they emerge from an all-encompassing system of exploitation – structured by state and capitalism – they are inseparable from it. The oppressions that result from the dynamic power relationships generated by capitalism and the state have the same moral status but they are felt more or less widely. Moreover, for Price, economic liberation is the constant or 'necessary feature' of non-class emancipation. Imagining a pile of pick-up sticks, he concludes that 'distinct oppressions' lean on each other and that some may be 'more central in the pile than others'. The centrality of class is shown in Figure 3.4 by the differential weighting of the 'sticks' representing familiar oppressions.[75]

A contrasting view, strongly influenced by poststructuralist theory, dislodges capitalism as the central plank that holds dissimilar oppressions together. Instead it looks at the formation of power relationships over time. This approach uncovers the institutional and cultural processes that

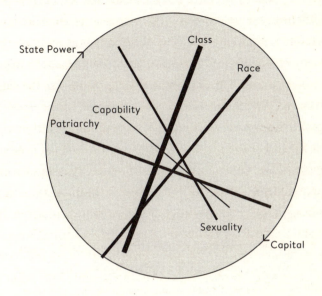

Figure 3.4
A view of intersectionality showing the relative weighting of class and randomized non-class oppressions within the framework of capitalism and the state

categorize individuals, whether Black, female, straight, able, young and so forth. Like the first approach, this analysis suggests that domination is felt materially – for example, in apartheid and segregation and as a result of a whole host of legal disqualifications (on property ownership, citizenship rights), arbitrary powers (to farm some species and not others) and prohibitions of various sorts (the selective criminalization of activities). Similarly, it rejects psychoanalytic analyses that take the 'metaphorical "intersection" of identities as its object of investigation'. This is the sort of strict pluralism that Price critiques.[76] Yet domination is said to emerge from the privilege and disempowerment that classification entails, a point that Price does not emphasize. The point is well made by the UK Anarchist Federation (Afed) Women's Caucus in a discussion of normalization and dominant white 'malestream' thinking. Their long statement is worth quoting in full:

> To talk about privilege reveals what is normal to those
> without the oppression, yet cannot be taken for granted
> by those with it. To talk about homophobia alone may
> reveal the existence of prejudices, stereotypes about how
> gay men and lesbian women behave, perhaps, or violence
> targeted against people for their sexuality. It's unusual
> to find an anarchist who won't condemn these things. To
> talk about straight privilege, however, shows the other
> side of the system, the invisible side: what behaviour is
> considered 'typical' for straight people? There isn't one,
> straight isn't treated like a sexual category, it is treated like
> the absence of 'gay'. You don't have to worry about whether
> you come across as 'too straight' when you're going to a job

Privilege and hierarchy:
Powers of certification (sanity, animality) and authorization (ordination, incorporation) create multiple intersecting oppressions

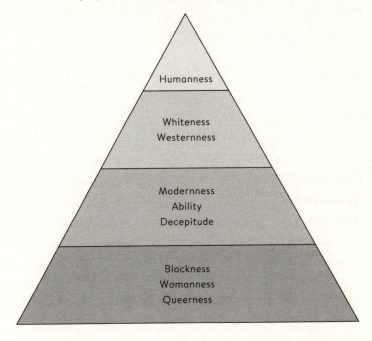

Figure 3.5
A view of intersectionality showing the complex hierarchies of oppression believed to develop through accidents of birth, social status and privilege

interview, or whether your straight friends will think you're denying your straightness if you don't dress or talk straight enough, or whether your gay friends will be uncomfortable if you take them to a straight club, or if they'll embarrass you by saying something ignorant about getting hit on by somebody of the opposite sex. This analysis goes beyond worries about discrimination or prejudice to the very heart of what we consider normal and neutral, what we consider different and other, what needs explaining, what's taken as read, the prejudices in favour of being straight aren't recognisable as prejudices, because they're built into our very perceptions of what is the default way to be.[77]

The capitalist-based and poststructuralist-inflected conceptions of intersectionality are not mutually exclusive. However, different strategies emerge from these debates about intersectionality. Price's analysis implies the need for unity of purpose and intersectional solidarities which allow activists to decide 'what is most important' at different times. Unlike orthodox Marxist theory, he does not predicate the liberation of women or people of colour on the prior emancipation of workers or simply assume that racism and every other form of oppression will disappear once the proletariat has put an end to capitalist exploitation. There is no straightforward class priority and therefore no duty to subordinate intersectional campaigns to the struggles of the urban working class. But intersectional oppressions appear to have a relative weight and this informs how activists should decide how to direct their energies at any given time. Reflecting on the choices, bell hooks argues:

if we move away from either/or thinking, and if we think, okay, every day of my life that I walk out of my house I am a combination of race, gender, class, sexual preference and religion or what have you, what gets foregrounded? I think it's crazy for us to think that people don't understand what's being foregrounded in their lives at a given point in time. Like right now, for many Americans, class is being foregrounded like never before because of the economic situation. It doesn't mean that race doesn't matter, or gender doesn't matter, but it means that . . . people are losing their jobs, insurance.[78]

By contrast the poststructuralist analysis suggests that there are tensions and trade-offs in struggle, which profoundly affect activism. The philosopher Ladelle McWhorter explains: 'some of the ways we try to fight racism reinforce sexual oppression; some of the ways we try to fight sexual oppression reinforce racism'. To give an example: a migrant solidarity activist in Calais safeguarding a squat being used by Black African women refused entry to Black men without papers. She felt uncomfortable doing this as a white woman even though the decision to safeguard had been made by a group in which Black African women predominated.

Tensions such as these may be exacerbated when the identities linked to intersectional oppressions become core to the analysis of domination and privilege. One response to the tension is for oppressed groups to organize independently in order to resist the 'networks of forces' that 'collude to keep us expending our energy separately' and prevent us from making 'much of a dent in the machinery of power'.[79]

The other is to attempt to build solidarities within diverse movements without denying the tensions that exist between their different constituents. This approach means addressing the power imbalances that stem from unearned privilege in order to combat the divisions that regimes of domination necessarily create. For Ernesto Aguilar, founder of People of Color Organize, it entails confronting the 'internalized racism of whites', and helping people of colour to work through 'their own internalized racism'. It is about unlearning 'the competitive, egocentric relations of the dominant society'.[80] Thinking about the Indigenous peoples' struggle on Turtle Island (the name given to North America by some Indigenous rights activists) the professor and activist Taiaiake Alfred presents a slightly different view, linking privilege more strongly with culture and tradition. For him, addressing privilege is about undoing the western biases underpinning domination. The 'vast majority of white people are cultured as individualists and cannot accept that they are not in charge and that they will not ever be in charge, and that they do not speak and impose their views on the situation they find themselves in'.[81]

Two major themes emerge from the anarchist discussion of class and intersectionality. One is about how the mass is constituted and the other is about its internal cohesion. Landauer once underscored the complexity of the changes anarchists wanted to see when he described the state as a condition, 'a certain relationship between human beings' and a 'mode of behaviour' that is destroyed 'by behaving differently toward each other'.[82] Debates about class and intersectionality show just how high anarchist activism sets its goals.

Anarchy in Action

In 1973 Colin Ward published his seminal text *Anarchy in Action*. Modestly describing the book as an updating footnote to Kropotkin, the book documented a vast array of anarchist practices in everyday life. Some resulted from social dislocation. For example, the spontaneous order of the Prague Spring or the community associations that typically mushroom in the wake of floods, fires and other disasters, often filling vacuums left by government ineptitude and/or neglect. Other cases stemmed from disaffection with existing orders, such as experiments in free universities or protest teach-ins. Some resulted in enduring projects like the Pioneer Health Centre in South London or the Anarchist Black Cross, and others were more fleeting everyday rebellions. Ward discussed the sabotage of local council regulations by tenants who over-painted their drab approved paintwork. 'Guerrilla gardening' – the planting of abandoned and privatized land – is a rebellion intended to build community and neighbourliness, as well as express defiance and beautify.

Ward's conception of anarchy as 'a mode of human organization, rooted in the experience of everyday life, which operates side by side with, and in spite of, the dominant authoritarian trends of our society'[83] begs important questions about the relationship between anarchist activism and anarchistic practice. Fans argue that by normalizing anarchism Ward showed how people who do not identify as anarchist nevertheless transform social orders or, at least, hold in check the worst excesses of state regulation. Critics contend that Ward overplayed the transformative power of on-going anarchistic experimentation and that his approach encouraged passivity. The worry informing Bonanno's insurrectionary anarchism was that his outlook was disempowering. It implied that you just had to scratch the surface to see anarchy working; there was no need for anarchists to egg others on, intervene or engage with particular initiatives or experiments. In the end there would be no incentive to change reality.

The questions that Ward's idea of anarchy prompts, then, are about the distinctiveness of anarchistic activism and the openness of anarchism to grass-roots initiatives. What divides anarchy in action from the vigilantism of the white militias, 'the Klan without the hats', that ostensibly protected white neighbourhoods in post-Katrina New Orleans and boasted the killing of Black Americans while the police turned a blind eye?[84] And how do anarchists ensure that their activism is relevant to the marginalized and oppressed?

Anarchism and feminism

The relationship of anarchism and feminism brings some of the questions about anarchist activism and anarchizing action into focus. Anarchism has a complicated relationship to feminism. On the one hand, anarchist women have been highly critical of dominant trends within feminism and called for the anarchizing of feminism. On the other, anti-feminist sentiments within anarchism have spurred anarchist feminists to challenge patriarchal behaviours. The first response led anarchist women to clarify the distinctiveness of their politics, usefully shining a light on two core concepts in anarchist activism: direct action and prefiguration. The second shows how feminist critique continues to drive transformative change within anarchist movements.

The mobilization of women to campaign for the vote at the end of the nineteenth century crystallized anarchist criticism. Feminism pre-dated the suffrage campaigns by some mark – the socialist labour activist Flora Tristan, described by her grandson Paul Gauguin as 'an anarchist bluestocking',[85] was an outspoken advocate for socialist feminism in the 1830s and 40s. But the struggle for the vote not only gave new prominence to feminist campaigning, it also helped narrow the definition of feminism as a movement directed to the extension of civil rights. In doing so, it also divided feminists along party-political lines and separated anarchists from non-anarchist feminists on issues of organization and strategy.

In many instances, anarchist women made the same arguments against male domination as their non-anarchist sisters. As advocates of free love, they rejected marriage as legalized prostitution and campaigned for rights over their own bodies and children. As 'hysterics', they fought to abolish the asylums built to cure them of 'moral insanity'. As muses, they rejected the suffocating supplications of their brooding suitors and the uninvited protection that was offered. As wives, they railed against their confinement in the home. As creative beings, they refused to accept exclusion from education and forms of industry arbitrarily reserved for men. As working women, they rejected the discriminatory regimes that left women vulnerable to intrusive, intimate searches and systematic police harassment. As impoverished workers, they attacked the punitive justice systems that incarcerated women for prostitution. As child-bearers, they flouted laws that restricted their ability to control their reproduction. As potential mothers, they celebrated the unique and special capabilities of women as nurturers and carers. As antimilitarists, they understood traditionalist appeals to motherhood as ideological manoeuvres designed to turn women into breeding machines and tag their male offspring as cannon fodder.

When it came to the suffrage campaigns, anarchist women often wrote admiringly about the protesters. They applauded the daring of their transgressions, the open defiance of the hunger strikes and the fortitude of the activists who put up with the punishments, both sanctioned and illicit, in defence of their cause. The suffrage campaign seemed to blur the boundaries between political and direct action which demarcated anarchists from all other party-political actors and excluded anarchists from the Second International. Yet anarchist women argued that the strategic logic of the suffrage campaign marked the parting of the ways for anarchists and non-anarchists. The principle of direct action was central to the anarchist case.

To explain the anarchist position Voltairine de Cleyre argued that all co-operative experiments involved direct action and that direct action was usually a spontaneous response to injustice or oppression. Quakers who refused to bear arms, unionists who downed tools to secure wage hikes and better working conditions, women who boycotted retailers to secure price reductions, tenants who withheld rents to check the power of landlords, activists who killed pro-slavers to disrupt slaving were all involved in this. On this score, so were feminists who disrupted social events to promote the campaign for the vote. Yet, de Cleyre argued, these suffragettes introduced a distinction between pragmatism and principle and she categorized them as fair-weather direct actionists. Like most other direct actionists, they weighed up the pros and cons of direct and indirect action and plumped for the former when it seemed more effective in the given circumstances. In contrast, anarchists were direct actionists as strictly 'non-resistants'. This meant rejecting indirect or political action – involvement in established channels of authority – altogether. Countering critics who conflated direct action with dynamiting and physical violence, de Cleyre argued that direct action was not merely a method, it was an approach to politics that was specifically anarchist:

> Direct action may be the extreme of violence, or it may be as peaceful as the waters of the Brook of Siloa[86] that go softly. What I say is, that the real non-resistants can believe in direct action only, never in political action. For the basis of all political action is coercion; even when the State does good things, it finally rests on a club, a gun, or a prison, for its power to carry them through.[87]

De Cleyre placed the construction of power and rights at the heart of non-resistant anarchist direct action. Whereas pragmatic direct actionists understood these as liberties and permissions to be granted by authorities, anarchist direct actionists saw them as assertions or demands. Direct actionists believed they 'had a right to assert, and went boldly and asserted it', alone or 'jointly with others'.[88] Applying this analysis to feminism she argued: 'I never expect men to *give* us liberty. No, Women, we are not *worth* it, until we *take* it. How shall we take it? By the ballot? A fillip for your paper rag! The ballot hasn't made men free, and it won't make us free.'[89]

The gist of de Cleyre's critique was that the suffragettes' direct action left mechanisms of domination intact. Feminists might secure the vote for women, but representative systems would be reinforced by this and women would remain enslaved. The early twentieth-century feminist and anarchist He-Yin Zhen drove this point home. Distinguishing 'active' calls for liberation 'initiated by women themselves' from 'passive' ones 'acted upon women and initiated by men' He-Yin Zhen warned that the latter would compound women's enslavement in both private and public realms. Male domination was rooted in the proprietary rights men claimed over women and the linguistically enforced philosophical differentiation and separation of male and female spheres. In the home, passive liberation would alter social relationships without upsetting the privileges and powers men enjoyed. Passive liberation was encouraged by men both because it demonstrated how enlightened they were and because it charged women with new responsibilities: passive liberation meant that women worked as breadwinners and household managers. No wonder men dangled 'the promise of liberation' in front of women's eyes, for the prospect was more money for concubines and diminished family duties.

The campaign for the suffrage, she argued, was another kind of permitted, passive liberation, even though it engaged women actively. Reflecting on feminism in Finland, Norway, Italy and Britain, He-Yin Zhen argued that the 'ultimate goal of women's liberation is to free the world from the rule of man and from the rule of woman', not to sustain the rule of men by adding women to patriarchy. '[D]id such powerful female sovereigns as Queen Victoria of the British Empire or Empresses Lü Zhi and . . . Wu Zetian in the dynastic history of China ever bring the slightest benefits to the majority of women?'[90] The goal of anarchist activism was non-domination, and direct action – active liberation – was the only possible means of its achievement.

Contemporary anarchists often describe the alignment of means with ends that de Cleyre and He-Yin Zhen tied to direct action as 'prefiguration'. As often as not, it is invoked to distinguish anarchist from Marxist revolutionary socialism and to establish a principled ground for the anarchist rejection of 'vanguardism' – the idea that the mass is incapable of emancipating itself without the help of an elite. In brief: if anarchists and Marxists are said to have the same ends, then prefiguration highlights the inconsistency of using dictatorial means to secure libertarian goals. Because anarchists also conceptualize non-domination in different ways, they also disagree about the repertoires of direct action that prefiguration allows.

For anarchists who associate dictatorship with violence, non-violence is a prerequisite for prefiguration. Valerie Solanas put the opposite view. Solanas's 1967 *SCUM Manifesto*, an untypical example of anarchist-feminist thinking, added a new spin to the anti-pacifist view by linking passivity to feminine legality and activism to violent feminist criminality. 'SCUM will not picket, demonstrate, march or strike to attempt to achieve its ends. Such tactics are for nice, genteel ladies who scrupulously take only such action as is guaranteed to be ineffective.' SCUM is 'opposed to a civil-disobedience . . . that is . . . opposed to openly violating the law and going to jail to draw attention to an injustice'. Civil disobedience acknowledges 'the rightness of the over-all system'. SCUM 'is out to destroy the system, not attain certain rights within it'. It therefore always operates on a criminal basis, though undertaking 'destruction and killing' selectively and with discrimination. Solanas's view was that direct action is prefigurative because it takes the fight direct-ly to the patriarchal master and, in doing so, eradicates the oppressor and kills the slave.[91]

In de Cleyre and He-Yin Zhen's analysis of direct action, prefiguration is understood as a broad principle. To borrow Saul Alinsky's framing, their concern was a general one about 'the question of means and ends' which arises whenever 'we think about social change', not the specific one about the re-lationship of this particular means to this particular end.[92] The conclusion they drew from their critique of the suffrage campaigns was that direct action is anarchist only when it is treated as a principle, that is, when it facilitates and pre-figures non-dominating practice. To return to the Ku Klux Klan, grass-roots supremacist white militias are direct action-ist, but their actions are reactive not anarchist or prefigura-tive, because they entrench existing cultures of domination.

As feminists, anarchist women borrow insights from femi-nist movement activists to shine a light on the patriarchal practices which are ingrained in anarchist movement politics. The response has not always been entirely positive. As Louise Michel wrote, 'even the socialist Proudhon' said that women 'can only be housewives and courtesans'.[93] Nevertheless, the injection of feminism into anarchism illuminates the dynamic relationship between anarchist and anarchistic politics.

Notwithstanding the anarchist commitment to non-domination, when it comes to women's liberation anarchists have a chequered record. Historians sometimes track the failing to the anti-feminist doctrines of the granddaddies of anarchism, particularly Proudhon, as well as to the conservatism of the many workers who joined anarchist movements. The notoriety of some anarchist women like Louise Michel, de Cleyre and Emma Goldman and the existence of women's associations like the Mujeres Libres, show that they were exceptions to the rule of male domination. Today, though some observers have argued that the anarchist milieu is comparatively women-friendly, hostility to feminism thrives.

At worst, unqualified opposition to 'feminism' leads to the comprehensive dismissal of all anarchist-feminist politics. 'Anarcho-feminism' is one of the anarcho-leftist fundamentalisms Bob Black condemns. He lumps it together with 'Third World nationalism (including indigenism)'; feminism is a 'particularist ideology' and one of the 'larger hunks of wreckage from the New Left' which have 'nothing to say'.[94] Less belligerent opponents claim that anarchist feminism is redundant by asserting the anarchists' principled opposition to all forms of domination. This response simultaneously closes down the space for the articulation of a feminist politics within anarchism and provides plenty of opportunity for misogynist behaviours. These have included the reproduction of 'sex-objectifying images' in the countercultural press[95] and the Machiavellian embrace of free love as a cover for rape. Ann Hansen's encounter with a professed radical is a harrowing example. Having just arrived from Canada in 1980 and keen to make contact with fellow radicals, she accepted the invitation to stay the night at the flat of a self-styled 'heroic revolutionary' and 'victim of the justice system' whom she met at the London Freedom bookshop. Naively thinking that he was a 'kindred spirit' she soon discovered the limits of his radicalism when he ignored her protests and forced her to have sex with him.[96] Her account suggests that little had changed in London in the ten years since the iconic *Anarchy* magazine used an Electric Ladyland-like collage of topless women to promote a special issue on female incarceration and delinquency.[97]

A copious zine literature on protest-camp protocols, street harassment, disrespect and consent indicates that feminists still have some way to go to combat habituated sexual violence in anarchist movements. Yet the 'feminist turn' in anarchism also reveals how a plethora of anti-oppression movements that do not identify as anarchist articulate anarchistic critiques of dominating practice. These should enable anarchists to confront current bad behaviours, review the limits of non-domination and modify anarchist cultures. Asking whether the anarchist is 'someone with a certain aesthetic' or 'someone who actually reflects on the values of patriarchy, class, race and sexuality that exist in society and within ourselves', critics of Spanish 'anarcho-machismo' describe how feminism transforms anarchism in Madrid:

It's funny that when you call some anarchist 'machista', they get all offended, and don't look within themselves . . .

If you really are an anarchist, you will look within when you are criticised . . .

The didactic role that we are required to play is one of the paradoxes . . . when anarchists around me don't understand feminist ideas . . . I get angry – since the ideas of feminism aren't exactly new, and if they're anarchists, they should have some idea of them! . . . If those who call themselves 'anarchist' truly opposed all hierarchies, we wouldn't need to call ourselves 'radical anarcha-feminists', just anarchists. But because the term 'anarchism' is used poorly, and just as a fashion, it loses its meaning.[98]

Anarchist engagements with gender, queer and trans-politics, Indigenous peoples' struggles and anti-colonial movements can engender parallel learning processes. As Taiaiake Alfred's critique of the western biases of anarchism indicates, the exchanges are often tricky. There are on-going disputes in anarchist movements about the extent to which new currents of ideas do in fact change anarchism. Nevertheless, they indicate how anarchists are able to benchmark anarchism against the non-dominating practices of grass-roots, anarchistic groups and movements.

Ever since Proudhon, anarchists have described anarchizing processes as disruptive and agonistic. His view was that anarchy was about the perpetual movement of social forces which operated through paradox or antinomy and the achievement of temporary equilibria. The destruction of harmony or, more positively, the conceptualization of harmony as a condition of permanent movement or agitation is a dominant theme in nineteenth-century writing. European anarchists were often inspired by atomic physics; neo-impressionist painters expressed the concept of unity-in-vitality visually in their vibrant, pixellated canvases. But the idea of finding order in disintegration, disaggregation and agonism has ancient roots. Ōsugi Sakae, the agitator and Esperantist, murdered in 1923 by Japanese military police, offered an aesthetic conception of this: 'Seeing the supreme beauty of life in the expansion of life, I see the supreme beauty of life today only in this rebellion and destruction. Today, when the reality of conquest is developed to its utmost, harmony is not beauty. Beauty exists only in discord. Harmony is a lie. Truth exists only in discord.'[99]

Anarchist activism develops through challenge and confrontation, because anarchists 'also have to take steps to realise how to act, how to educate themselves, how to critique themselves'.[100] Anarchist feminism shows how the destruction of anarchist truths can be accomplished through troubling encounters which can also be constructive.

The ripples of nineteenth-century debates continue to be felt in movement subdivisions and debates about tactics and strategy. Anarchists have attempted to extend cultures of non-domination by mobilizing the disadvantaged – the mass structurally dominated through capitalist class relations and/or by oppressions linked to privilege. This relationship is fundamental to anarchist activism. It requires anarchists to remain open to the non-dominating activity of non-anarchists, while they seek to explain and extend anarchist practices through their own associations. Anarchists work with not for the marginalized and oppressed.

CHAPTER 4

Conditions

It would be unusual to find either decolonization or feminization described as conditions for anarchy even though these demands are now frequently heard: a condition seems too rigid, threatening to fix relationships in ways that most anarchists would consider un-anarchist. However, the term can be used more loosely: lots of anarchists have set certain minimal tests for their own interactions. Manifestos and safer spaces policies are examples of the sorts of conditions anarchists propose. And some anarchists have devised complex regulatory rules for proposed alternatives.

In this chapter I explore anarchist constitutions, showing how anarchists who sorted themselves into individualist and communist camps envisaged the functioning of anarchist societies. This leads us to a consideration of anarchist utopias as well as of anarchist conceptions of democracy.

Anarchist constitutions

In 1909 Max Nettlau, often considered the first great historian of anarchism, discovered an article written in 1860 by the botanist and economist P. E. de Puydt entitled 'Panarchie'. It described the convention that everybody submit to one form of government as fundamentally illiberal. By 'government', de

Puydt did not mean the parties or factions that competed for control of institutional power but the foundational principles of governance. Whether government was 'constituted upon a majority decision or otherwise', he believed that existing restrictions on choice were prescriptive. Short of emigrating, dissenters had no means of expressing their dissatisfaction with the systems of government preferred by the majority. But the majority, too, were denied real choice once a social order had been established, though they might consent (tacitly or explicitly) on the basis of the advantages they derived from it.

De Puydt, Nettlau explained, had been a free-market liberal, a supporter of laissez-faire economics, and he had attempted to extend the same principles of liberty he saw in the market to the political realm. The freedom de Puydt wanted was 'the freedom to be free or not free, according to one's choice'. His proposal was 'panarchist'. He wanted to give each person the right to 'select the political society in which they want to live'.

How would panarchy work? The de-territorialization of government was the central principle. Government, or social organization (the term Nettlau preferred), would be based on subscription not prescription. The model was the 'civil registry office':

> In each municipality a new office would be opened for the Political Membership of individuals with governments. The adults would let themselves be entered, according to their discretion, in the lists of the monarchy, or the republic, etc.
>
> From then on they remain untouched by the governmental systems of others. Each system organizes

itself, has its own representatives, laws, judges, taxes, regardless of whether there are two or ten such organizations next to each other.

For the differences that might arise between these organizations, arbitration courts will suffice, as between befriended peoples.[1]

Surprisingly, de Puydt was willing to include anarchy in his choice-set. In fact, he was as critical of Proudhon's federalist proposals as he was of the various statist options proffered by republicans, liberals and monarchists. From his perspective, anarchists crossed a pluralist panarchist line when they recommended a limited set of political models. For him, anarchy was an option as restricted as monarchy or republicanism. In contrast to anarchists, panarchists offered a full range of governance models, marketing them to meet the claimed demands of political consumers.

From an anarchist perspective, de Puydt mistakenly conflated government with state. He either misunderstood or wrongly rejected the anarchist idea that there was a fundamental difference between statism and anarchy. De Puydt placed anarchy and statist forms of government on a single spectrum whereas anarchist taxonomies of government – monarchist, republican, liberal – assumed this basic division. Admittedly, this also meant that anarchists were offered fewer choices than de Puydt proposed. They were clearly unable to sanction forms of governance that facilitated and legitimized uneven distributions of power, exploitation and domination. Yet beyond this basic point there was no agreed view about the constitution of anarchy. Anarchists disagreed about the sort of power that should be constrained and how best to institutionalize those constraints to safeguard anarchist principles.

Some anarchists argued that it was impossible to devise a constitutional framework for anarchy. Émile Armand, a free-love, antimilitarist propagandist, was one. Describing life as an experiment, he argued that anarchists should seek to live it 'constantly . . . outside of the "law" or "morality" or "customs"'. Life as experiment 'cuts programs to shreds, tramples over properties, smashes the windows, descends from the ivory tower. Vagabond, it deserts the city of the Acknowledged Fact, leaving through the gate of Final judgment, seeking adventure in the countryside, open to the unexpected.'[2] The only rule this seemed to allow was the end of all rules. In fact, Armand's politics was more complicated: he combined his exhilarating notion of experiment with a conception of self-organization and he expected that experimenters would spontaneously arrange their collective affairs:

> The individualist knows that relations and agreements among men will be arrived at voluntarily; understandings and contracts will be for a specified purpose and time, and not obligatory; they will always be subject to termination; there will not be a clause or an article of an agreement or contract that will not be weighted and discussed before being agreed to; a unilateral contract, obliging someone to fill an engagement he has not personally and knowingly accepted, will be impossible. The individualist knows that no economic, political or religious majority – no social group whatever – will be

able to compel a minority, or one single man, to conform against his will to its decisions or decrees.[3]

Armand's response speaks to a deep and long-held anti-constitutional bias in anarchist thinking. Yet his rejection of the plans that other anarchists formulated was based on a refusal to recognize the constitutional status of the rules he hardwired into experimenters' brains. Although anarchists have been largely reluctant to use the language of constitutionalism to explore their proposals, those less squeamish about rule-making have argued that greater specification of anarchist social relations, perhaps even extending beyond men, is both necessary and desirable.

In the face of the question 'Which forms of social organization are best suited to realize anarchist principles?' anarchists developed two broad constitutional models. As we will see, the constitutions such as those designed by David Andrade and Victor Yarros were individualist while those coming from Platformists and Spanish anarchists were communist.

Individualist constitutional experiments

AN ANARCHIST PLAN OF CAMPAIGN

David Andrade was a prominent member of the Melbourne Anarchist Club active from the 1880s. He learnt about Bakunin's and Proudhon's ideas reading Benjamin Tucker's paper *Liberty* and Moses Harman's paper *Lucifer the Light-bearer*. These were among the most celebrated individualist-anarchist papers in America; *Lucifer*'s profile was raised after the censorious Comstock Laws were used to prosecute Harman for daring to discuss marital sex and rape within marriage. Andrade shared Tucker's view on law and government, though his view on capital and profit was less relaxed. Like Tucker, he described himself as an individualist and socialist. For Andrade, individualist anarchism was not at odds with socialism. It was just a non-communist version of it.[4]

In 1888 Andrade published his constitution: *An Anarchist Plan of Campaign*.[5] It was designed to foster the spread of anarchist social principles in Australia and beyond by appealing to the workers of the world. His idea was that workers would establish co-operatives to purchase goods in bulk and run anarchist economies selling to the public within the capitalist state system. Co-operatives would generate their own capital, purchase their own land, set up their own factories and stores and construct their own living spaces. The expansion of the movement over time would depend both on the economic success of the ventures and the robustness of their political arrangements.

Andrade's chief concern was to secure economic equality or, as he put it in his dedication, to 'better our sad condition' by pointing to 'a method of escape from . . . intolerable slavery'. Insofar as the constitution was designed to curtail power, Andrade most wanted to curb the power to accumulate individual profit through the exploitation of labour: 'Profit-making is the first form of exploitation that the labourer must understand.' This constitution, then, was an agreement between workers to organize themselves as equal co-operators. Yet it also had a positive, empowering aspect. The Plan would ensure that 'laborers are no longer expropriated slaves, competing on a capitalistic labor market for employment; but free men, possessing their own property and capital, and employing themselves.'

With thirteen articles, Andrade's model constitution was short and simple. There was no preamble and no grandiose sentiments. The wording was similarly plain and clear. The egalitarian norms of the constitution were embedded in institutional provisions and regulatory rules. It was also meant to deal with two problems which Andrade anticipated. One was the necessity of complying with 'statute law' and being 'amenable to, and tied down by the regulations and restrictions of, the very laws and legal institutions which we are striving to abolish'. The other was to protect the co-operative from 'intriguing schemers' and internal collapse.

Andrade proposed a number of measures to guard against this possibility. The constitution guaranteed all members access to collectively owned property 'free of all change, no rent being demanded of its use'. Each member would be an equal shareholder in the co-operative, insofar as the law allowed, and would be 'equally remunerated, on a time basis, for any services performed'. Labour notes would be issued to run the economy independently of the state and guard against individual capital accumulation. The commitment to equality was also written into the constitution: 'To guard against any possible violation of this principle, it should be a fixed understanding, introduced into the constitution of the cooperation at its inception' that the constitution was 'only alterable by the *unanimous* consent of the members'. Profiteers who entered the co-operative in order to exploit it would have to secure the support of all members to change the rules of co-operation. The Plan gave members the right to withdraw from the co-operative at any time but otherwise obliged them to adhere to its terms. Anyone who violated the agreement could be expelled without the possibility of readmission by majority vote.

Most of the rules Andrade proposed were written into the Plan. His general view that '[f]ree men require no rulers' meant that non-constitutional rules could be kept to a minimum: individuals could determine for themselves how they wanted to live within the framework of the co-operative. At the same time, it was important to introduce rules to regulate the institutions the co-operatives would have to run. Andrade imagined the establishment of a Mutual Bank which would free the co-operative from reliance on 'privileged bankers' and support loans for expansion, particularly house-building. He also recommended that the co-operative produce its own 'journal and general literature' to 'educate the public concerning the principles and methods adopted' by the co-operative and counteract the lies likely to be spread in the capitalist press. The smooth management of these institutions would require other sets of rules. Co-operation required co-ordination and administration. The Plan included rules about the appointment of managers and the conduct of business meetings. In addition, Andrade empowered managers to introduce by-laws to oversee the day-to-day running of the co-operative (time-keeping, accountancy and distribution of goods produced by the members through warehouses), as long as these did not contravene the constitution.

Andrade's hope was that the economic independence achieved by co-operation would foster a spirit of political independence. For example, the constitution guaranteed that there was to be 'no recognized inequality or other distinction, on account of sex'. Andrade added that the habit of co-operation would breed new norms, enriching and improving the quality of interpersonal relations. Thus the constitutional *Plan of Campaign* would prompt a cultural change. Having become 'the equal of man' woman's 'wretched dependence upon him will have vanished, and she will be sovereign over her own body, her own mind, and her own passions, instead of being the *property* of a husband and subject to all the right or wrongs he may inflict upon her'. Once released from 'matrimonial bondage' women would become happier and healthier, breeding happier, healthier children, too. 'The nation will become healthier, happier, and freer; and the miserable, puny, vicious, licentious generation of the present will make way for a higher and nobler humanity than the world has yet seen'. For good measure, Andrade argued that crime would become a thing of the past as the realm of freedom expanded. The 'toiling millions who . . . have groaned in misery under the yoke of law, authority, plunder, and crime, will feel a new life within them as they step out into the full light of liberty'. Clearly, Andrade was an optimist, yet his hopes were not limitless: the criminality that co-operation eradicated was only the idlers' advantage of reaping a reward from others' toil. And the anarchist freedom he described was grounded in the respect for anarchist rules and the sanctity of the constitution.

CONSTITUTION OF THE BOSTON ANARCHISTS' CLUB

Victor Yarros unusually began his chequered political career as a communist before embracing individualism under the influence of Benjamin Tucker. Born in Kiev in 1865, he arrived in America in the 1880s already a seasoned activist. He became a leading contributor to Tucker's *Liberty* and ended life as a social democrat, convinced that the state had an important role to play in bringing about equality.[6] Nonetheless, in 1887, six years after Tucker started *Liberty*, Yarros delivered an address at the first meeting of the Boston Anarchists' Club. This was later published as *Anarchism: Its Aims and Methods*. It included a formal constitution which was adopted by the Club.

The 'abolition of all government imposed upon man by man' was the central theme of Yarros's extended preamble and the major substantive principle of what followed. Subscribing to Proudhon's view that 'liberty is the mother, not the daughter of order' he proclaimed government 'is the father of all social evil'. Quoting copiously from the first issue of *Liberty*, he argued that the anarchists' 'chief battle' was with the state 'that debases man', that 'prostitutes woman . . . corrupts children . . . trammels love . . . stifles thought . . . monopolizes land . . . limits credit . . . restricts exchange' and 'gives idle capital the power of increase and allows it, through interest, rent, and profits, to rob industrious labour of its products'. The abolition of government was also enshrined in the second article of the constitution. Indeed for Yarros, it was 'the definition of the term *An-archy*'; it was the 'central affirmation underlying our philosophy and system of thought'. Casting about for a positive term to describe it, Yarros chose '*Individual Sovereignty*, or Egoism'. In contemporary language it was libertarian anti-capitalist.[7]

Like Andrade, Yarros listed thirteen articles. With the

exception of the second, all referred to the internal organization of the Club and the conduct of its business meetings. Any signatory to the constitution could become a
member. All members had equal voting rights. There was
no membership fee; members made monthly contributions
to the Club's expenses as 'circumstances will allow'. Members elected a Chair at each monthly meeting by majority
vote. The only 'regular official' was the Secretary-Treasurer.
This was also an elected position which could be held for
as long as a year. The Chair had significant powers. Article
V gave the Chair power to 'preside . . . at all meetings of
the Club, public or private' that may be held between regular monthly meetings. Article IX specified that the 'conduct
of each meeting shall be vested solely in the chairman, and
from his decisions there shall be no appeal'. Sensitive to
potential abuse, Yarros ensured that there were checks on
these powers. Ten members of the Club could request the
Secretary-Treasurer to call special business meetings and
article X provided that the Chair could be removed by a 75
per cent majority vote. Yarros also limited the powers of the
Secretary-Treasurer, but the checks here were weaker: not
only were the 'duties . . . incumbent upon such an official'
left unspecified, but the membership could remove and replace the incumbent only on condition that 'each member of
the Club has been notified by the Secretary-Treasurer that
such a proposition is to come before the meeting'. Members
could leave the Club at any time but had to resign formally
by notifying the Secretary-Treasurer in writing. All decisions
on ordinary business, as well as the removal of the Secretary-
Treasurer, were made by simple majority vote. Dissenters

had the right to have their views recorded on request. Exceptionally, changes to the constitution had to be agreed unanimously. Proposals for constitutional change could only be debated at regular business meetings and although they could be tabled at special meetings, Club members had to be notified by the Secretary-Treasurer in writing prior to any vote. No amendment could be 'offered twice within a period of three months'.[8]

Yarros included two extensive notes to explain the powers of the Chair and the use of majority voting. While he argued that the difference between the anarchist and government principle was 'too plain and striking not to be perceived and admitted', their inclusion indicated that he recognized the possibility of there being some confusion between the anti-government position he outlined in the preamble and the constitutional provisions he made.

The difficulty was resolved by recourse to Yarros's conception of voluntaryism. Here he looked to another prominent individualist, the abolitionist Stephen Pearl Andrews, who had used the example of the parlour to model the best kind of social interaction. In the beautiful laissez-faire parlour the '[i]ndividuality of each is fully admitted. Intercourse is . . . perfectly free. Conversation is continuous, brilliant, and varied. Groups are formed according to attraction . . . continually broken up, and re-formed through the operation of the same subtle and all-pervading influence'. It was a place of liberty and equality. Any 'laws of etiquette . . . are mere suggestions of principles admitted into and judged of' by each person. Andrews contrasted this to the 'legislated gathering'. Here, the time each had to speak was 'fixed by law'. The positions of the participants were 'precisely regulated'. And their topics of conversation 'and the tone of voice and accompanying gestures carefully defined'.[9] The legislated parlour was intolerable slavery.

Yarros applied Andrews's analogy to the relationship of anarchy to the state. The state was a special kind of legislated organization, a 'war-institution' that was built on aggression and a class institution that produced inequalities by granting privileges and creating distinctions. Government 'set men against men and classes against classes by their favouritism . . . and special opportunities'. Once established, it used force to compel obedience to these arrangements. But anarchists refused to consent to the government's abuses.

Like de Puydt's panarchists, Yarros argued that anarchists had no intention of forcing governmentalists to relinquish their preferred order in favour of anarchy. But in contrast to the panarchists, he characterized government as monopoly and argued that the state was crushing alternative forms of governance. Since the state was tyranny, he also argued that anarchists had the right to use any means necessary to resist it. While he believed that propaganda by the word was more effective than impulsive revolutionary action, he also held that in war all was fair. Indeed, in a nod to John Most, one of the most celebrated communist advocates of propagandistic action, he urged anarchists to gen up on the science of revolutionary warfare to ensure their own security.

Yarros was unimpressed with the argument that majority rule was the same as government by consent. Democracy might be the 'least objectionable form of rule', but he refused to accept that individual consent could ever legitimately be set aside on the basis of a majority decision. If A and B had no 'rightful authority' over C when acting separately and independently, how was it possible that C's preferences could be overridden when they acted conjointly? Either A, B and C had 'natural rights to life and liberty', or they did not.[10]

Two important points emerged from Yarros's discussion. First, the anarchy of the parlour was not an unregulated order but one that promoted 'another *kind* of regulation'. Second, the rules that anarchists adopted to self-regulate their societies were entirely voluntary. Admitting that government was vastly more complicated and considerably larger than a parlour, Yarros contended that 'the question of the scope and proportions of government power is a subordinate and purely practical question'. The difference between government and anarchy was one of principle: only the latter ensured that 'members have the right to withdraw at any time' and that 'no limit be put beforehand to the limit of its operations'. Members can 'increase and diminish its functions at will, and experience may safely be relied upon for demonstrating just what the amount of benefit there is to be derived from associative effort'.[11]

Having once decided to combine voluntarily, Yarros argued, anarchists were free to adopt majority decision-making to conduct their business. He included the provision in the constitution for reasons of efficiency. Nobody could possibly 'confound this with the system of majority rule obtaining under democratic forms of government', for there was nothing voluntary about the submission that government decisions involved. Similarly, if anarchists decided to invest one or some of their number with greater decision-making powers than the rest, this was because they reserved the right to 'choose any mode of practical organization' to carry out their wishes. They could abandon or modify these working arrangements at any time. Thus the Chair of the Club did not function as an authority, even though it was possible for the Chair to exercise discretion in 'extraordinary cases'. Members could not be coerced to accept the Chair's rulings for an anarchist principle was that the Chair followed the members' instructions.

Like Andrade, Yarros expected that anarchist orders would be more stable and peaceful than government, simply because anarchists would be free to conduct their business without coercion. His aim was to carve out anarchist spaces for anarchists and his constitution was intended as a model for others to adopt. Like Andrade, he believed that the success of anarchy depended on building relationships between small, resilient clubs and societies. Yet unlike Andrade, Yarros did not anticipate the extension of the model to the workers of the world, even though this was conceivable. Indeed, his elitism helped explain his confidence in his constitutional scheme. As he put it, he was not interested in rescuing 'half-starved' 'blind slaves' who worshipped the 'power which grinds them to powder' and stood ready 'to defend it with their last drop of blood'.[12] The anarchist constitution protected the rights and liberties of the enlightened and intelligent few, able to resolve their differences over a glass of wine. Everyone else was free to put up with the evils of the legislated order.

Communist constitutions

THE ORGANIZATION OF THE PLATFORM

Following the Bolshevik defeat of the anarchist campaign in the Ukraine, the insurgent leader Nestor Makhno and some of his group went into exile in Paris. They set up a paper, *Dyelo Truda*, and in 1926 published the *Draft Organizational Platform of the General Union of Anarchists*. This stirred a lot of controversy in the anarchist-communist movement and some leading organizationalists, including Malatesta, were quite critical of it. Its leading idea was that anarchism lacked a 'homogeneous program' and a 'general tactical and political line'.[13] For the *Dyelo Truda* group, this lack helped explain the success of Bolshevism and the marginalization of anarchism in Russia, in both urban and rural areas. But critics found the proposed remedy too strict and protested that it imposed a party line. The Platformists – the name that Maknno's supporters now took – responded that anarchists would never be able to disseminate their message to the oppressed for as long as their ideas remained unclear and undefined.

The Platform was anarchist but called itself libertarian communist. The change in language reflected its founders' desire to distance themselves equally from the Bolsheviks, who also called themselves communist, and individualist anarchism. Platformists embraced the 'principle of individuality in anarchism' but rejected the individualists' distortion of this principle to mean egoism, which showed a 'cavalier attitude, negligence and utter absence of all accountability'.[14] Libertarian communists by contrast held that 'social enslavement and exploitation of the toiling masses form the basis upon which society stands'. They saw violent social revolution as the 'only route to the transformation of capitalist society'. And they recognized that 'free individuality' develops 'in harmony' with 'social solidarity'. The egalitarianism of the libertarian communist model rested on the equal moral worth and rights of each individual. The realization of this right demanded the abolition of exploitation and this was to be achieved through socialization of property and the means of production and the 'construction of economic agencies on the basis of equality and self-governance of the laboring classes'.[15] The Platform was formally committed to the communist principle of distribution according to need and distinguished itself from authoritarian communism by also specifying a commitment to workers' 'liberty and independence'. This was an 'underlying principle' of the 'new society'.[16]

To overcome the authoritarianism of the state a federal system was proposed. That involved the establishment of special, dedicated libertarian communist organizations and the organization of free workers' and peasants' co-operatives. The former had an educative function, disseminating libertarian communist ideas. The latter were the foundational units of libertarian communist organization. They would be organized locally, uniting from the bottom up, to construct larger units:

> There will be no bosses, neither entrepreneur, proprietor nor proprietor state (as one finds today in the Bolsheviks' State). In the new production, organizing roles will devolve

upon specially created administrative agencies, purpose-built by the laboring masses: workers' soviets, factory committees or workers' administrations of firms and factories. These agencies, liaising with one another at the level of the township, district and then nation, will make up the township, district and thereafter overall federal institutions for the management of production.[17]

Federalism was defined as the 'free agreement of individuals and organizations upon collective endeavour geared towards a common objective'. It was coupled with ideological and tactical unity and so required self-discipline and the acknowledgement of individuals' rights and duties. The 'right to independence, to freedom of opinion, initiative and individual liberty' was part of it. The other part was the acceptance of 'specific organizational duties', the insistence that 'these be rigorously performed, and that decisions jointly made be put into effect'. This provision was in line with the commitment to collective responsibility or, as Platform put it, the idea that 'operating off one's own bat should be decisively condemned and rejected in the ranks of the anarchist movement'.[18]

The proposals outlined in the Platform assumed that libertarian communists would be organizing in preparation for a revolutionary war or during one. The formation of military units was therefore integral to the Platform. These were to be run on a voluntary basis, but according to strict rules: no conscription, free 'revolutionary self-discipline' and political control by the workers' and peasants' organizations.[19] Expecting to operate in war conditions, the Platform contained all sort of plans to cover contingencies: production failures and shortages resulting from economic dislocation. Perhaps recognizing the tension between the commitment to communism and the principle of liberty, it also took a cautious approach to the collectivization of land. This policy was not to be pursued as systematically as the collectivization of industry. Should land workers who were used to working the land 'self-reliantly' object to communist principles, it was better to run a mixed economy rather than impose communism, even if this meant allowing some private cultivation while collectivization spread. There was a degree of vagueness, too, in the administrative proposals the Platform made and about the role of the Executive Committee of the Anarchist General Union, and indeed, how this Union was to function. The authors openly admitted these gaps. For them, the Platform was only a beginning, a groundwork for general organization. It was up to the General Union of Anarchists to 'expand upon and explore it so as to turn it into a definite program for the whole anarchist movement'.[20] It was an ambitious plan and typically anarchist in the way it embraced its own fallibility.

COLLECTIVES IN TERUEL IN THE SPANISH REVOLUTION

In 1936, when General Franco launched his military coup against the Spanish Republican government, anarchists across the country rose in revolution, taking control of significant areas of the territory within the Republican zone. In Aragon, in the north-east of Spain, about three-quarters of the land mass were collectivized. It is estimated that in February 1937, just over six months into the revolution, there were 275 collectives with around 80,000 members. Three months later 175 more were added to this total, together with another 100,000 members. The process of collectivization, often spontaneous and sometimes driven by anarchist militias, can be understood as a constitutional one. The collectives represented 'an attempt to create a model, an example for the future of what, once the war was won, a new libertarian society would be like'. They were designed to abolish 'the exploitation of man by man'. Moreover, a federal structure linking 'each village at the district and regional level' was introduced. First producing for themselves, the collectives channelled surpluses to the Council of Aragon to 'sell or exchange it with other regions or abroad'.[21]

Collectivization varied from place to place. Naturally, there were disagreements about putting it into practice. A scene in Ken Loach's film *Land and Freedom* depicts land workers discussing how property should be collectivized and disagreeing about the rewards that should go to individual cultivators. Rather than illustrating anarchist 'chaos', it showed how the commitment to 'anarchy without adjectives', the idea promoted by Tárrida del Mármol the engineer and survivor of the Monjuich tortures, was supposed to operate on the ground and be promoted.

In Mas de las Matas, a commune in Teruel, the process was reasonably smooth: a specially formed committee proposed the collectivization of the existing small and medium-sized holdings. Smallholders and artisans handed over their land, tools, livestock and wheat to the collective. Labour groups were then organized and assigned to one of the twenty-odd new land sectors and assorted workshops. The principles of the collective were egalitarian. Money was abolished and the communist principle of distribution according to need was adopted for all collectively produced goods. In the absence of money a rationing system was used for distribution.

There was no formal plan. Assemblies, which included women, were held to discuss special matters, but the fundamental point for the collective's success was the commitment to reconstitute social relations through collectivization. Not everybody subscribed to the new egalitarianism, so in order to ease the tensions that collectivization caused, concessions were made. Small portions of irrigated land were set aside for each collectivist to grow crops for personal use and each was allowed to keep chickens and rabbits. Agreeing these rules, the collective sought to institutionalize new social norms. Taverns were closed (though wine was included in the ration). Gambling was banned. Resources were found to send a villager to Barcelona to undergo a medical treatment that he otherwise would never have afforded. A threshing machine was procured from the surplus the collective produced. Schools were re-opened, staffed by students and stocked with 'rationalist' teaching materials from Barcelona. New schools opened to provide education to those formerly excluded from education.

The canton of Alcorisa, about fifteen kilometres to the north-east of Mas de las Matas, was also collectivized. It was a relatively wealthy canton of nineteen villages with a population of 4,000. After driving out the Francoist rebels and Civil Guard, a hastily constituted Defence Committee, made up of republicans and anarchists, decided to take control of production and prohibit private commerce. In parallel, locally syndicated agricultural workers set about organizing a new system of production, as in Mas de las Matas, assigning teams to work twenty-three sections of collectivized land. Machinery was redistributed and land surveys were completed. Unlike Mas de las Matas, Alcorisa was 'definitively constituted'.[22] Two lawyers were instrumental in drawing up the terms of the agreement. Its main articles related to property in goods, usufruct, membership, withdrawal and administration.

Property and assets owned by families and individuals, the Municipal Council and the agricultural syndicate were placed in common ownership, to be held on the basis of use. All members of the syndicate were automatically considered members of the collective. New members were admitted by decision of a General Assembly. This was the main decision-making body of the collective and its role, along with the rights and duties of the collectivists, was also specified in the constitution. Withdrawal from the collective was possible, but the collective then reserved the right not to return goods and property, in order to guard against speculation. A five-member commission was set up to take charge of the administration. One served as secretary and the others had briefs to manage food supplies, agriculture, labour and public education.

The collective subscribed to libertarian socialist values. The abandonment of legal marriage was one indicator. In addition the General Assembly adopted the communist principle of distribution according to need. Vouchers were issued by the Defence Committee and these could be exchanged for goods in the local food stores. Services were free of charge. Money was abolished and Alcorisa introduced a point system instead of providing a standard ration, as was done in Mas de las Matas. This meant that individuals and families could choose what they wanted from the available stocks. The collective ran a cinema from a converted church and transformed a convent into a school. It had four grocers and four butchers, a textile co-operative, a haberdashery and tailor's shop, various hairdressers and barbers, a joinery and smithy. It set up a salt factory, ran a hotel and stud farm and managed a herd of cows. According to Gaston Leval, the administration 'was responsible for providing accommodation and furniture for all new domestic set-ups'. Everything else 'was distributed in specially organized shops where the purchases of each family would be entered in a general register with a view to attempting a detailed study of the trends in consumption'.[23] Had the collective been operating without the constraints of war, it may well have organized the envisaged statistical committee to 'scientifically balance production and consumption' and manage local provision of goods to meet needs, as James Guillaume's 1876 *Ideas on Social Organization* had proposed.[24] Instead a 'system of compensatory mutual aid'[25] was used for exchange in the canton and a barter system was set up to organize exchanges with neighbouring regions. This extended across Aragon and to towns and villages in Levante, Catalonia and Castile.

What really separates individualists from communists? There are perhaps two nagging problems that each identifies in the constitutions of the other. Individualists worry that anarchist-communism seems to demand that individuals curtail their rights to satisfy the communists' moral commitment to common ownership. But individualists consider it is both reasonable and possible to estimate what each person contributes separately to collective well-being and that justice demands that each is rewarded for their time or labour. That makes it hard for individualists to imagine how communism could be implemented without coercion.

On the other hand, communists reject the elitism of individualists like Yarros and question the basis of the rights individualists rely on to protect equality. They dispute Yarros's claim that the abolition of the state provided the solution to 'the labor problem' or that the legal guarantee of 'rent, interest, and profits' was its cause. While communists accept that the state and capital were co-constituted, they did not share the individualists' view that respect for equal rights would keep differentials in check. They also feared that individualism bred acquisitive cultures. The communist view was that Yarros's 'state of freedom' had a limited shelf life for as long as labour continued to 'command a price'.[26] The most advantaged would eventually attempt to resurrect a state to enforce their rights and guarantee their property. There was another objection, too. Communists questioned the individualists' assumption that the abandonment of the constitutional guarantee of private property would result in the collapse of capitalism. They thought that individualists tied the persistence of economic slavery too narrowly to the state and this badly underestimated the monopolizing tendencies of capitalism and the power of financial systems. Tucker eventually admitted the miscalculation and Yarros's turn from individualism to social democracy was another kind of acknowledgement of the problem.

Individualists and communists shared some common

Figure 4.1
The principles distinguishing anarchist-individualist and anarchist-communist constitutions and their degree of overlap

ground, but their shared principles – mutual aid, co-operation, freedom and equality – took on different meanings and the nuances were reflected in the constitutions they devised. While it may be hard to imagine Yarros ever having a long conversation with the Platform, it is possible to place Andrade close to the Spanish collectives because of the primacy he gave to equality and the collectivists' flexibility on issues of individual rights.

Arguments between anarchist individualists and communists have been complicated by the historical development of anti-statism and egoism in twentieth-century political thought. For many anarchist communists, anarchist individualism, egoism in particular, provides a ground for anti-statist capitalism or anarcho-capitalism. The archetypal individualist is Fernando Pessoa's anarchist banker: a man who gives up collective struggle for fear of creating new tyranny and chooses instead to amass vast wealth in order to free himself from enslavement to social fictions like the common good or justice.[27] Linked to authoritarian forms of free-market liberalism, anarchist individualism thus becomes anti-socialist. Yet the central point is that there is a significant difference between anarchism, whether individualist or communist, and the liberal and republican alternatives. The sociologist Franz Oppenheimer explained the liberal position. Oppenheimer accepted the anarchist analysis of the state as a colonizing force. The 'villain in the process of history is the Class-State', he argued. Yet as a 'real liberal', he argued that anarchists were wrong to think that it was possible to 'dispense with a public order which commands the means necessary to maintain the common interest against opposition dangerous to the commonwealth'. Oppenheimer continued: 'No great society can exist without a body which renders final decisions on debatable issues and has the means, in case of emergency, to enforce the decisions. No society can exist without the power of punishment of the judge, nor without the right to expropriate property even against the wish of the proprietor, if the public interest urgently demands it.'[28] Individualists and communists vehemently disagreed. Anarchist constitutions had no such final point of authority as liberals like Oppenheimer believed.

Utopias

There is a strong utopian current in anarchist political thought. Yet many anarchists are wary of the label. As critics of liberal and republican constitutions and opponents of historical materialism, many anarchists have felt impelled to imagine anarchies, but a highly divisive, bad-tempered nineteenth-century debate between anarchists and Marxist social democrats has led many anarchists to associate utopia with blueprints and vain hopes: social conformism, inflexible systems, perfectibility and certainty on the one hand, but escapism and whimsy on the other. Even though it was anarchists like Engländer who condemned the abstract utopias associated with the French Revolution, 'utopianism' was the charge that their socialist opponents laid at their door. To a degree, the charge stuck. Today many anarchists defend anarchy as a good idea because it is not a utopia. The anonymous statement *Anarchy Against Utopia!* is an example:

Anarchy doesn't have any platform or vision for society.
There is no ideal to strive for; no image of what is perfect.
As anarchists, we recognize nothing is perfect, not even
nature. And it is the imperfections that we embrace,
because it is the opposite of striving for an external ideal.
Imperfection means diversity and beauty. We realize that
whatever type of life we lead, we will not be perfect; and
that no matter what type of community we make, it will
not be perfect. Whether in a perfect or imperfect society,
problems will arise – both large and small. In a perfect
society, these problems are all addressed with the same
ideal; however, in an imperfect society they can be dealt
with as they really are: each problem is different, needing
a different solution.[29]

Anarchists who endorse utopianism typically do so as 'anti-
utopian utopians', that is as critics of utopian blueprints. This
was the argument Marie-Louise Berneri put when she distinguished authoritarian from anarchist utopias. A member
of the inter-war London Freedom group and a leading anti-
fascist, she argued that anarchists were 'not concerned with
the dead structure of the organization of society, but with the
ideals on which a better society can be built'.[30] While the reference to 'dead structure' describes one anarchist concern,
Berneri's distinction seems too stark. Colin Ward's later discussion of utopias is more sensitive to the diversity of the
utopias anarchists have produced. The straightforward question that utopias pose is 'How could we or should we live?'[31]

Responses to this question can take almost any form. A few
anarchists have played with the idea of good place/no place

central to the literary genre. Louisa Bevington's *Common-sense Country*, published in 1896, is a poetic, gently satirical and romantic depiction of a communist utopia that deploys anarchist common sense to deride the incoherence of the existing world order. In 'Common-sense country', there is no property market, just housing. People enjoy their daily activities, goods are distributed fairly and everybody lives well:

> You never came to a place in any Common-sense city
> where . . . you could see . . . a lot of grain or fish being
> destroyed on the lunatic excuse that it could not be sold
> for more than it cost, while . . . men and women (with
> their children) [were] hungry, worried, and constantly at
> their wits' end, only because they could not buy back the
> comestibles they had ploughed, reaped, milled, fished, and
> otherwise laboured to bring within human reach.

Common-sense country is a secular and anti-disciplinary, non-punitive society. It has no churches or temples and no prisons. '[T]he sky was holy enough to "sit under", and even to sing spiritual songs under.' Life moves at a leisurely pace because time is not money. Schools have been abandoned so that education can flourish. Children's 'little, honest, ignorant, simple questions received honest, accurate, and simple answers, in language which they could understand.' They 'never needed to unlearn afterwards'. Money has been abolished, too. And this means that there are no kings, police, armies or arsenals, 'no poorhouses: no brothels, no divorce courts, no nunneries, no confessionals: no "rings", no strikes, no infernal machines, no gallows'. Nor is anyone in a position to lord it over 'two, or five, or ten cities, or markets, or communities'. It is a place of honesty and authenticity. '[E]ven newspapers expressed real opinions, and conveyed real information.' And it is libertarian: 'Every shade of individuality was respected and made welcome, variety being suggestive as well as interesting. No one wheedled, no one canted, no one flattered, or equivocated, or slandered; because none of these were necessary expedients.' This was indeed a lovely place. Bevington concluded her narrative: 'There was Peace in Common-sense Country, and Goodwill among men; and Happiness and Fullness of Life had become the Natural Order of the day.'[32]

One of the best-known anarchist visual images, Paul Signac's *In the Time of Harmony: The Golden Age is not in the Past, it is in the Future*, plays with similar ideas. Completed in 1894–5, when anarchist violence reached a peak in Paris and Signac left the capital for the South, the painting uses the Mediterranean landscape to depict 'anarchist ideals of social harmony, ample leisure and natural beauty'.[33] The reference to the Golden Age is an allusion to Eden, but the images are recognizably modern.

These perfected images would doubtless have irritated Yarros, who had no time for 'utopias, sentimental effusions, and fanciful ideals'.[34] Yet it is difficult to paint them either as anarchist ready-mades or what philosopher Martin Buber referred to as a 'wish-picture', an expression of unconscious desire, 'a dream, a reverie' or 'seizure' that 'overpowers the defenceless soul'.[35] Nor were they merely political-programmes-dressed-as-art. Admittedly, Bevington set out many of the principles that underpinned life in *Common-sense Country* in her 1895 *Anarchist Manifesto*.[36]

Following Thomas More, whose sixteenth-century master-piece *Utopia* gave rise to the genre, Bevington's *Common-sense Country* imagines a not-impossible future.[37] Yet unlike More with *Utopia*, she writes from the position of the no-place that reality obstructs, exemplifying Buber's conception of utopia as 'the truth of to-morrow'.[38] Her story expresses her personal investment in anarchist goals and it is melancholy and morally charged. *Common-sense Country* and *In the Time of Harmony* creatively capture an idea of a better life that millions of people have associated with anarchy. For Bevington and other anarchist utopians, breathing life into anarchist principles is a way of showing that the not-impossible is just that.

The line between a plan and a utopia is hard to draw, but a comment in the Platform hints at the relationship: 'Anarchism is not some beautiful dream, nor some abstract notion of philosophy: it is a social movement of the toiling masses.'[39] There is a practical element in anarchist utopianism as well as a visionary aspect. This was also Martin Buber's view. In 'utopian socialism' he detected 'an organically constructive and organically purposive or planning element which aims at a re-structuring of society'. In his view, the indicative marker of utopian socialism was that the restructuring would not 'come to fruition in an indefinite future after the "withering away" of the proletarian dictatorship, but beginning here and now in the given conditions of the present'.[40]

Enduring utopia

One version of the anarchist utopia is designed to endure. This type is usually projected onto the future and has a strong organizational element. The aim is to imagine viable anarchies that empower individuals while avoiding the 'dead structures' Marie-Louise Berneri warned against. As a result, anarchists have tended to be critical if friendly towards Robert Owen, Charles Fourier and Saint-Simon, labelled 'utopians' by Marx and Engels. Kropotkin, for example, championed Fourier's approach to organizing. Shaking a box of stones and letting them organize themselves seemed like a good principle to Kropotkin. Yet he was distinctly unenthusiastic about the regimented communities that Fourier proposed. He thought Fourier's 'phalanstery' (the communal unit of association) was an artificial grouping of representative personality types rather than an organic community. Moreover, Kropotkin thought that Fourier wanted to regulate the activities of its inhabitants too closely.[41]

It is unusual in anarchist politics to have a comprehensive double-faceted model such as Kropotkin's. He focused on two issues: first, the need to ensure that struggle resulted in flexible, self-organizing and self-sustaining systems; second, that anti-capitalists had the capacity to conduct protracted revolutionary campaigns against the bourgeoisie. On both counts decentralization and integration were essential.

In *Fields, Factories and Workshops* Kropotkin outlined his macro-economic plan. It called for the decentralization of production, the abandonment of the division between mental and manual labour, and the amalgamation of agriculture and industry on a regional level. Socialism depended not only on abolishing capitalist production for profit but also on abandoning trade based on the fiction of the free market and the principle of division and exchange.

Kropotkin's foil here was Adam Smith's *Wealth of Nations*.

He argued that it had proposed the disaggregation of production tasks and minute specialization in order to improve efficiency, increase surpluses and boost investment. Kropotkin believed that this model dehumanized workers locally for the sake of a global common good that was ultimately unsustainable. It appeared to Kropotkin that Smith had no sense that labour could and should be fulfilling, even therapeutic. Efficiency trumped all. Implemented in each locality, specialization would condemn workers to a lifetime of mindless, repetitive tasks. Applied internationally, it would encourage clientelism: the supposition that industrialization created a permanent territorial division would transform non-industrialized regions into service economies for 'advanced' European states. Efficiency also meant the spread of monocultures and the intensive exploitation of natural resources. The obvious contradiction was that the export of industrial kit by the 'workshops of the world' in the medium- to long-term militated against specialization. The spread of industrialization was not only inefficient but unstable. It would inevitably bring sharper rivalry and competition for markets.

In *The Conquest of Bread*, Kropotkin concentrated on questions of micro-economic change and revolutionary resilience. He called for communes – towns and cities – to prepare to meet the demands of anarchist struggle. The premise of his argument was that supply lines could be secured only by expropriation: the abolition of private property, production for profit and the wages system. In the medium and long term, anarchist communism required the restructuring of production to meet needs. In the immediate short term, it demanded the introduction of systems of distribution based on free exchange. All goods and services – housing, clothing and food – would need to be distributed on the basis of need. With the example of the Paris Commune still fresh in his mind, Kropotkin argued that Parisian workers could withstand a year or two of siege imposed by the 'supporters of middle-class rule' if they learned how to draw on their own resources, co-operate and reorganize 'economic life in the workshops, the dockyards [and] the factories'.[42] Witnessing the complete meltdown of the Russian economy after 1917, he realized that this had been far too optimistic. Yet he remained convinced that the prospects for anarchy depended on the ability of local communities to meet their own needs. In 1942 George Woodcock, Kropotkin's biographer, reiterated the case: 'if adequate food can be produced only after the economic and social revolution, it is equally certain that a revolution cannot be maintained . . . A country in revolt, even more a country at war, must provide against a blockade of the most ruthless kind. Revolution without bread is doomed.'[43]

Kropotkin's plans were an anarchist response to liberal and conservative forms of internationalism that prevailed at the turn of the twentieth century. The most bullish of these called for the internationalization of markets through the extension of free trade and the corporate globalization of the economy. Liberals saw these moves as guarantees of perpetual peace. The American journalist Harold Bolce, for example, advocated the 'financial and commercial amalgamation of the nations', praising the 'magnates denounced as international pirates' for giving 'stability to a world divided by political anarchy'. Where nation states urged 'races to conflict', corporations called for 'combination'. The promise of liberal market internationalism was 'world-unity greater even than the sovereignty of nations'.[44]

For Kropotkin, Bolce's arguments were flimsy. He pointed out that states and corporations worked hand-in-hand and their buccaneering collaboration was the primary cause of inter-state rivalry, instability and war. As an internationalist, he understood anarchy as an outlook and a process, just as Bolce did. But his aim was to push economic forces towards decolonization and to construct non-dominating trans-national global communities. *Fields, Factories and Workshops* opened with an exposé of the colonizing logic of international trade and division:

'Why shall we grow corn, rear oxen and sheep, and cultivate orchards, go through the painful work of the labourer and the farmer, and anxiously watch the sky in fear of a bad crop, when we can get, with much less pain, mountains of corn from India, America, Hungary, or Russia, meat from New Zealand, vegetables from the Azores, apples from Canada, grapes from Malaga, and so on?' exclaim the West Europeans. 'Already now,' they say, 'our food consists, even in modest households, of produce gathered from all over the globe. Our cloth is made out of fibres grown and wool sheared in all parts of the world. The prairies of America and Australia; the mountains and steppes of Asia; the frozen wildernesses of the Arctic regions; the deserts of Africa and the depths of the oceans; the tropics and the lands of the midnight sun are our tributaries. All races of men contribute their share in supplying us with our staple food and luxuries, with plain clothing and fancy dress, while we are sending them in exchange the produce of our higher intelligence, our technical knowledge, our powerful industrial and commercial organising capacities! Is it not a grand sight, this busy and intricate exchange of produce all over the earth?'[45]

For Kropotkin, this exploitative exchange, rooted in domination, could never be altered by the globalization of the international capitalist market, or any rebalancing of corporate over state control. By contrast, anarchist internationalism would mean that regions and nations (understood in the 'geographical sense' rather than the geopolitical) would exchange only 'what really must be exchanged'. The restriction would reduce the volume of trade while 'immensely' increasing 'the exchange of novelties, produce of local or national art, new discoveries and inventions, knowledge and ideas'.[46] The emergence of global scientific knowledge or *Erdkunde* from local practice and experience or *Heimatkunde* would enable peoples in each region to determine how they wanted to live, applying insights gained from non-dominating exchanges to reduce the burdens of labour. Like many nineteenth-century socialists, Kropotkin expected the working day to be slashed by the intelligent use of technology. But he also thought that the mode of production would change. Anarchy would reinvigorate the petty trades – artisan crafts – because this kind of work was more rewarding than factory labour. The expansion of market gardening was one of his particular hobbyhorses; greenhouse technologies would enable year-round production and extend growing seasons in harsher climates.

The use of wind and solar power would facilitate the creation of industrial villages. Kropotkin did not promise universal happiness, which, he said, was well beyond the scope of anarchy. Anarchist internationalism was a more modest rational plan, just and sustainable. It encouraged peoples to work co-operatively with 'their own hands and intelligence' and with the 'aid of the machinery already invented and to be invented' to 'create all imaginable riches'. Its ethic was do not 'take . . . bread from the mouths of others'.[47]

Kropotkin's utopia is controversial among some post-left and postanarchists, both because it assumes that technologies can be detached from the conditions of their production, and because it seems teleological. Kropotkin not only outlined a programme for change, but also appeared to suggest that his integrated economy was already progressing. The future, he argued, is 'already possible, already realisable' for 'the present' was 'already condemned and about to disappear'.[48] Even if he left room for the exercise of will, Kropotkin seemed to indicate that history was on the anarchists' side.

The distinction between probability and possibility drawn by sociologist Deric Shannon offers a different interpretation. Probability speaks to existing configurations of power and possibility is about resistance to them. 'It seems much more *probable*', he argues, 'that capitalists will either bring us to ruin through some nuclear disaster or through environmental devastation, than that humanity will wage a successful war on capitalism's institutions of profit-making-at-all-costs and end the separation of humanity into competing nations based on glorified lines drawn on a map.' Yet it is still *possible* to find 'plenty of reasons to support anticapitalist efforts and engage in those efforts ourselves'.[49] By insisting that economic trends were as supportive of anarchist internationalism as of its regressive forms, Kropotkin invited his audience to weigh one utopia against the other and consider which was really the most enduring.

Transitory utopias

The world has changed dramatically since Kropotkin's time. As the political philosopher Takis Fotopoulos notes, the 'present internationalization is qualitatively different from the earlier internationalization'. The latter had been based 'on nation-states rather than on transnational corporations'. Commodity and financial markets are now much larger and play a 'crucial role in determining the "agent" of internationalization' and the 'degree of the state's economic sovereignty'.[50] Similarly, while Kropotkin was in the forefront of early twentieth-century debates about climate change and its associated migratory pressures, looming ecological collapse was not at the top of his agenda, as it is today for many anarchists. It is not surprising, then, that most influential modern anarchist utopias differ to Kropotkin's, especially when it comes to ecology and technology, and that some are imagined as fleeting possibilities rather than enduring alternatives.

Published in 1983, Hans Widmer's anti-capitalist utopia, bolo'bolo, is an example. The framing and language seem designed to highlight the fantastical, otherworldly quality of the utopia he imagines. Writing under the pseudonym P.M., Widmer opens the work with a critique of civilization. This is presented as a story and it plots the shift from nomadic ways of living during the Old Stone Age 50,000 years ago, to horticulture, animal-farming, land protection, settlement and ritual. Hierarchy and domination and the regulation of work followed. Heightened by industrialization, the repressive tendencies of civilization centre on the expanding 'Work-Machine' and 'War-Machine'. These have wrought planetary destruction: 'jungles, woods, lakes, seas' are 'torn to shreds'; 'our playmates', non-human animals, have been endangered or 'exterminated' and the air has been polluted by 'smog, acid rain [and] industrial waste'. The machines have emptied the 'pantries' of their 'fossil fuels, coal, metals' and prepared for 'complete self-destruction' through nuclear holocaust. The inability of the Work-and-War Machine (also called the Planetary Work-Machine) to provide for the earth's human populations has made some people so 'nervous and irritable' that they are ready for the 'worst kind of nationalist, racial or religious wars'. War appears a 'welcome deliverance from fear, boredom, oppression and drudgery'.[51]

The Machine is 'planned and regulated' by corporations and international trade and finance. There are no central organs of power. Instead, the Machine exploits the tensions between workers and capital, public and private provision, sexes and genders in order to 'expand its control and refine its instruments'. Workers employed as 'cops, soldiers, bureaucrats' run the 'truly oppressive organs of the Machine'. Mostly white, male technical-intellectual workers, concentrated in the US, Europe and Japan, are placed at the apex of the Machine. Industrial workers, both male and female, who predominate in eastern Europe and Taiwan, are parked in the middle. Fluctuant workers, those without regular employment or income, composed mainly of women and non-whites living in African, Asian and South American shanty towns, are slumped at its foot. The Machine also runs international chain gangs. 'Turkey produces workers for Germany, Pakistan for Kuwait, Ghana for Nigeria, Morocco for France, Mexico for the US'. Division and specialization mean that each cog daily serves as its own slave-master:

> You spend your time to produce some part, which is used by somebody else you don't know to assemble some device that is in turn bought by somebody else you don't know for goals also unknown to you. The circuit of these scraps of life is regulated according to the working time that has been invested in its raw materials, its production, and in you. The means of measurement is money. Those who produce and exchange have no control over their common product, and so it can happen that rebellious workers are shot with the exact guns they have helped to produce. Every piece of merchandise is a weapon against us, every supermarket an arsenal, every factory a battleground. This is the mechanism of the Work-Machine: split society into isolated individuals, blackmail them separately with wages or violence, use their working time according to its plans.[52]

Resistance is possible and within limits allowed, but it is futile. Oppositional forces are either neutralized through recuperation or repression. 'The Machine is perfectly equipped against political kamikazes, as the fate of the Red Army Faction, the Red Brigades, the Monteneros and others shows. It can coexist with armed resistance, even transform that energy into a motor for its own perfection.'[53]

Utopian planning might seem an obvious route out of

this wretchedness, but Widmer disagrees. Instead he seeks to learn from the past. Utopia is the last resort of the miserable, destined to replicate the conditions of their own misery. Remembering how the industrial horrors of the nineteenth century spurred on utopian hopes for the future but only extended enslavement, he warns: 'Even the working-class organizations became convinced that industrialization would lay the basis of a society of more freedom, more free time, more pleasures. Utopians, socialists and communists believed in industry.'[54] Widmer concludes that the limits of utopia are inescapable because our alternatives are constrained by our reality. 'Dreams, ideal visions, utopias, yearnings, alternatives' are 'just new illusions'. If we rely on these, we will only be seduced 'into participating in a scheme for "progress"'. History teaches that any projected futures we dream up will be 'the primary thought of the Machine'.[55]

The answer is to create a second reality. This reframes Colin Ward's question by asking 'How would I really like to live?' in an entirely subjective way. We should think about the immediate future, not some prospective alternative and it is not a question about reality but about understanding individual desires, regardless of their practicality.

bolo'bolo is the second reality. It works globally and locally through subversion (rather than attack) plus construction: a strategy Widmer calls substruction. Its success depends on the development of 'dysco knots' through three forms of direct action: 'dysinformation', 'dysproduction' and 'dysruption'. These take shape outside workplaces in spaces that the Machine does not completely regulate and through encounters between people who are otherwise divided. They 'attempt the organization of mutual help, of moneyless exchange, of services, of concrete cultural functions in neighborhoods' and 'become anticipations of bolos'.[56] These expand into macro-level 'trico-knots', bringing geographically dislocated neighbourhoods into direct relation with each other. Trico-knots have a moneyless exchange function, first for 'necessary goods' like 'medicine, records, spices, clothes, equipment', but also for cultural enrichment. For example, those involving predominantly Technical and Fluctuant workers 'will give a lot of material goods (as they have plenty), but they'll get much more in cultural and spiritual "goods" in return; they'll learn a lot about life-styles in traditional settings, about the natural environment, about mythologies, other forms of human relations.'[57]

The 'bolo' is the principal social unit emerging from all this activity. The bolo expands to create a 'patchwork of micro-systems' ('bolo'bolo'), each with 300–500 'ibus', imperfect beings tortured by the reality of the Machine. The bolo is an ecological survival strategy underpinned by an agreement or 'sila' for 'living, producing, dying'. It guarantees survival, conviviality and hospitality to each ibu by abandoning money as the medium for social interaction and it uses 'asa'pili', an artificial language, to facilitate universal communications without domination.

The sila guarantees each ibu with 'taku'. Widmer contends that individuals have a need for private property and the taku satisfies this. It is a 250 litre volume storage container for personal items, 'unimpeachable, holy, taboo, sacrosanct, private, exclusive, personal'. The sila also provides 'yalu' (a daily ration of 2,000 calories-worth of local food), 'gano' (a minimum of one day's housing in any bolo) and 'bete' (medical care). To facilitate movement, each bolo must provide hospitality for up to fifty visitors, each ibu being a potential guest. The adoption of 'fasi', or borderlessness, means that ibus are free to come and go as they please and cannot be expelled. Ibu also have 'nugo' – a suicide pill for use anytime and a right to demand aid to dispatch themselves.

Sila includes 'nami', the right of ibus 'to choose, practice and propagandize for its own way of life, clothing style, language, sexual preferences, religion, philosophy, ideology, opinions, etc., wherever it wants and as it likes'. In turn, nami is realized through the diversity of the 'nima' or the 'territorial, architectural, organizational, cultural and other forms or values' of the bolos.

> As any type of nima can appear, it is also possible that brutal, patriarchal, repressive, dull, fanatical terror cliques could establish themselves in certain bolos. There are no humanist, liberal or democratic laws or rules about the content of nimas and there is no State to enforce them. Nobody can prevent a bolo from committing mass suicide, dying of drug experiments, driving itself into madness or being unhappy under a violent regime. bolos with a bandit-nima could terrorize whole regions or continents, as the Huns or Vikings did. Freedom and adventure, generalized terrorism, the law of the club, raids, tribal wars, vendettas, plundering – everything goes.[58]

Widmer contends that bandit-nima are unlikely: the possibility is explained as part of the hangover of the Machine. 'Alcobolo', 'Indio-bolo', 'Krishna-bolo', 'Sado-bolo', 'Soho-bolo' are among the nima he imagines taking shape. He labels nima 'pluralistic totalitarianism' but they give bolo'bolo a panarchistic flavour. In practice, of course, nami depends on the nima of the bolos. Because no bolo and no ibu is like any other compromises have to be made. 'Every ibu has its own conviction and vision of life as it should be, but certain nimas can only be realized if like-minded ibus can be found.'[59]

There are a number of other limits on sila. 'Munu', honour or reputation, ensures compliance with the hospitality rule, but there is an exception here, too. Where guests constitute more than 10 per cent of the bolo, the bolo can refuse sila. In addition, the freedom of 'yaka', a carefully regulated code allowing ibu to challenge other ibu or groups of ibus to duels, suggests that all the terms of sila are limited. Widmer argues that the survival of bolo'bolo depends principally on a critical mass of ibus deciding to take part. If too many decide not to, then money economies are likely to return. There are no other serious social threats because the personal contacts fostered by bolo'bolo. Once money is abandoned, the Machine's unnatural enforcement agencies 'police, justice, prisons, psychiatric hospitals' also 'collapse or malfunction'. Widmer comments that nobody remains to 'catch the "thief"' and 'everybody who doesn't steal is a fool'.[60] At the same time, he also observes that bolo'bolo encourages self-policing and the adherence to local moral norms.

Bolos take root in existing spaces – towns, across rural settlements – and across geographical areas – groups of islands, for example. They can also emerge from fluid interactions of seafaring or other nomadic folk. Forming a 'patchwork of micro-systems' collections of ten to twenty bolos can combine to form larger co-ordinating bodies at local, sub-regional and autonomous regional levels. These larger units, 'tega', 'vudo' and 'sumi', are organized by a set of formal rules to ensure accountability to the bolos. For example, tega take responsibility for infrastructural projects and run 'dala' or decision-making assemblies composed delegates from the bolos and external observers or 'dudis' from other tega.

Self-sufficiency in basic foods underwrites the self-determination and self-governance of the bolos. Each bolo practises a general culture of 'kodu', or agricultural production. The priority attached to kodu, as a means of establishing the ibus' relationship with nature, tends towards the integration of urban and rural areas, the depopulation of larger cities and the repopulation of villages. Bi- or multilateral agreements facilitate the procurement of foodstuffs that bolos either cannot produce or prefer not to. Kodu depends on ibu commitment, approximately 10 per cent of each ibu's time. This may be experienced psychologically as work or pleasure, depending on the proclivities of individual ibu. The potential burdens kodu entails are offset by 'sibi', the production of non-foodstuffs, which is typically an expressive, creative, pleasurable activity. Gift-giving and carefully controlled markets are used for exchange, enabling ibus to satisfy their need for personal property.

Bolos benefit from integrated energy systems and ecological waste recycling. In cold zones, Widmer estimates that bolos achieve between 50–80 per cent energy independence. Water consumption is reduced by changes in industrial production and the shift from the 'disciplinary functions of washing' that white-collar work and suburban living foster.

Other gains are made as a result of the changes in knowledge production. The disappearance of 'centralized, high-energy, high-tech systems' makes 'centralized, bureaucratic, formal science' redundant but it does not result in the end of science. There is 'no danger of a new "dark age"'. The time that ibus have at their disposal means that 'the scientific, magical, practical and playful transmission of capabilities will expand considerably'. Everyone will be a professor. 'There will be more possibilities for information and research; science will be in the reach of everyone, and the traditional analytical methods will be possible, among others, without having the privileged status that they have today. The ibus will carefully avoid dependency upon specialists, and will use processes they master themselves.'[61]

Much of the detail of bolo'bolo resonates with Kropotkin's utopianism. The fundamental difference is that Widmer builds instability into his projections. bolo'bolo ultimately fails and domination returns. The problem stems from a mutation in the cultures of non-domination that bolo'bolo fosters. After 358 years an epidemic ('the whites') spreads, overwhelming the other bolos. A period of contemplation and chaos lasting just over 400 years ensues until 'Tawhuac puts another floppy disc into the drive.'[62]

How is bolo'bolo a transitory utopia? In many ways it looks as enduring as Kropotkin's revolutionary commune model. Unlike Kropotkin, Widmer does not include a lot of statistics to support the feasibility of the project but the utopia is described in extraordinary detail. Widmer also includes a provisional schedule: bolo'bolo is projected to come into being within three to five years. The substraction starts in 1983. The first planetary convention, 'asa'dala' meets in 1987. bolo'bolo begins in 1988.

In part, the difference is stylistic. *bolo'bolo* is written as fantasy. *Fields, Factories and Workshops* is social science. A second difference is the relationship of the utopia to the practice. Hakim Bey calls bolo'bolo a permanent autonomous zone (PAZ), that is, a temporary autonomous zone (TAZ) that has succeeded in 'putting down roots'. More than a thought-experiment but less than a plan, bolo'bolo is an insurgency that exists in time and space while avoiding all 'permanent solutions'.[63] It is about liberation for a while, not revolution and restructuring for good. Kropotkin's utopia was for keeps, in the sense that the practice of communism was intended to support a system of self-regulation that would prevent the return of capitalism and the state.

Bey prefers the transitoriness of bolo'bolo. It conforms to Stephen Pearl Andrews's idea of the unlegislated dinner party that also inspired Yarros and it imagines spaces that exist within the legislated parlour.[64] Bey uses two examples to illustrate where the line between enduring and transitory utopias should be drawn. On the one hand, he finds features of TAZ in the 1919 Munich Soviet. Here, the expectation of its crushing (which right-wing paramilitaries soon made certain) encapsulated the aims of the rising more exactly than the revolutionaries' professed aim, which was to achieve lasting change. On the other hand, Bey contends that Makhno's revolution was 'meant to have *duration*'. It did not last a long time, but it was 'organized' for this purpose.[65] No features of TAZ were present here. The intentionality Bey describes points to a third difference, namely about the quality of space that enduring and transitory utopias are designed to create. In his history of German-American anarchism, the historian Tom Goyens comments that anarchists 'did not simply occupy space; they consciously *produced* it by appropriating places for themselves and inscribing them with meaning that reflected their ideology and identity'.[66] The anarchists who created these spaces in a plethora of bars and clubs typically looked outwards. Their visions were unrestrained. *bolo'bolo* describes the possibility of survival for everyone but it is constructed as an inward reflection on the control that the Planetary Work-Machine exercises on spaces of liberation.

Democracy

Anarchists have often been ambivalent about democracy. Their doubts arise from the power inequalities that democracy regulates. Even in genuinely liberal regimes, where democracy is defended both as a value and a process, many anarchists argue that it serves essentially repressive ends. This is Yarros's argument and it is also presented in the Makhnovist Platform. A section titled the 'Negation of Democracy' distinguishes the liberal principles which democrats promote from the reality of democracy's institutional operation. Democracy lauds 'freedom of speech, of the press, of association, as well as equality before the law' but it 'leaves the principle of capitalist private property untouched'. It thereby 'leaves the bourgeoisie its entitlement to hold within its hands the entire economy of the country, all of the press, education, science and art'. Democracy 'is merely one of the facets of bourgeois dictatorship, concealed behind the camouflage of notional political freedoms and democratic assurances'.[67]

Anarchist misgivings are also explained by the principle of representation that democratic government institutes. George Woodcock rejected representation on the grounds that it required individuals to abdicate 'sovereignty'. 'No conception of anarchism is further from the truth than that which regards it as an extreme form of democracy,' he argued. While democracy 'advocates the sovereignty of the people', anarchism 'advocates the sovereignty of the person'. Representation infantilizes individuals, as well as coercing them. Citizens are by turns treated as incapable of determining their own interests and forced to accept the judgements of those supposedly best placed to make them. Decisions are made in the name of electors even though representatives are institutionally detached from them. 'Not in my name' has become a familiar rallying cry of those who feel aggrieved by the outcomes of particular policy decisions. Woodcock turned to Proudhon to describe the anarchist critique underpinning this grievance: 'Universal Suffrage is the Counter-Revolution.'[68] Saul Newman's version of this thesis is that representation is based on a notion of rational consensus that militates against 'wilful' autonomy. Individuals have to accept the rationality of rules they have had a hand in making and, therefore, the justness of the norms, laws and practices that ensure compliance. Representation treats the individual as an autonomous being but in fact denies any the space to explore creative practices of individual 'self-making'.[69]

The normalization of liberal democracy since 1945 and

the reduction of democracy with a particular western system
of government have prompted some anarchists to revisit
these critiques. They have attempted to rescue the principle of democracy from its institutional expression in the
liberal capitalist state. Noam Chomsky's critique of capitalist democracy is not just that it provides a smokescreen
for concentrations of corporate power, that it institutionalizes a division between leaders and led through ritualistic
electoral competitions, or even that its success in the US has
consecrated a system of international state terrorism and
exploitation. His chief insight is that capitalist democracy
'manufactures consent' through media control and propaganda. According to this analysis, democracy is a powerful
force of the people for self-government which has been co-
opted and corrupted by elites in order to maintain minority
rule. Arguing that democracy is deterred by liberal democratic regimes not protected by them, Chomsky defends the idea
of free, popular self-government and argues for the extension of grass-roots democracy – in workplaces, schools and
other public institutions.[70]

In the same vein, anarchists involved in the global justice
movements of the noughties painted representative government, electoral competition, periodic free and fair elections,
and universal adult suffrage as elitist and hierarchical. Yet
they also identified as democrats and sought to promote distinctive forms of 'real democracy'. As Rebecca Solnit argues,
real democracy means that 'everyone has a voice, that no one
gets away with things just because of their wealth, power,
race or gender'.[71] On these measures, liberal democracy per-
forms badly. It fairs even less well in terms of the latitude

for dissent it achieves. Distinguishing democracy from dictatorship Solnit argues that the existence of formal rights is one measure of democracy; dictatorship means prohibition of 'public gatherings and groups'. Yet rights are not the be-all and end-all of democracy because democracy is above all 'a bodily, tangible life'. Those inured to liberal democratic systems defend 'freedom of speech, the press, and religion' and even rights of assembly. But, she argues, they tend to forget about its dynamic aspects.[72] This forgetfulness shows where liberal democracy shades into dictatorship and it provides the spur for real democracy. Real democrats know that 'democracy must be exercised, regularly and on foot' and that 'the life of crowds . . . the vitality of the streets . . . the potential for revolt that always hovers there' are its essential components.

While this re-casting of democracy is consistent with the anti-democratic critique, it provides a more solid defence of democratic principles. Anarchists emerge from it as pro-democracy critics of liberal-democratic regimes rather than averse to democracy as opponents of their constitutional arrangements. Murray Bookchin's 'communalism' is one of the best known pro-democracy anarchist models. More recently, not least because it was widely practised in the Occupy movement, the idea of consensus decision-making has taken centre stage in anarchist thinking about democracy.

Bookchin understood democracy as a principle of both self-management and collective decision-making, integral to anarchist decentralized federation, and, ethically, as a process for social freedom. For advocates of consensus decision-making, democracy is principally an anti-elitist action that directly challenges hierarchy and privilege in order to construct new social relationships. It is almost a synonym for anarchy rather than a component of it.

Democratic communalism

Bookchin's anarchism was arguably constructed around the notion of conditions. A sympathetic critic of Marx and Engels, he distinguished himself as an anarchist early in his career by jettisoning earlier talk about the 'preconditions' for socialism and pressing a new agenda. This centred on the realization of the '*conditions* of freedom'. For Bookchin, writing in 1969 when the damage caused by industrialization was becoming clearer, it was time to set aside Marx's survivalist theories. Marx's vision of harnessing the power of technology to secure material abundance was also outmoded. We had entered 'the realm of *life*', Bookchin declared.[73] The task now, was to make that realm real by adopting a new approach to social transformation.

Bookchin called his outlook social ecology and argued that it involved both moral regeneration and social reconstruction along ecological lines.[74] Social ecology revolved around the idea that 'the natural world and the social are interlinked by evolution into one nature that consists of two differentiations'. The first, which Bookchin called 'biotic nature', was the world as non-human beings inhabit it. The second, social nature described the effects of human habitation and the changes that humans wrought on the world. Prevailing cultures of domination, engendered by human hierarchies, had resulted in an artificial separation of the biotic from the social: nature was wrongly conceptualized as something to be dominated and the economy was organized accordingly. Social ecology brought first and second nature back into alignment by instituting far-reaching structural and cultural change.

Anarchist principles of decentralized federation provided Bookchin with the appropriate model for harmonization. In coming to this conclusion, Bookchin referenced Kropotkin, but indicated that William Morris, Herbert Read and George Woodcock were the more profound influences. Yet in one important sense Bookchin clearly followed Kropotkin: turning to anarchism from Marxism in the 1950s and 1960s and, conscious of the right-ward drift of international politics in the 1980s, his work repeatedly probed the question of how to build mass movements.

If Bookchin's aim was to re-articulate a critical ecological politics that addressed the problems of the post-war (western) world, his notion of communalism also resonated with the anarchist-communist politics advocated by Kropotkin and Reclus. Indeed it was animated by 'the vision of a "Commune of communes"' that had stirred the nineteenth-century anarchist imagination and it built on the ideas of autonomous self-government and decentralized federation that anarchists had advanced since Proudhon's time. That said, Bookchin clarified and refined the earlier model in two regards.

First, he advocated a confederal constitutional model. Confederalism is usually understood to entail a commitment to the autonomy of the units that comprise a federation and it is often linked to political centralization. Bookchin gave the concept his own slant. Confederalism was 'a network of administrative councils whose members or delegates are elected from popular face-to-face democratic assemblies in various villages, towns, and even neighborhoods of large cities'. Mutualism and interdependence defined the relationship between the composite units and the confederal network, for if 'one community is not obliged to count on another or others generally to satisfy important material needs and realize common political goals in such a way that it is interlinked to the greater whole, exclusivity and parochialism are genuine possibilities'.[75] As far as the members' powers were concerned, Bookchin imagined that each would be 'strictly mandated' and 'recallable' and responsible only for 'coordinating and administering the policies formulated by assemblies themselves'. In contrast to representatives in conventional legislative bodies, they would have no policy-making role.[76]

Bookchin's second refinement was to place the city at the heart of his model. Taking a long view of the city, he conceptualized it as a 'uniquely human, ethical, and ecological community that often lived in balance with nature and created institutional forms that sharpened human awareness of their sense of natural place as well as social place'.[77] This characterization bore some similarity to Kropotkin's conception of the medieval city-state. But like the Situationist Guy Debord, Bookchin recognized the power of those social trends that Kropotkin had wanted to halt and the mid- to late-twentieth century spread of urbanization. Just as the Debord had associated urbanization with the 'explosion of cities which cover the countryside', the 'dictatorship of the automobile', the 'domination of the freeway' and the 'enormous shopping centres built on the bare ground of parking lots',[78] Bookchin argued that urbanization was 'engulfing' the countryside and the city and that both were under siege.[79]

Bookchin's social ecology was designed to reverse the damage done to the city by the cancerous dehumanization of modern life.[80] While he recommended similar 'rounded eco-technologies that rescale the most advanced elements of modern technology' such as wind and solar power 'to local dimensions', he called for the restoration of the equilibrium between town and country rather than the integration of agriculture and industry, as Kropotkin had done. Moreover, the revival of the city spelt the restoration of 'urbanity as a meaningful terrain for sociation, culture, and community'. Bookchin's city was a civic community designed to revive citizenship. This imagined the city in a very different to way to Kropotkin.

For Bookchin the city was defined by the quality of its social relations and, as the primary unit of communalist social organization, he visualized it as an eco-community. The city's ecological community transformation thus went hand-in-hand with its political resurrection. As he put it, 'the rounded citizen' could only thrive in a 'rounded environment'.[81] To accomplish the shift from 'anemic parliamentarism' to what he called 'libertarian municipalism' Bookchin took his lead from classical Greek democracy.[82] His aim was to invest the city with 'the best features of the *polis*'.[83] Of course, as an egalitarian, he stripped the Athenian model of its institutionalized forms of domination: chattel slavery and the exclusion of women. What remained in this non-party, anti-parliamentary and anti-representational ideal were directly democratic, open, participatory citizen's assemblies and, above all, the idea of public space and an 'abiding physical arena of politics'.[84]

The democratic politics Bookchin had in mind sought 'to create a vital democratic public sphere', empowering citizens to regulate municipal institutions – schools, workplaces, leisure facilities and public spaces – while leaving citizens to conduct their social lives as they pleased. Delineating the social from the political realm, Bookchin called for citizens to exercise power directly in their communities while prescribing the policy that assemblies could legitimately enact. As private individuals, citizens would be free to determine what they 'do in their homes, what friendships they form, the communal lifestyles they practice, the way they make their living, their sexual behavior, the cultural artifacts they consume, and the rapture and ecstasy they experience on mountaintops'.[85] As citizens, they had a duty to consider how any of these practices would affect the municipality. The resulting tension between the social and the political realms was the lifeblood of anarchist democracy.

Consensus

Consensus decision-making is a type of value-based democracy. It emphasizes the importance of sharing power, resolving differences, active participation, trust and transparency. There is no set process for consensus but it typically involves the working and reworking of proposals until everyone directly affected by the proposal is able to accept the result. The point is not to 'convert others' to a single point of view or exert power by mobilizing support for preferred options. In this sense, it breaks with standard electoral models.

Some anarchists reject consensus decision-making, considering it a deeply flawed organizational process. Bookchin died before the Occupy movement 'enacted the impossible' and introduced processes of consensus decision-making in mass public assemblies.[86] But familiar with its adoption in activist movements in the 1970s, he rejected it as unanarchist. His practical objection was that consensus decision-making 'permits an insidious authoritarianism and gross manipulations'. Consensual processes took root where organizational structurelessness reigned. The resulting fluidity was disastrous. Consensus enabled 'small tightly knit' factions to press their own 'hidden agendas'. 'Minority dissenters were often subtly urged or psychologically coerced to decline to vote on a troubling issue, inasmuch as their dissent would essentially amount to a one-person veto'.

Bookchin also had a philosophical objection: consensus silences 'that most vital aspect of all dialogue, *dissensus*'. The 'ongoing dissent, the passionate dialogue that still persists even after a minority accedes temporarily to a majority decision' is replaced 'by dull monologues – and the uncontroverted and deadening tone of consensus'. Where anarchists adopt majority decision-making, 'the defeated minority can resolve to overturn a decision on which they have been defeated – they are free to openly and persistently articulate reasoned and potentially persuasive disagreements'. Consensus 'mutes' minorities 'in favor of the metaphysical "one" of the "consensus" group'.[87]

Not surprisingly, advocates of consensus decision-making take a different view. The highly influential guide produced by the UK-based workers' co-op and advocacy group Seeds for Change addresses Bookchin's philosophical concerns directly. Consensus is designed to overcome factionalism and discourages participants from expressing narrow self-interest, but it does not stifle disagreement. This is part of the process. The advice on achieving consensus is:

- If you don't understand something, don't be afraid to say so.
- Be willing to work towards the solution that's best for everyone, not just what's best for you. Be flexible and willing to give something up to reach an agreement.
- Help to create a respectful and trusting atmosphere. Nobody should be afraid to express their ideas and opinions. Remember that we all have different values, backgrounds and behaviour and we get upset by different things.
- Explain your own position clearly. Be open and honest about the reasons for your view points. Express your concerns early on in the process so that they can be taken into account in any proposals.
- Listen actively to what people are trying to say. Make an effort to understand someone's position and their underlying needs, concerns and emotions. Give everyone space to finish and take time to consider their point of view.
- Think before you speak, listen before you object. Listen to other members' reactions and consider them carefully before pressing your point. Self-restraint is essential in consensus – sometimes the biggest obstacle to progress is an individual's attachment to one idea. If another proposal is good, don't complicate matters by opposing it just because it isn't your favourite idea! Ask yourself: 'Does this idea work for the group, even if I don't like it the best?' or 'Does it matter which one we choose?'

- Don't be afraid of disagreement. Consensus isn't about us all thinking the same thing. Differences of opinion are natural and to be expected. Disagreements can help a group's decision, because with a wide range of information and opinions, there is a greater chance the group will find good solutions. Easily reached consensus may cover up the fact that some people don't feel safe or confident enough to express their disagreements.

Some of the strongest defences of consensus decision-making have been made by anarchists who champion particular forms of anti-oppression politics. Anarchist feminists involved in grass-roots anti-authoritarian politics in Quebec value consensus as part of a toolkit that constructively tackles intersectional oppressions and unrecognized privilege by fostering 'freedom, solidarity, collective autonomy, social justice, respect, spontaneity, and mutual aid'. Practised with 'skill sharing, resource sharing, horizontal organizing without leaders, mutual emotional caretaking, no official membership lists or fees, joining by doing', consensus contributes to the construction of the non-hegemonic social relationships that enable self-government.[88]

These ideas also infused the politics of the Occupy movement of 2011, where consensus decision-making was practised by large numbers of people. For David Graeber, one of the leading lights in Occupy, consensus not only described a participatory decision-making practice but an alternative system of self-government. As it was enacted in Occupy camps, consensus emerged as a political practice that enabled participants to take decisions at General Assemblies transparently and directly. It empowered them to make rules about their living spaces and social relations and to charge working groups or spokes-councils with formulating policy recommendations without resorting to representation. By practising democratic consensus decision-making as a protest against the elitism and corporate corruption of existing representative institutions, Occupy demonstrated their redundancy. Consensus democracy, then, promoted self-government – rule by the people – as an anti-capitalist activity.

In this setting, consensus democracy is not only an instrument to address privilege and oppression, it also represents a revolutionary challenge to liberal constitutionalism. Plotting a parallel history of conventional and resistance politics from the eighteenth century, Graeber contrasts constitutional rule to 'communal self-governance'.[89] The first has its origins in the historic re-attribution of sovereignty from monarchs to the people. This transferred power to an educated elite – not coincidentally, all white men who enjoyed significant economic advantages and thought themselves 'wiser and better able to understand the people's true interests than the people themselves'.[90] At the same time, it kick-started in the 1790s Tom Paine's popular campaign against political and economic corruption. For Graeber, this was an instance of a transnational, transhistoric campaign for democracy and against the constitution. Occupy gave it new expression and in doing so created a model for self-government that also challenged hierarchy, privilege and domination. Speaking about the Occupation of Zuccotti Park in New York in 2011, A. J. Bauer notes:

Much has been made of the movement's official embrace of consensus democratic practices through routine General Assembly meetings, and later more controversially through the Spokes Council, but the occupation's ability to generate speech and action, and thus democratic power, extended far beyond official meetings and even the boundaries of the park. In a way, it was these myriad smaller, undocumented conversations among new acquaintances where the Occupy movement realized its democratic potential. That is, the occupation of Zuccotti Park enabled not only a working space for the movement to conduct its official business, nor only a living space for those who chose (or were forced by circumstance) to reside in the park. Rather, the occupation's appropriation of physical space enabled the kind of politics . . . where people approached one another as equals, recognized one another's distinct humanity and common interest, and drew up plans to act upon that interest.[91]

Consensus points to a conception of democracy that is quite different to the Hellenic idea championed by Bookchin. Consensual democratic processes stress the need to transform our existing social relations to enable us to re-imagine our local communities. Bookchin emphasizes the re-creation of the public sphere, for this is essential for the exercise of citizenship. Many of the values of anarchist self-organizing are common to both, but the institutional modelling and the aspirations for social transformation are distinctive.

Conditioning anarchy

One of the persistent themes running through anarchist discussions of conditions is the degree to which the very specification of anarchist self-organizing automatically limits its possibilities. In 1840 Proudhon observed that anarchists were culturally disadvantaged by assumptions about hierarchical leadership that demonstrated (apparently incontrovertibly) the inevitability and desirability of typically centralized, top-down rule. Defining anarchy as 'the absence of a master, of a sovereign', he related a story of 'a citizen of Paris in the seventeenth century' who 'having heard it said that in Venice there was no king . . . nearly died from laughter at the mere mention of so ridiculous a thing'. 'Such is our prejudice,' Proudhon commented.[92]

To overcome it, anarchists have repeatedly tried to describe how power can be distributed to ensure 'the greatest possible number of sovereigns'. Yet in doing so, they appear to lay down rules for others. This implies that anarchists are caught in a trap. Midnight Notes, the loose, avant-garde collective which began publishing in the 1970s, once argued the case against Bookchin: 'radical and "anarchist" anti-plans such as Bookchin's proposals . . . which want to cut back society and economy to small, humane, self-sufficient units, without state, capital and money, suffer from the same basic vice: anticipating and planning a future for "others".' The group provided a class explanation for Bookchin's failing: 'The ecological and anti-plan ideology is an expression of the fears of intellectual workers in confronting less valuable labour power. They are not ready to devaluate themselves, to renounce their planning and managing function.' Yet the collective's more compelling conclusion was surely that Bookchin's apparent 'failing' actually points to an intractable tension in anarchism. Whether or not he and other anti-planners were guilty of '[h]iding behind the concept of "responsibility for humankind"', the anarchist concern with '"ifs" and "buts" (will we have enough energy? who will clean the streets?)' was 'neither surprising nor vicious'. The lesson was that 'we just have to be aware'.[93]

CHAPTER 5
Prospects

In two significant regards, the prospects for anarchism seem to be no better today than in the 1840s when Proudhon told his story about the incredulous seventeenth-century Parisian. The cultural bias for authority seems to be as strong as ever and the problem of distributing power among 'the greatest number of sovereigns' remains unresolved. There are a large number of anarchist groups and associations (libraries, unions, social centres, worker and housing co-ops, journals, publishers, newspapers and study groups) and these are well networked.[1] Yet anarchists frequently inhabit largely anarchist-exclusive spaces. In this sense, the dinner-party model predominates, even though the vast majority of anarchists would reject Victor Yarros's elitist disdain. While the prospects for anarchism may seem bleak, I want to suggest the possibilities for anarchism should not be evaluated by the spread or reach of anarchist groups but by the adjustments anarchists can foster in non-anarchist organizations. In this last chapter, I argue that the way we frame anarchist success is key to the evaluation of its prospects.

Success and failure

Anarchism is sometimes called a colossal disappointment. The Communards, the Makhnovists and the Spanish anarchists are cast as starry-eyed champions of noble but doomed causes. Political scientists can also look at anarchism's 'second and third waves' – the New Left, the 'alterglobalization' social justice movement and Occupy – and find examples of quixotic failure. Those who are not left scratching their heads, wondering what the actual results of these movements were, sometimes suggest that the only real legacy is one of state or capitalist recuperation. The Amsterdam white bike scheme is an example. In the 1960s Dutch police confiscated the bikes that anarchists made freely available for public use: today officers are duty-bound to arrest those who tamper with bank-sponsored cycles that can only be hired at cost. To give another example: Jerry Rubin's 1960s message of empowerment, 'Do It!' now comes with corporate swoosh – *Just Do It*.

A swathe of recent research shows that the European anarchist experience is not definitive. That means that glib pronouncements about the health or significance of a global movement cannot be based on the appraisal of its European fragments. There's another objection, too: which criteria of success and failure can be used to judge anarchism, a movement that explicitly rejects the goal of winning power? Is it fairer, then, to judge anarchism for its failure to deliver what its ideals promote? If so, it might be argued that anarchists have not managed to denuclearize the world, secure global peace, deliver women from everyday violence or eradicate famine. Yet non-anarchists have not fared any better and it is unfair to focus on anarchism without judging liberalism, Marxism, republicanism or conservatism in the same way: if the criticism is valid in principle, it is generally applicable. Perhaps a better test is to consider how anarchist norms have become institutionalized: for example, the eight-hour day, access to contraception, the relaxation of marriage laws or conscientious objection. These are not universally accepted or successful, nor are they purely anarchist achievements. But anarchists have spent a lot of jail time advancing these causes and have undoubtedly played a role in their accomplishment.

Anarchists have often bypassed conventional measures of success and failure and instead of drawing up balance sheets they have focused on issues of capacity and endurance. In 1979 David Porter noticed that significant numbers of 60s activists were burnt out. 'To their despair, the struggle for change drained too much energy, too fast, and with no source of replenishment.' He also noticed that this was nothing new. Bakunin had felt it, too. Porter concluded that '[d]espite such depression, many anarchists *did* persist'.[2] Resilience is one of the mainstays of anarchist success, even though this is more usually associated with chest-thumping Churchillian patriotism. The quote recently attributed to Churchill at the end of Joe Wright's film *Darkest Hour*, 'Success is not final, failure is not fatal. It is the courage to continue that counts', also expresses well an anarchist conception of victory and defeat. Perhaps the judges should have thought twice before locking up an ex-soldier who turned Winston Churchill into a punk by adding a turf Mohican to his statue in 2000. For the same sentiment was encapsulated by Emma Goldman as she began to confront the end of her life of long struggle:

> Regardless of the present trend toward the strong-armed man, the totalitarian states, or the dictatorship from the left, my ideas have remained unshaken. In fact, they have been strengthened by my personal experience and the world events through the years. I see no reason to change . . . As in the past, so I do now insist that freedom is the soul of progress and essential to every phase of life . . . My faith is in the individual and in the capacity of free individuals for united endeavor.
>
> The fact that the Anarchist movement for which I have striven so long is to a certain extent in abeyance and overshadowed by philosophies of authority and coercion affects me with concern, but not with despair . . .
>
> Considered from this angle, I think my life and my work have been successful. What is generally regarded as success – acquisition of wealth, the capture of power or social prestige – I consider the most dismal failures. I hold when it is said of a man that he has arrived, it means that he is finished – his development has stopped at that point. I have always striven to remain in a state of flux and continued growth, and not to petrify in a niche of self-satisfaction. If I had my life to live over again . . . I should work for Anarchism with the same devotion and confidence in its ultimate triumph.[3]

Patience in the face of setback and failure were the criteria that Goldman (like Bakunin) used to evaluate anarchist progress. The defeats of revolutionary action are significant and they cannot be ignored, but neither can anarchist persistence be overlooked. The fact is that anarchist movements have endured and have risen above setbacks and compromises, to continually push for libertarian change.

The fortitude shown by anarchists may explain why anarchism is now generating more interest than ever. Repeated waves of popular non-party, horizontal activism since the late 1990s have helped attract closer attention to anarchism than at any time in its past. Assessments of the anarchistic sensibilities of the radical and revolutionary left and the anarchist influences on the values, attitudes, practices and creative aesthetics of contemporary activists are many and multiplying. Anarchism also has a significant online presence and the libraries of academic literature are rapidly expanding. Anarchists argue about the ideological soundness of the newest social movements, but there's little dispute that there has been a change in grass-roots activism, particularly since the destruction of the Berlin Wall and the collapse of the Soviet bloc. Significant movements of the left – from Antifa to the Zapatista uprising – are routinely discussed with reference to anarchism. In 1968, contrary to Marxist orthodoxy, Daniel Cohn-Bendit suggested that anarchism deserved recognition as an important current within leftism. Yet even with this fillip, anarchism remained largely under the radar. In the 1970s Carol Ehrlich commented on its invisibility: coverage 'veered between a bad press and none at all'. No surprise, then, that the 1971 statement *Blood of the Flower* (written by Cathy Levine and Marian Leighton for the Black Rose anarchist-feminist collective) was also an excavation. Defending the supposed naivety of Black Rose's decision to reject the staples of the mainstream left – patriarchal, van-guardist movement organizing – Levine and Leighton called on their readers to discover 'another entire radical tradition which has run counter to Marxist-Leninist theory and prac-tice through all of modern radical history'. This tradition ran 'from Bakunin to Kropotkin to Sophie Perovskaya to Emma Goldman to Errico Malatesta to Murray Bookchin'. It was 'less familiar to most radicals because it has consistently been distorted and misrepresented by the more highly organ-ized State organization and Marxist-Leninist organization'.[4] Anarchism still routinely gets a bad press, but fifty years on, radicals can at least tap into the traditions that Levine and Leighton helped uncover.

In this context, Abdullah Öcalan, leader of the Kurdish Workers' Party, has raised anarchism's star to new heights. His adaptation of Murray Bookchin's democratic communal-ism has been central to the constitutional project that has been initiated by Kurdish forces active in Northern Syria. In 2014 a provisional constitution was declared in the Rojavan cantons of Efrin, Kobane and Cizire. The declaration of the Rojava-Northern Syria Democratic Federal System followed in 2016. This was agreed by 200 delegates from the Rojavan cantons and the Arab, Assyrian, Syriac, Armenian, Turkmen and Chenchen peoples living in neighbouring regions of Girê Spî/Tal Abyad, Shaddadi, Aleppo and Shehba. Both breathed life into Bookchin's concept of social ecology, animating 'groundbreaking' knowledge through action, as Öcalan put it.[5] Öcalan enjoys cult status within the Kurdish movement and although he is no mere Bookchin acolyte he has effectively initiated a sweeping experiment in anarchy, demonstrating that anarchism's influence extends far beyond the circles of its adherents. Of course, the Rojavan revolution is far from secure and the peace plan, 'The Project of a Democratic Syria',[6] proposed by the TEV-DEM (the coalition administering the region of the Democratic Federation of Northern Syria) is being roundly ignored by the dominant military powers. Yet for all this, there is a significant multicultural, grass-roots, self-governing confederal project working on the ground and a project for its extension across a wide geographical area. Is this anarchy in action? Öcalan's comment, that 'alternative free life is neither a form of production nor a society but a life that can be constructed daily by communities', certainly reverberates with anarchist thinking. And the anarchistic reality being constructed on this ground can be imagined elsewhere, too.

What does anarchism's staying power tell us about the futures of anarchy? In this final section, I consider this question by describing the conundrum that anarchists face and the strategies they use to solve it.

The conundrum

The anthropologist and political scientist James Scott argues that the practical and theoretical 'conundrum' facing anarchists is how to provide the 'relative equality' necessary for democracy, 'mutuality and freedom' in the absence of the state. Though acknowledging that the history of the state is one of repression, intolerance and genocidal violence, he also argues that states play a positive role in people's lives. In particular, they safeguard the rights of individuals who suffer prejudice and hate and protect them from neighbours who want to inflict harm or perpetuate their disadvantage. As an anarchist 'fellow-traveller', Scott regrets that this seems to suggest that we appear stuck 'with Leviathan'. But he gives only two cheers for anarchism because the reality of the state's existence means that its abolition 'is not an option'.[7]

Scott's conclusions show how dramatically the political context has altered since anarchism's early history. Less than 150 years ago the Haymarket anarchists demanded that governments show how the legal and constitutional arrangements they preferred could ever realize the principles of liberty, equality and fraternity that legitimized them. Today the tables have turned and the state seems so all pervasive that the anarchist complaint seems obsolete. Whether the case is made in terms of sociological inevitability, historical achievement or political desirability, state organization seems both stable and permanent: anarchy looks unfeasible not just because it has been largely superseded by the state but also because anarchists cannot show how they would manage or provide the goods on offer in states. How will rubbish collections be organized in anarchy? Who will run the schools? How will crime be tackled? The default anarchist response, that these kinds of questions cannot be answered precisely because people must decide and act for themselves, rarely satisfies those looking for concrete solutions to specific organizational problems.

The familiar retort to Scott's conundrum is that the amenities that states provide only mitigate the worst excesses that they perpetuate. This is scott crow's response: the state institutionalizes the prejudices of dominant minorities and prioritizes its own protection over the interests of its citizens.

scott crow was a co-founder of the Common Ground Collective, a community crisis-response initiative in New Orleans that provided healthcare and housing in the aftermath of Hurricane Katrina. He recalls the context in which the group established its operations:

> Then the police drew guns on us constantly. This is something that people in these communities have to go through every day, but this was happening to white people who didn't live here. And the police kept saying that we're going to overthrow them. But they weren't doing anything to help people; they wanted to restore law and order. You have to understand – there's people trapped in their attics, on their rooftops. We're not talking about a few hundred people. We're talking tens of thousands of people are going to die, and all they want to do is restore law and order, and they're turning a blind eye to all the white militia in this neighborhood.[8]

A second response to the conundrum is that the amenities that states provide are purchased at an unacceptably high price. Chomsky adds up some of the costs. Freedom of speech is an 'achievement' and a right 'protected more in the United States than in any other country I know', but it functions in a political culture marked by 'colossal' inequality and the repression of independent thought.[9] The trade-offs become starker as states decide to offer the same benefits to other citizens. As Chomsky puts it, US foreign policy is geared to the delivery of US freedoms to others 'whether they like or not'. America is not unusual in assuming this role. It just happens to be the dominant power in the twentieth and early twenty-first century international system. 'What's called "American exceptionalism",' Chomsky observes is 'uniform across states, to the extent that they have power'. States typically 'find a way of making themselves exceptionally "good" and justify what they're doing'. Before the US assumed hegemonic power at the end of 1945, the French and British busily pursued their 'civilizing missions'. The Japanese similarly brought 'what they called – an "earthly paradise" to China . . . defending the population from . . . Chinese bandits'.[10] Even if the brutality of these colonial adventures was not uniform, Chomsky's point is that brutality is the relevant measure.

A third response is that the amenities on offer in states are not provided as a matter of course. In 1944 George Woodcock argued that the 'homes for heroes' promised by inter-war governments only appeared in the UK once demobbed soldiers and their families took direct action against landlords and organized rent strikes. Tenants had to make concerted efforts to secure homes and fight off eviction.[11] Chomsky generalizes this to argue that citizens are forever obliged to struggle to safeguard the benefits won by their forebears. Returning to the US, he argues that 'popular movements democratized the country', compelling 'the government . . . to create significant welfare measures, social security, labor rights and so on'. Likewise, the protection of freedom of speech has less to do with the Bill of Rights than with the public pressure exerted in the 1960s. Current legislation was enacted on the back of 'the wave of the civil rights and other popular movements: women's rights . . . the rights of ethnic minorities'.[12]

For those prepared to give anarchy three cheers, this last counter perhaps describes the political and theoretical conundrum anarchists face more precisely than Scott's worry: that anarchy cannot provide the protections guaranteed by states. The implication of Chomsky's view is that the resolution to Scott's conundrum does not depend on showing how anarchy will replicate the state. It comes from acknowledging that the best arrangements available in states have come from the pressure exerted 'from below' and imagining the plasticity of Leviathan. This has a philosophical as well as a practical aspect.

The philosophy can be traced back to Proudhon and the qualms he expressed about abstract utopian thinking and Bakunin's contention that philosophers should theorize from experience. Paul Goodman restated the case when he defined philosophy as a 'concrete' and 'central' art. Goodman understood philosophy as he understood science: as a mode of thinking rather than an academic discipline. Properly construed, it meant 'directly attending to the human beings, the citizens of the city, their concrete behavior and their indispensable concerns'.

He also believed that the effects of poor philosophy were felt in everyday life. Asking hypothetical questions meant getting bogged down in 'traffic problems, housing problems, tax problems, and problems of law enforcement'. These were important issues but the manner of their investigation was even more important. Giving someone a brief to find out how a particular service could be introduced or regulated led to poor design. Planners and designers were being tasked with resolving problems of co-ordination by delivering goods to people without being asked to consider patterns of social interaction. The results were usually fussy and over-elaborate, and the effects were rarely libertarian. The art of philosophy,

Goodman argued, required a holistic approach. It was best to plan by thinking first about the how people lived. This meant considering 'work, residence, and transit as one problem' and not a series of separate concerns to be parcelled up from the whole.[13] The causes that anarchists have persistently promoted, about work, housing and prisons, typically have this character. While they might look like single-issue campaigns, they are actually about capitalism, property and justice.

Goodman believed that the realignment of philosophy from the concrete to the hypothetical had skewed perceptions of the depth of the problems that modern societies faced and resulted in the exclusion of whole bundles of knowledge from the search for possible remedies. To re-invigorate philosophy he constructed a set of fictional ideal-type social orders. These models enabled him to imagine how different social arrangements might practically function to tackle common problems.

He sketched three social forms: the 'city of efficient consumption', the 'new community' and the 'community of planned security with minimum regulation'. The first resembled post-war America but centred on the metropolis and Goodman described it as a department store. The second was rooted in an artisan, arts and crafts ethic and was intended to close the gap between production and consumption. The third was an egalitarian welfarist society which guaranteed security of subsistence as the springboard for creative political experimentation. Each was sketched in some detail but Goodman emphasized that they represented possibilities, not choices. They were more or less feasible in particular geopolitical contexts.

Goodman's approach resonated with Rocker's idea of culture: if there were stark sociological models, there were also gradations within the spectrum that history had marked out. Social orders were more or less nationalistic not straightforwardly nationalist or naturalist. So feasibility was about the shades of grey that came out of black and white alternatives, such as the stark choice between order and chaos. The multiple possibilities depended on the ways that people articulated their desires, how they conceptualized their ideas, how they understood apparently shared concepts, what ethics they adopted, what sort of technologies they considered useful or appropriate, and so on. The two principles Goodman brought into his philosophy were that 'the thousand places that one plans for have mixed conditions and mixed values' and that '[d]ifferent people in a place want different things, and the same people want different things'.[14]

How did Goodman reformulate the anarchist conundrum? He turned it towards the complexities, uncertainties and imperfections of concrete philosophy – philosophy practised as popular art. Like Scott, he agreed that most of us are stuck in states but he argued that this sociological reality was not the last word on social organization. Goodman's final reflection took the form of a riddle worthy of Proudhon: 'the people are not philosophical, they do not know the concrete and central facts. Yet only the people *can* know them. The answer is in the remarkable and thought-provoking sentence of Michelet: "Initiation, education, and government – these are three synonymous words."'[15]

So restated, the anarchist conundrum is not about forcing a political choice between two modes of living – state and anarchy – but about motivating popular political, social and cultural projects within the framework of the state system. It entails the replication and mimicry of alternatives that transform the services that states provide, not the replication of those services using different methods. As the *L'En-dehors* group associated with Émile Armand and Zo d'Axa argued in their 1926 Manifesto, anarchy is about 'anarchization'.[16]

The practical puzzle is how to encourage groups and individuals to alter arrangements that they may well consider beneficial, even while acknowledging that they operate in imperfect and often alienating ways. As we will see, there are two responses to this conundrum: one treats anarchism as a form of common sense while the other sees it as a special insight and presumes a gap between anarchists and non-anarchists.

Approaches to Anarchization

ANARCHIZATION THROUGH CONVERGENCE

Malatesta's 1884 *Fra Contadini, or A Talk About Anarchist Communism Between Two Workers* points to an early example of convergence:

> *Bert:* Ah! George, is that you? I'm glad to see you. I've been wanting to talk to you for a while. O, George! George! I've been hearing so many things about you! When you lived in the country you were a good lad, quite an example to the young people of your age . . . If your poor father were alive . . .
>
> *George:* Bert, what's wrong? What have I done to deserve this? And why would my poor father have been dissatisfied with me?

Bert: Don't be offended, George. I'm an old man, and speaking for your own good. Besides, I was a close friend of old Andrew your father and it upsets me as if you were my own son to see you turned out so badly, especially when I think of the hopes your father had of you and the sacrifices he made to give you a good upbringing.

George: But what are you talking about? Am I not an honest worker? I've never done anyone any harm. On the contrary, I've always done what little good I could, so why should my father have been ashamed of me? I do my best to learn and improve, and try together with my comrades to do something about the evils that afflict us all. So why are you getting at me like this?

Bert: Ah, that is just it! I know quite well enough that you work and help your neighbours. You're a good lad, everybody in the area says so. But haven't you been in prison several times, and it's said the police keep an eye on you and that only to be seen talking to you is enough to get one in to trouble. But I'm fond of you, and I'll speak to you in spite of that. George, take the advice of an old man: leave politics to the gentry who have nothing to do, and think of getting on in life. That's the only way to get on in peace and in the grace of God; if you don't you'll lose body and soul. Listen: stop hanging around in bad company. Everybody knows they're the ones that are leading the sons of the poor astray.[17]

In the end, Bert brings George round to his way of thinking: Malatesta's narrative provides a commonsensical response about injustice to a misinformed but fair-minded protagonist. Taking the part of George, Malatesta does not promote anarchism as much as give it a fair hearing. The dialogue emphasizes the reasonableness of anarchism and reveals the partial, narrowly ideological character of the anti-anarchist critique. After reassuring Bert that his activist mates are neither degenerates nor criminals, George convinces him of the virtues of anarchism simply by dispelling the myths about anarchists perpetuated by elites.

Francis Dupuis-Déri and Thomas Déri's *Anarchy Explained to My Father* follows a similar pattern, though Francis's father Thomas comes to their conversation much more positively predisposed to his son's politics. Like Bert, Thomas is also persuaded that anarchy is not quite what he thought it was:

> *Thomas*: We've come a long way from my first innocent question, 'What is anarchy?' Your answers have led me off the beaten path, into terrain I never knew existed. I've read pamphlets and books I'd never heard of before, and you've motivated me to think for myself about a lot of things, not just anarchy. I'm happy to say that I've shed a lot of my old prejudices about anarchy. I no longer accept the stereotypical view of anarchism as a negative force, and see now that it is actually full of hope. Anarchism aspires to abolish authority, or power, to establish a free and egalitarian society. Freeing ourselves from parental authority comes naturally, if we've had a good upbringing. We can try to free ourselves from the authority of the state by creating systems of mutual aid. To counter the authority of religion, we can insist that it remain in the private domain and that society make space for atheists. To fight

the patriarchy we can encourage and support feminism.
We can oppose capitalism with mutual aid and by joining
the alter-globalization movement. We can fight racism
in all its forms by remaining vigilant and deconstructing
theories that extol the superiority of one race over another.
And when people ask us why we bother, why we carry on
this utopian struggle without end, we can answer: to try to
achieve a society whose motto could be 'Freedom, equality,
mutual aid and justice'.[18]

Dialogues like these are popular vehicles for anarchist propaganda because through them anarchists promote the level-headedness of anarchist politics. They show how apparently extreme, radical ideas speak to ordinary intuitions. The dialogue is plain and obvious. It is conducted with friends and family, neighbours and colleagues, with those who may not identify as anarchist, mix with anarchists or spend much time thinking about anarchist politics. Dialogues show that anarchist principles – however labelled – are widely shared. As bell hooks puts it, 'in practice, many more Americans are anarchists than would ever use that term'.[19] Dialogue has the power to demonstrate the convergence between 'American' and 'anarchist' values.

The story Stuart Christie tells about his granny making him an anarchist indicates how this convergence works. Christie's emphasis is not on the everyday practices of Colin Ward's 'anarchy in action': it is the ethical thrust of anarchist critique. As Christie explains, his granny profoundly influenced the way he understood justice and injustice. Indeed, though an atheist he has also acknowledged that his

'Presbyterian upbringing' had an important effect 'inasmuch as it was rooted in the principles of popular sovereignty, the perfectibility of man, and the belief that it was neither safe nor right to act against one's conscience'.[20]

Behind convergence is the idea that it is possible to decouple what Steven Pinker calls the 'primary colors of our moral sense' from the political theologies that institutionalize them. Recent research suggests that

> [p]eople everywhere, at least in some circumstances and with certain other folks in mind, think it's bad to harm others and good to help them. They have a sense of fairness: that one should reciprocate favors, reward benefactors and punish cheaters. They value loyalty to a group, sharing and solidarity among its members and conformity to its norms. They believe that it is right to defer to legitimate authorities and to respect people with high status. And they exalt purity, cleanliness and sanctity while loathing defilement, contamination and carnality.[21]

With some exceptions, anarchists would agree. The disputes between them turn on the legitimacy of authority, the status of particular occupations or roles, and what constitutes 'carnality'. Just debating these issues is a route to anarchization. When the *L'En-dehors* group reflected on anarchization it promised to shout its messages from the rooftops and whisper quietly in people's ears, to use reason and sentiment, appeal to intelligence and instinct to help people to break free of authoritarian practice. The aim was to give a fresh tint to morality. Similarly, Kropotkin's *Appeal to the Young* called on ordinary ethical intuitions to push anarchization.

In exhorting newly trained professionals to use their skills and talents to support workers' struggles, he not only invited the young to set aside calculations of self-interest and utility to determine moral good. He also asked them to attack institutions that debased shared moral values. For example, he exhorted teachers to take to task parents who pushed their offspring into 'reputable' business or military careers. That was to prioritize status over ethics and promote social conservatism. The teacher's role was to expose the underlying moral choice and encourage the anarchist alternative.

Above all, anarchization through convergence is about bridge-building. *L'En-dehors* aspired to talk to everyone – workers, communists, individualists, even other anarchists who ignored them. Kropotkin wanted to reach an even wider constituency. He once imagined 'Conservative, or Liberal, Nationalist or Internationalist, Social Democrat or Anarchist' workers together confronting 'Conservative, Liberal, Jingo or anti-Jingo' capitalists.[22] Read as a statement about anarchism, his eclecticism seems remarkable. But his comment was about the relationships he thought anarchists could forge, not the nature of anarchist politics or anarchist ideology. Kropotkin was looking for co-operators not converts, and anarchization meant finding opportunities to introduce non-anarchists to alternative practices.

The Common Ground initiative in post-Katrina New Orleans provides a good example of this type of anarchization in action. When asked the question 'why do [social movements] . . . start with so much vigor and end in so much despair', the co-founders replied: 'people don't ever take into account their common ground'.[23] By standing with the local

African-American population, scott crow and others helped alleviate the racial tensions that had been heightened by the National Guard. Malik Rahim, co-founder of the Collective recalled the action:

> It did more to unite this community than anything. It showed the African Americans here that not all whites were exploiters or racists. And it showed the white folks coming in that all the African Americans here weren't like how the government said. We weren't all criminals. We were just hard working people that didn't have the means to escape. I had over 19,000 volunteers working some of the most dangerous parts of New Orleans, and we never had any incidents of anyone being robbed, or raped, or god forbid murdered. That's because any person, I mean any person, can respect the hand that has reached in need.[24]

As it developed, the distinguishing feature of the project was the principle of 'solidarity not charity'.[25] Reporters and participants record that this set Common Ground apart from the dysfunctional Federal Emergency Management Agency and ineffective Red Cross. It was embraced consistently by those who took part in the emergency work and it brought down the barriers between 'service providers' and 'users'. A news story filed at the time reported that Kropotkin's principle of mutual aid had been quickly adopted in the volunteer-run emergency communities that mushroomed:

> Take Amie Roberts. She used to cut hair at a St. Bernard salon before it flooded. When she started coming to eat at the Made With Love Café, it didn't take long for her

to realize that was what was left of the parish citizenry needed to get their hair cut. She mentioned the ideas to the volunteers at the café, and they provided her with a tent and some chairs. She brought her own scissors and a donation can. 'I wanted to do it for the residents,' she told me while snipping way at the head of a Red Cross worker from Arkansas. By all accounts hers was the only functioning hair salon in the entire parish, attracting dozens of residents, contractors, and relief workers a day.[26]

Some political philosophers argue that crisis mobilizes morality and that the idea of 'wartime spirit' is a perennial feature of disasters. People come together, help each other out, organize temporary infrastructural support while government agencies try to work out what to do. The anarchist response to Hurricane Katrina bears this out. The surprising logic of crisis morality is that the behaviours that statists observe when disaster strikes are the same that anarchists promote for 'normal' times: when states break down, the anarchy that reigns is often more like the condition anarchists describe than the chaos statists warn against. Finding convergence does not assume that all decent people are anarchists, to quote Eric Gill. Nor does it assume that all anarchists are decent people. It means that every policy proposal, every debate about control, ownership, participation and fairness can be rethought concretely from an anarchist perspective by anyone.

ANARCHIZATION THROUGH DISJUNCTURE
While convergence is about emphasizing the connections between anarchists and non-anarchists, disjuncture assumes

that these connections are buried and need to be exposed, usually through acts that draw attention to the iniquities of domination. It is rooted in the belief that most people are incapable of breaking with dominant value systems that inhibit independent judgement. While it may still be possible to talk about the 'primary colors of our moral sense', disjuncture assumes that these are significantly diluted by social pressures to conform.

Étienne de la Boétie's *The Politics of Obedience: The Discourse of Voluntary Servitude* is an exemplar for this model. His 1549 treatise has been revived by Murray Rothbard and Saul Newman. Rothbard sums up its fundamental insight: 'every tyranny must necessarily be grounded upon general popular acceptance . . . the bulk of the people themselves . . . acquiesce in their own subjection'.[27] Illusion, habit, mystery, the hierarchy of privilege and propaganda combine to ensure compliance and to forestall the mass withdrawal of consent which is fatal to tyranny.

Rothbard and Newman understand the implications of La Boétie's thesis quite differently. For Rothbard, its central message is that 'not *all* the people will be deluded or sunk into habitual submission'. Amid the 'brutish mass' there is always a 'more percipient elite' blessed with 'clear and far-sighted minds'.[28] Newman, by contrast, concentrates on the idea of will. La Boétie's observation that we 'will our own servitude', he notes, 'means that our own freedom is also a matter of the will'. The implication is that we have no need for elites to deliver us from obedience: we just need to take a deep breath and be brave. The 'joyous realization' is that 'freedom is simply a matter of willing differently, of turning

away from power and investing in ourselves and our own autonomy; simpler still, it is a matter of breaking with certain
patterns and behaviours of obedience that sustain power'.[29]
Whereas Rothbard recommends the formation of a 'valiant
knowledgeable elite' to act as the 'vanguard of the revolutionary resistance movement against the despot',[30] Newman
calls on each of us to draw on our inner resources.

The psychological constraints that La Boétie observed
were explored early on in anarchist history. Proudhon, for
example, saw that individual conscience was vulnerable to
the social roles that individuals were required to play (as
teachers, judges, soldiers and so on). Adapting Proudhon's
idea, Tolstoy argued that 'thoughtful and conscientious
people' were hypnotized by the edicts of Churches, newspapers and Emperors and by vaguer notions of patriotism and
national belonging. Emma Goldman used a version of Proudhon's idea to explain the failure of the women's movement to
uproot patriarchal oppression. The most advanced women,
she argued, set their sights on 'external emancipation'. This
narrow aim had turned 'the modern woman' into 'an artificial
being, who reminds one of the products of French arboricul-
ture with its arabesque trees and shrubs, pyramids, wheels,
and wreaths; anything, except the forms which would be
reached by the expression of her own inner qualities'. Warm-
ing to her theme, Goldman added that trailblazing women

> never truly understood the meaning of emancipation. They
> thought that all that was needed was independence from
> external tyrants; the internal tyrants, far more harmful to
> life and growth – ethical and social conventions – were

left to take care of themselves; and they have taken care of themselves. They seem to get along as beautifully in the heads and hearts of the most active exponents of woman's emancipation, as in the heads and hearts of our grandmothers.[31]

In the 1960s Angry Brigade changed the tenor of the analysis. It linked submissiveness and voluntary obedience to the ability of the corporate media to incentivize conformity and the power of capitalism to structure compliance through exploitation. In an address to 'unemployed brothers and sisters', Communiqué 11 read:

> Do not be fooled by the army recruiting campaign. An army career isn't fun in the sun and learning a useful trade, if you join you'll be trained in Belfast, Derry and all the other working class ghettos in Northern Ireland to murder and brutalise ordinary working class people. The training will come in useful when the boss class sends the troops into Clydeside, Merseyside, Tyneside, Birmingham, London and all the working class districts throughout Britain. To any unemployed worker thinking of joining up we ask you one question:
>
> WHICH WAY WILL YOU POINT YOUR GUN WHEN THE OFFICERS ORDER YOU AGAINST THE PEOPLE OF YOUR OWN TOWN?[32]

The analysis of recuperation presented by the insurrectionist Invisible Committee provides another take on the idea. It uses the concept of destitution to describe the power to break 'the circle that turns our contestation into a fuel for what dominates us'. Destitution is the answer to revolution, understood by the Invisible Committee as 'the desire to change everything and the desire that everything stays the same'.[33]

All these commentaries share the same insight: that the capacity to withdraw consent and/or to assert autonomy is universal but voluntary submission is far more common than disobedience and insubordination. From this point of view the expectation that anarchists can anarchize by correcting slurs about anarchism, entering into dialogue about ethics or even forging solidarity through action seems hopelessly optimistic. Disobedience is not routine for most people most of the time. And where disobedience occurs, it is often partial. Even rebels tend to focus on the opportunities that exist to extend the benefits that privileged groups enjoy. They rarely question the worth of the privileges themselves or the institutional mechanisms that are required for their delivery. As Goldman might have argued, when women fight to enter the boardrooms they reinforce the status of the corporations and stock markets.

Instead of prioritizing the search for common ground, advocates of disjuncture usually aim to expose the internalized social norms that act as brakes on transformation and shock or jolt people from their habits. Actions are typically dissonant and transgression is deliberately cultivated. Visual and performance arts have become favourite media, both strongly influenced by Dada, Surrealism and, more recently, the standards of cultural production and reproduction set by anarchist punks. The network Liberate Tate, which operates against corporate art washing and green washing promotes disobedient performance to uncover and attack the nefarious power relationships between oil corporations and cultural institutions. Past performances include 'Licence to Spill', an audacious, controlled oil release at a champagne reception celebrating twenty years of BP's sponsorship of the Tate, and 'Human Cost'. This was an 87-minute performance to commemorate the first anniversary of the 2010 Deepwater Horizon disaster and it involved dousing a human participant in a viscous black liquid brewed from charcoal and sunflower oil.[34]

The integrity and internal coherence of aesthetics, delivery and design are keys to these dissonant acts. For Yekaterina Samutsevich, one of the participants in the 2012 Pussy Riot performance of 'Punk Prayer: Mother of God Drive Putin Away', the artist 'is a person who is constantly analysing critical thoughts, always working out an independent opinion regarding everything'. For Samutsevich art is fundamentally about critique not technique. 'Art gives a breath of fresh air and a different way to protest.' In order to accomplish this task, artists must avoid participating in the systems they seek to disrupt. Thus while Pussy Riot was appreciative of the support that the group received when their arrest sparked an international outcry, it turned down invitations from various celebrities to join them on stage. Critique entails the rejection of 'commercial forms . . . legal performances . . . We can't do something by agreement . . . it contradicts our struggle with commercialization.'[35] Anarchization relies on the reception of the messages that these artists and activists communicate and a willingness to act upon them.

Convergence and disjuncture are preferences rather than alternative responses to the conundrum of anarchist change.

	Character	Stance	Barrier	Priority
Convergence	Inclusive	Solidaristic	Habit, complaisance	Shared moral intuitions
Disjuncture	Exclusive	Discordant	Internalized norms, social hypnosis, compliance	Recovery of conscience

Figure 5.1
The convergence and disjuncture models of change contrasted

Both are in fact optimistic and hopeful, but they operate in different ways. In convergence, the demonstration of a shared sense of injustice acts as a trigger for change. In disjuncture, the spur comes from the negativity of the critique.

Clearly, there are dangers in both: convergence risks falling into conservatism (the critique Bonanno makes of Colin Ward and the English anarchists) and disjuncture can result in aristocratic disdain and the kind of vanguardism that Rothbard endorsed.

Anarchization and sacrifice

In 1891 the Stirnerite John Henry Mackay published a fictionalized account of London anarchist life. It featured a long discussion between two anarchists, the communist Otto Trupp and the individualist Carrad Auban. The story follows Auban's disillusionment with communism and his turn to egoism. As a young man, he had been taken with the idea of the old world's destruction and had 'found refuge' in communism's 'first principle': 'To each according to his needs, from each according to his powers!' It had worked as an elixir.

> And his dreams reared the structure of the future of humanity: they built it high, broad and beautiful . . . Everybody would be contented: all hopes fulfilled, all desires satisfied. Labor and exchange would be voluntary; nothing henceforth to determine their limits, not even their value. The earth belongs to all equally. Each has a right to it as he has a right to be a human being. And he reared the proud structure of his thoughts – reared it into the heavens.[36]

However, after a good deal of soul-seeking Auban comes to the conclusion that anarchist communism is repressive, hypocritical and wholly destructive. It demands that its advocates commit everything to the cause. In doing so, it imposes intolerable duties on them. The promise of universal liberation becomes a form of moral blackmail, incentivizing the faithful to kill others in suicidal actions. At a meeting to commemorate the execution of the Haymarket anarchists, Auban 'thought of the heroic forms of those martyrs, of their silent sacrifice, and of their single-hearted devotion to an idea'.[37] Their cause was no longer his. He tells Trupp, 'I am beginning more and more to live for myself . . . What can I do in the clubs? These long speeches, always on the same subject: what are they for? All that is only tiresome.'[38]

Talking through Auban, Mackay equated sacrifice with submission. One way or another it meant being duped. He associated anarchy with self-assertion and the rejection of sacrifice.

How far does anarchization entail sacrifice? Uchiyama Gudō, the Sōtō Zen Buddhist priest executed for conspiracy to harm the Emperor in 1911, had a different view. Sacrifice, he argued, was not about subordinating the self to some reified goal, phantasm or spook, it was about living according to ones principles. From prison he wrote:

A religious man like Śākyamuni [the Buddha] gave up the throne and became a mendicant; a philosopher like Diogenes spent his entire life in a tub. Both lived lives full of joy and gratification that couldn't be taken away from them even by the emperor. Jesus Christ was killed on

the cross, but nonetheless, by claiming that by doing so
he was compensating for everyone's sins, he rejoiced in
death. People who have acted according to their principles
are happy people. Thus, participating as much as one
can in various movements with the goal, as all people
equally desire, that everyone in this society can work
in just conditions and receive fair supplies of clothing,
food, and shelter – isn't this a form of acting according
to one's principles? One can live calmly as they do in
normal conditions even though, just because one has acted
according to one's principles, one will become like dew
on the scaffold or be insulted on the cross, or again finish
his life in a subterranean prison in Hokkaido with the cold
winter wind piercing one's bones; this is what is called
happiness in life.[39]

Anarchists still argue about the idea of sacrifice, usually in
order to show that anarchism is not the cause that Mackay
took it to be. Yet if anarchists attempt to deny sacrifice,
they risk losing sight of the kinds of changes that anarchy
demands. Anarchization is not just about desiring alternatives but about taking up projects to realize them. Clearly
it would be un-anarchist to set anyone else's programme,
but surely it is disingenuous to suggest that anarchization
does not ask people to give things up. This might take the
form of giving up time to take part in solidarity actions or
exchange knowledge or share skills; providing food, shelter,
medicine, clothes or maps to people who need them, driving
people without papers across borders, writing to prisoners
or supporting resistance against the police.[40] It might involve

relinquishing opportunities for self-enrichment or the desire to consume limitlessly. And if in the end it is to fully respect the plurality of aims, goals and desires, anarchization also requires unremitting pragmatism.

The chances of anarchizing our social relationships and institutions are a lot higher than the likelihood of replacing the state with anarchy. Building confidence is one of the essential ingredients and here anarchism excels. To borrow Paul Goodman's phrase, anarchism offers utopian visions and practical proposals in abundance. It has a host of inspiring role models, a toolbox stacked with ideas about how to act and why and, as Voltairine de Cleyre argued, bridled optimism about the prospects of change. Anarchism tells us that present injustice is the justice of the past, made plain by fearless denunciation and capable of redress through direct action.

Anarchist Biographies

Introduction: Anarchism – Myths and Realities

ERIC GILL (1882–1940)

Gill was a social theorist, essayist and artist: sculptor, carver, engraver, and typeface designer. Strongly influenced by John Ruskin and William Morris, he adopted an arts and crafts ethos and strove to integrate work, faith and community. He converted to Catholicism in 1913 and became a member of the lay order of Dominicans. While he formally committed to chastity, he sexually abused his daughters, had a number of affairs and conducted an incestuous relationship with his sister. As well as producing village war memorials, he received commissions for a large number of public sculptures, including for BBC Broadcasting House.[1]

VLADIMIRO MUÑOZ (1920–2004)

Born in Gijon, Spain, and educated at the Arts and Crafts School in San Sebastian, Muñoz fled to France in 1936 after the fall of Irún at the start of the Spanish Revolution. He became an anarchist pacifist and individualist under the influence of the philosopher and novelist Jacques Ambroise Ner (aka Han Ryner), a contributor to Émile Armand's journals and noted campaigner for anarchist individualists and communists alike. Having returned to Tarragona, Muñoz was conscripted in 1937 for service on the Aragon front. In 1938 he was sent to a French concentration camp and, after the fall of France, he was forced to work at La Rochelle, then commandeered by the Nazis as a U-boat base. In 1947 Muñoz moved to Uruguay and became a regular contributor to the Uruguayan anarchist press. His biographical histories included work on Chinese and Romanian anarchism. Muñoz documented the lives of leading individuals, their heritage, key publications, interconnections and activities. He died in Montevideo in 2004.[2]

Chapter 1: Traditions

STEPHEN PEARL ANDREWS (1812–1886)

An essayist, lawyer, lecturer and reformer born in Templeton, Massachusetts, Andrews promoted a range of radical causes. Abolitionism, Fourierism, spiritualism, women's rights, free love and communism all had a place in his politics. He graduated from Amherst College in 1829 and was admitted to the Louisiana Bar in New Orleans in 1833. Relocating to Houston in 1839, he was driven out of Texas after proposing an abolitionist scheme. He found sanctuary in England until moving back to New York. Andrews was involved in the utopian communities Modern Times (1851) and Brownstone Utopia or Unitary Home (1855). His work *The Science of Society* was published in two volumes in 1851.[1]

MICHAEL BAKUNIN (1814–1876)

The son of a wealthy ex-diplomat, Bakunin was sent to St Petersburg to train as an artilleryman in 1829, graduated in 1832 and renounced his commission in protest at the repression of the Polish uprising of 1830–31. He began to read German philosophy, studying Hegel with his friend, the literary critic Vissarion Belinsky in the 1830s. Bakunin went to study in Berlin in 1840, sharing digs with Ivan Turgenev. In 1842, disillusioned with philosophy, he moved to Dresden and he published *Reaction in Germany*, which contains the immortal phrase: 'The passion for destruction is a creative passion, too!' In the next few years, he travelled to Zurich, Brussels and Paris, establishing contact with Karl Marx, Friedrich Engels and Pierre-Joseph Proudhon. In 1846 he declared himself an anarchist. Bakunin left Paris in 1848 after the February Revolution and travelled back to Germany to take part in revolutionary activities there. Arrested and condemned to death for supporting insurrections in Prague and Dresden, he was eventually returned to Russia and imprisoned in St Petersburg's Peter and Paul Fortress. In 1857 he was granted internal exile and deported to Tomsk. He married Antonia Kwiatkowska, leaving her on his escape in 1861. Arriving in London, having travelled via Japan, San Francisco and New York, he re-established contact with Marx and Alexander Herzen, the writer and socialist whom he had first met in 1839. He also met Giuseppe Mazzini and Giuseppe Garibaldi. Visiting Paris in 1864, Bakunin established contact with Élie and Élisée Reclus. Two years later he founded the Universal Brotherhood in order to propagate anarchist ideas and in 1867 he published *Federalism, Socialism and Anti-Theologism*. The same year, he joined the international League of Peace and Freedom, using this to agitate for anarchism. This was a short-lived association and in 1868 Bakunin established his own anti-authoritarian group, the International Alliance of Social Democracy. Élisée Reclus became a member. The Alliance was dissolved when Bakunin pursued membership of the First International. After taking part in the Lyon insurrection in 1870 he started to write *God and the State* (1882), and published *The Knouto-Germanic Empire and the Social Revolution* (1871). *Statism and Anarchy* was published in 1873, by which time Bakunin was settled in Locarno, in Switzerland. He moved to Lugano in 1875, too ill to continue with his revolutionary activities. He died in the Swiss capital, Berne, and he is buried there.[2]

CARLO CAFIERO (1846–1892)

Cafiero is credited with being one of the pioneers of anarchist communism. Born into a wealthy family in Puglia he studied law at the University of Naples. Treading a path towards the diplomatic service, he mixed in republican circles and began to study Islamic and Eastern thought. He went to Paris in 1870 and from there travelled to London, joining a colony of Mazzinian exiles. In London he was exposed to free thought and the squalor of the East End. After the Commune he assumed a leading role in the Naples section of the IWMA. Working with Bakunin, he organized Italian sections of the International into a national federation when the IWMA collapsed. In 1872 he attended the St Imier conference which Bakunin had called to promote anti-authoritarianism. In 1873, after a brief spell in prison, he bought a villa near Locarno to use as a refuge for Bakunin and a centre to plot anarchist revolutionary action. The tension between meeting Bakunin's needs and those of the Italian movement led to a break with Bakunin in 1874. Cafiero played a role in the Bologna insurrection in 1874 and the rising at Benevento in 1877. In 1879 he published a compendium of Marx's *Capital*. To escape repression in Italy, he settled in France and then Lugano. He attended the London Anarchist Congress of 1881. In 1882 he was arrested in Milan and attempted suicide. In 1883 he was admitted into a mental asylum.[3]

GUSTAVE COURBET (1819–1877)

An artist and a Communard, Courbet was born in Ornans, not far from Besançon, the home of his friend P.-J. Proudhon. Courbet established a reputation for radicalism in the late 1840s and early 1850s when he produced a series of canvases that shocked and perplexed the Academy. He continued to scandalize the Salon during the period of the Second Empire, honing his realist style. His correspondence with Proudhon was published along with Proudhon's reflections on realism as *Du principe de l'art* (1865). At the fall of the Second Empire, Courbet was elected President of the Federation of Artists and then elected to the Council of the Commune. In April 1871 he played an instrumental role in the toppling of the Vendôme column, symbol of French imperial power. He served six months for his participation in the Commune and was also held responsible for the costs of the column's reconstruction. He died impoverished in exile in Switzerland and his works were auctioned in a public sale.[4]

VOLTAIRINE DE CLEYRE (1866–1912)

The daughter of an abolitionist, Voltairine de Cleyre was radicalized while still at school by the campaigns for the eight-hour day in the 1870s. In 1889 she started to read translations of Proudhon's work in Benjamin Tucker's paper *Liberty*. A year later, having met Dyer D. Lum (author of *The Economic Aspects of Anarchism* (1893)), she began to take part in anarchist activities in Philadelphia. In the mid-1890s she contributed to anarchist journals and lectured in Paterson, an anarchist centre in New Jersey. In 1893 she wrote *In Defence of Emma Goldman and the Right of Expropriation*, protesting Emma Goldman's arrest and imprisonment. In London in 1897, Voltairine met a number of leading anarchists, including Louise Michel and Fernando Tárrida del Mármol, one of the survivors of the tortures at the Monjuich fortress in Barcelona. Taking up the Spanish cause, she published the pamphlet *The Modern Inquisition in Spain* (1897). Back in America, she went on lecture tours with Emma Goldman and translated Jean Grave's *Moribund Society and Anarchy* (1899). In 1902 Voltairine was shot by a former student, Herman Helcher. Although she survived, the injury contributed to her early death. A number of her lectures were published as pamphlets during her lifetime, notably *Anarchism and American Traditions* (1909), *The Mexican Revolution* (1911), *Direct Action* and *Francisco Ferrer*. She died in Chicago.[5]

GEORGE ENGEL (1836–1887)

One of the 'Haymarket anarchists' Engel was born in Cassel, Germany. In Bremen just prior to the outbreak of the Danish-Prussian War, he joined one of the volunteer forces organized to support the demands of ethnic Germans in Schleswig-Holstein, then under Danish rule. He emigrated to America in 1873 and started work in a sugar refinery in

Philadelphia. From there he went to Chicago where he was introduced to socialism. In 1878, he joined the Socialistic Labor Party of North America, which campaigned to secure votes for labour candidates. Disillusioned by electoral corruption he joined the International Working People's Association. He attended the strike meetings before the Haymarket demonstration but was at home on the evening of the bombing. He was executed because he was a known radical together with Adolph Fischer, Albert Parsons and August Spies.[6]

FRANCISCO FERRER (1859–1909)

Ferrer was born in Barcelona and grew up in a devout Catholic family. He rebelled, becoming a Freemason in 1883 and a radical republican. He moved to Paris in 1885, met with Louise Michel, Charles Malato and others and leaned towards anarchism. His interest in education was sparked by his involvement in anarchist politics. In 1901 he established a Modern School in Barcelona. Ferrer also set up a publishing house and commissioned translations of libertarian writings to provide his own teaching materials. Following two attempted assassination attempts on King Alfonso XIII, he was arrested in 1906. The would-be assassin, Mateo Morral, committed suicide, but because he was associated with the Modern School the authorities took the opportunity to implicate Ferrer. Acquitted for lack of evidence, he was released in 1907 but the School was closed. In 1908 he founded the International League for the Rational Education of Children and became editor of its paper *L'École Rénovée*. Following protests in Barcelona in 1909 ('The Tragic Week'), Ferrer was re-arrested and charged with orchestrating rebellion. The trial was conducted by court martial. The spectacle of his show trial and the death sentence the court passed sparked international protests and widespread condemnation of the Spanish government, but there was no commutation and Ferrer was executed by firing squad at Monjuich fortress.[7]

SAMUEL FIELDEN (1847–1922)

Fielden was one of the three Haymarket anarchists who escaped the death sentence for the 1886 bombing. He was born in Todmorden in Lancashire to a Chartist father and Methodist mother. He was sent to work in a cotton mill when he was eight years old, turning full-time when he was eighteen. He went to America in 1868 as a Methodist and freethinker. A trip to Louisiana convinced him that the gains secured in the Civil War were illusory and that slavery endured. He became a socialist in 1884 and joined the Labor League. This opened Fielden's path to the International Working People's Association and he became secretary of the English-speaking 'American' section in Chicago. On the night of the Haymarket bombing Fielden was due to give a lecture and was unaware of the meeting that had been called in Haymarket Square. Lucy and Albert Parsons persuaded him to change his plans and address the crowd. Wounded after the bomb was thrown, Fielden was arrested for conspiracy the next day. He was tried for incitement to riot. His death sentence was commuted and he served six years of the sentence. On his release he bought a ranch in Colorado. He withdrew from labour activism. He is the only one of the Haymarket anarchists not to be buried in Waldheim cemetery.[8]

ADOLPH FISCHER (1858–1887)

Executed in 1887, following the bombing of the public meeting in Chicago's Haymarket Square, Fischer was born in Bremen. He described his childhood as uneventful and unremarkable. By implication, his life started when he was fifteen when he left Germany for America. He was apprenticed as a compositor in Little Rock, Arkansas, and worked on the weekly German-language journal there. He joined the German Typographical Union in 1879 in St Louis. In 1883 he moved from Nashville to Chicago and worked as a compositor in the offices of the *Arbeiter Zeitung*, run by August Spies and Michael Schwab. Fischer had become a socialist in Germany, encouraged by his socialist father and the aggressively patriotic, anti-socialist teaching that prevailed during the Franco-German War. In Chicago he was an active member of the International Working People's Association and the armed defence group the Lehr-und-Wehr Verein.[9]

WILLIAM GODWIN (1756–1836)

Born in Wisbech in Cambridgeshire, Godwin trained to become a Protestant pastor but gave up his position under the influence of French republicanism. In 1793 he published *An Enquiry Concerning Political Justice, and Its Influence on General Virtue and Happiness*, a response to Edmund Burke's *Reflections on the Revolution in France*. In 1794 he published *Things as They Are; or, The Adventures of Caleb Williams*. Two years later, Godwin married Mary Wollstonecraft and in 1797 he published *The Enquirer. Reflections on Education, Manners, and Literature*, just before Wollstonecraft's death. He subsequently published *Memoirs of the Author of A Vindication of the Rights of Women* (1798).[10]

EMMA GOLDMAN (1869–1940)

Born in Lithuania, then part of Imperial Russia, Goldman was educated in Kaliningrad (then Königsberg) and moved with her family to St Petersburg in 1882. Radicalized there, she left Russia for America in 1886 and settled in Rochester, New York. She entered into revolutionary activity after the executions of the Haymarket anarchists in 1887. Working with John Most she met Alexander Berkman. They became life-long companions. She fell out with Most in 1892, when he condemned Berkman's attempted assassination of the Carnegie industrialist Henry Frick. After spending a year in prison for inciting riot in 1894, she established a reputation as a leading anarchist thinker and activist, earning the label Red Emma. She made two trips to Europe in 1895 and 1899, studying nursing and midwifery in Vienna. In 1901 she was re-arrested in connection with the assassination of President McKinley by Leon Czolgosz. In 1906 she founded the paper *Mother Earth*, co-editing it with Berkman. Goldman lectured widely throughout her career, reaching an estimated 25,000 people in a tour of thirty-seven US cities in 1910 alone. An opponent of the war in 1914, she helped establish the No-Conscription League and organized anti-war rallies across America. In 1917 she and Berkman were charged with conspiracy to obstruct the draft. Stripped of citizenship, Emma was deported in 1919 to Bolshevik Russia. Initially enthusiastic about Revolution, she was struck by the repression and corruption she witnessed. In 1921, after the Kronstadt uprising, she adopted a strongly critical stance. In 1923 she published *My Disillusionment in Russia*. After Berkman's suicide in 1936 she went to Spain to support the anarchist revolution. She died in Canada and was buried in the Waldheim cemetery in Chicago with the Haymarket anarchists.[11]

JEAN GRAVE (1854–1939)

Grave was born in Puy-de-Dôme and grew up in Paris, having moved there in 1860. Prevented from joining the Communard militia, Grave helped construct barricades in the Commune's last days and witnessed the savagery of the government reprisals, recording the events in his novel *La Grande famille*. In 1875 he was drafted and served in Brittany. He returned to Paris in 1877 and worked as a shoemaker. In 1879 he started to read *Le Prolétaire*, the paper of the Parti des Travailleurs Socialistes de France, and to attend socialist meetings. He adopted an anarchist position and in 1880 co-founded the anarchist Social Study group of the Fifth and Thirteenth Wards of Paris. Malatesta and Cafiero attended meetings. In 1882 he began writing and the following year became editor of Kropotkin and Reclus's paper *Le Révolté*. He remained in charge when it changed its name in 1886 to *La Révolte* and when it was reborn in 1895 as *Les Temps nouveaux*. In 1892 Grave was arrested and prosecuted under the *Lois scélérates* ('wicked laws') introduced in response to anarchist violence and designed to crush the anarchist movement. He had briefly flirted with bomb-making in the 1880s but was detained for his written propaganda. In the early years of the twentieth century, Grave maintained a sympathetic but critical stance on anarchist syndicalism. He kept up a close correspondence with Kropotkin for much of his life and in 1914 supported Kropotkin's position on the war. His vocal criticisms of the Bolshevik coup in 1917 further alienated him from sections of the French anarchist-syndicalist movement. After resigning the editorship of *Les Temps nouveaux*, he started a new venture, *Les Publications*. This failed to attract readers and was wound up in 1936. He left Paris, fearing Nazi occupation, and died in the Vienne-en-Val in the Loiret Department after a short illness.[12]

EZRA HEYWOOD (1829–1893)

A graduate of Brown University, in Rhode Island, Heywood campaigned against segregation in schools and churches and adopted the abolitionist cause, giving his first public address in 1858. Rejecting political action as a means of securing abolition, he prioritized individual behavioural change. He regarded the Union and the Constitution as instruments of slavery. Between 1859 and 1864 he delivered over 200 speeches for the Massachusetts Anti-Slavery Society. The Civil War precipitated his split with the abolitionist movement: Heywood could not accept war and violence as a legitimate means to end slavery. He was a founder member of the Universal Peace Society, established as the Universal Peace Union in 1865, and drafted its preamble and constitution. In the 1860s and 70s he threw himself into campaigns for labour reform, setting up the New England Labor Reform League in 1869 and publishing *The Word: A Monthly Journal of Reform* to promote economic change and individual freedom from 1872. He worked closely with Benjamin Tucker but was also supportive of the Chicago-based social revolutionaries and he published several of John Most's speeches in *The Word*. Heywood championed women's rights, including the suffrage, campaigned with Moses Harman for free speech and to promote free love: he was tried for obscenity and imprisoned several times as a result. He served his final term in 1891. He died a year after his release on his way to the convention of the American Reform League.[13]

JOE HILL (1879–1915)

Songwriter and activist for the Industrial Workers of the World (IWW), Hill was born Joel Hägglund in Sweden. He left Sweden for America in 1902 and changed his name to Joseph Hillstrom. He joined the IWW in 1910, five years after its founding. He became one of the leading contributors to the IWW's *Little Red Songbook*, writing a slew of songs that were regularly sung on picket lines. Hill fought at the Battle of Mexicali alongside Magonistas and was badly beaten at a free speech rally in 1912. In 1913 he went to Utah, responding to a call to support local workers engaged in bitter labour disputes with the Utah Copper Company and the Utah Construction Company. He was arrested for murder after a shooting at a grocery store in Salt Lake City in January 1914. He had been shot the same night, the injured party in a love triangle. There was no evidence to link him to the grocery killing but the coincidence of the shooting, coupled with his reputation as an IWW agitator, ensured that he was charged. Refusing to divulge the details of his whereabouts on the night of the shooting, and already excoriated by the press in advance of the trial, Hill was found guilty and sentenced to death. A defence campaign was mounted. His case was appealed and efforts were made to have the sentence commuted. Mass petitions, Swedish diplomatic and Presidential interventions all failed and Hill was executed by firing squad.[14]

PETER KROPOTKIN (1842–1921)

Kropotkin was born into an aristocratic family in Moscow. Introduced to radical ideas by his private tutors, he decided to drop his princely title in 1854. Three years later he went to St Petersburg to be educated at the elite Corps of Pages. Exposed to the work of Bakunin's contemporary Herzen and the radicalism of Voltaire, he began to advocate the abolition of serfdom in Russia. In 1862, a year after the Emancipation of the Serfs, he graduated and opted for a posting in Siberia, eager to avoid the parades and court balls that high rank promised. He spent five years exploring Siberia, travelling over fifty thousand miles, and was radicalized by his encounters with the local inhabitants. During this time he also met Bakunin's wife, Antonia Kwiatkowska, and read Proudhon's *System of Economic Contradictions*. Kropotkin left the military in 1867 to resume study at St Petersburg University, undertaking geographical research in Finland and Sweden. In 1871 Kropotkin travelled to Switzerland, where he helped James Guillaume edit the *Bulletin of the Jura Federation*. Now an anarchist Kropotkin joined the Bakuninist Geneva Federation before returning to Russia and joining the revolutionary Tchaikovsky Circle. Arrested, he was incarcerated in the Peter and Paul Fortress but escaped from the prison infirmary in 1875. Moving quickly between Edinburgh, Switzerland and London, Kropotkin met leading figures in the anarchist movement, including Élisée Reclus, Malatesta and Carlo Cafiero. In 1879 he founded the highly influential anarchist paper *Le Révolté*. He attended the 1881 London Anarchist Congress before returning to France, where he was arrested for having been a member of the First International. Released in 1886, Kropotkin settled in the UK where he took a leading role in the newspaper *Freedom*. Kropotkin lectured widely in the UK and travelled twice to the US to lecture. He regularly took part in protest meetings, notably for the Haymarket anarchists and the prisoners at Monjuich but is best known for his books and pamphlets. In 1914 Kropotkin attracted the wrath of the majority anarchist movement when he sided with the Entente against the Central Powers. In 1917 he ended his exile to return to Russia. Invited to meet Lenin after the Bolshevik coup, Kropotkin defended anarchism against Bolshevism. Kropotkin's vocal opposition to the Bolshevik revolution restored his reputation with anarchists in Russia and his funeral in Moscow attracted a huge crowd. It was the last anarchist demonstration in Russia.[15]

LOUIS LINGG (1864–1887)

Lingg was born in Mannheim, in Germany. Apprenticed to a carpenter, he completed his training in 1882. He became a socialist after joining a socialist workers' education society. On a tour of Switzerland in 1883, he witnessed debates between anarchists and social democrats and adopted an anarchist position. Lingg advocated the use of physical force to resist state repression. In order to avoid conscription in Germany, he went on the run in 1884 and booked his passage to America in 1885. He joined the Carpenters' and Joiners' Union in Chicago and took an active role in the eight-hour day movement. Lingg was not present at the Haymarket Square meeting. However, when bomb-making paraphernalia was found in his home he was charged with being the bomb-maker. Frank Harris's fictionalized account of the Haymarket Affair, *The Bomb* (1908/2008), also points to Lingg as the manufacturer. Paul Avrich's research implicates his comrade Rudolph Schnaubelt, who had fled Chicago. The combination of false witness statements, Lingg's union activity and his open advocacy of defensive violence delivered the death sentence for criminal conspiracy. A blasting cap was smuggled into his prison cell and he set this off in his mouth before he could be executed.[16]

FREDERICK LOHR (1909–1961)

A member of the London Freedom group, Lohr contributed to the magazine *Why?* and campaigned with the Freedom Defence Committee to protest the prosecutions of the editors of *War Commentary*. Born in London, he acquired British citizenship when his German-born father was naturalized in 1910. In his youth he ran a garage and worked as a Lancia agent. Agitated by the prospect of war, he joined the Peace Pledge Union and was a member of the Forward Group, which argued for social transformation through non-violence. Discovering a talent for oratory at London's Speakers' Corner, he started the London Forum, a radical discussion group which met at Endsleigh Gardens, in Bloomsbury. Lohr was imprisoned for three months for breaching the peace after a brawl erupted there. In the 1940s Lohr moved with his second wife Mary Rebekah ('Molly') to a three-storey house at 170 Westbourne Terrace, in Paddington, sharing the property with a group of anarchists. He introduced the gay rights activist Sharley MacLean to anarchism but gradually detached himself from the movement and moved towards Christianity. He wrote several pamphlets, including *The Meaning of Total War* (c. 1939), *The Grand Inquisitor* (1945), *Greek, Roman and Jew: Reflections on the Psychology of History* (1952). He died in Roehampton.[17]

JOHN HENRY MACKAY (1864–1933)

Writer, poet and Stirnerite anarchist and pederast, Mackay was born in Greenock, near Glasgow, Scotland. After his father died his German mother took him to Saarbrücken. He studied at Kiel, Leipzig and Berlin universities. He spent the 1880s and early 1890s travelling in Germany, Europe and America, eventually settling in Berlin in 1894. He turned to radical politics after visiting London in 1887. He read Stirner's *The Ego and Its Own* (1844) and a translation of Benjamin Tucker's *State Socialism and Anarchism* (1886) shortly afterwards. Mackay and Tucker met in 1889, after which Mackay became an advocate of anarchist individualism and critic of anarchist communism. The fictionalized account of his time in London, *The Anarchists*, published in 1891, sets out his positions. He produced a biography of Stirner in 1898. In the early twentieth century Mackay started to campaign for pederasty, what he called 'nameless love', writing under the name Sagitta. In the course of his life, he published volumes of poems and wrote several novels, including *The Hustler*, published in 1926. He died in Berlin.[18]

RICARDO FLORES MAGÓN (1873–1922)

Magón was born in a period of intense anarchist agitation in Mexico and grew up during Porfirio Díaz's dictatorial rule. He was imprisoned in 1892, after taking part in an anti-government student protest. The following year he began to study law and became one of the editors of the newspaper *El Demócrata*. He became acquainted with anarchist ideas in 1900 when he read Kropotkin's *The Conquest of Bread* and works by Malatesta and Jean Grave. The same year Magón founded the libertarian paper *Regeneración*. This soon became a lightening rod for anti-government activism. *Regeneración* was temporarily shut down, only to be circulated covertly. Magón was imprisoned again in 1902 and on his release in 1904 went into exile in Texas. He survived an assassination attempt after re-circulating *Regeneración* against Díaz's wishes. In 1905 Magón became the president of the Mexican Liberal Party. Adopting the slogan 'Reform, Freedom and Justice', the party was committed to the overthrow of the Díaz regime. To escape the repressive action of the government, Magón moved first to Toronto and then to Los Angeles. In 1907 he founded a new paper, *Revolución*. On Díaz's orders, he was arrested once more but managed to avoid deportation. From 1908 to 1910 he agitated for anarchism in the Liberal Party. *Regeneración*, the party's paper, adopted the slogan 'Tierra y Libertad', borrowing the title from the nineteenth-century Castilian anarchist newspaper. After Díaz fled Mexico during the revolution of 1911, Magón continued to advocate anarchism, pressing the case against the new liberal government headed by Francisco Madero. Having been freed in 1910, he was jailed in 1912 and again in 1916. With the help of Emma

Goldman and Alexander Berkman he was bailed in 1918 but re-arrested the same year after publishing an anti-war manifesto. He was given a twenty-year sentence. Magón died in Leavenworth penitentiary, Kansas, apparently suffering from heart disease. Anarchists suspected that he was assassinated.[19]

ERRICO MALATESTA (1853–1932)

Malatesta was the driving force of Italian anarchism from the 1870s. Sentenced to death on more than one occasion, he spent several years in prison and was constantly under police surveillance. The son of an affluent landowner, he was born in Caserta, in the south of Italy and studied medicine at the University of Naples. Gravitating from republicanism to socialism, Malatesta was profoundly influenced by Bakunin, who took up residence in Italy in the 1860s. In 1872 he played a key role in the establishment of the Italian Federation of the IWMA and in the anti-authoritarian St Imier conference, called after Marx's split with Bakunin. He was involved in insurrections in 1874 and 1877 in central and southern Italy. Together with Cafiero, he helped develop the concept of propaganda by the deed. Malatesta went into exile in 1878 and spent the next two years in Egypt, Romania, Switzerland and France. He attended the 1881 London Anarchist Congress and led the charge against anarchists in the Italian movement who advocated parliamentary tactics. In 1885 he went to South America, returning to Europe in 1889. Throughout this period he edited influential papers in Buenos Aires, Florence, Nice, London and Ancona. He wrote extensively for the anarchist press and produced a series of important pamphlets. In 1899 Malatesta went to the United

States and played a role in setting up a journal with anarchists in Paterson, New Jersey. He spent thirteen years in London from 1900. His arrest in 1912 on the flimsiest suspicions sparked a massive campaign for his release. Highly critical of Kropotkin's decision in 1914 to support the Entente powers, Malatesta advocated revolutionary war and became one of the leading voices in the majority anarchist movement. He returned to Italy in 1919 and after Mussolini's seizure of power in 1922 he was kept under house arrest in Rome until he died.[20]

CHARLES MALATO (1857–1938)

Journalist, essayist, editor and movement chronicler, Malato was the son of a Communard brought up in exile in New Caledonia. He returned to France in 1881 and gravitated towards anarchism six years later. Malato was imprisoned in 1890. The expulsion order that followed prompted a temporary move to London. He found a home in the Italian, French and British anarchist communities and resumed his work as a writer, famously defending some of the leading practitioners of propagandistic actions: Ravachol and Émile Henry. Back in France, he took an active part in the campaign to defend Dreyfus and promoted anarchist syndicalism. Suspected of involvement in a 1905 bomb plot against the Spanish king, Malato was arrested but acquitted after a high-profile defence campaign. In 1914 he sided with Kropotkin and supported anarchist intervention in the war, adding his name to the Manifesto of the Sixteen. At the end of the war he found work in offices of the French Chamber of Deputies. He continued to advocate anarchist politics. He is buried in the Père-Lachaise Cemetery.[21]

FRANCESCO SAVERIO MERLINO (1856–1930)

Born in Naples, Merlino was the son of a magistrate who graduated in law from the University of Naples. He joined the anarchist movement while he was still studying and in 1881 attended the London Anarchist Congress. Sentenced to four years for conspiring against the state in 1883, he went into exile in London, making frequent trips to other European countries and the United States. Returning to Italy illegally in 1894, he was promptly arrested and served two years of the outstanding sentence. Merlino was an important theorist of libertarian socialism and leading opponent of terrorist methods. He moved away from the anarchist movement after a public dispute with Malatesta about the virtues of parliamentary action. In 1899 he joined the Italian Socialist Party – however in 1900 he defended Gaetano Bresci, the anarchist assassin of King Umberto, falling out with his socialist party colleagues. In 1907 he withdrew from politics to practise law. He re-established his links with the anarchist movement after the war. Common opposition to Bolshevism and fascism facilitated the rapprochement and Merlino published his work in the anarchist press, including Malatesta's *Umanità Nova*. He also defended anarchists and anti-fascist workers. He died in Rome.[22]

LOUISE MICHEL (1830–1905)

Michel was a novelist, playwright, poet and educator, brought up in a strongly republican household. She began teaching in 1853, employing experimental methods to foster revolutionary values. After being denounced for her methods she moved from Vroncourt in north-eastern France to

Paris in 1856. She was by then in correspondence with Victor Hugo, a vocal critic of Napoleon III, and speaking out publicly against the regime. In 1871 she took up arms in defence of the Commune. Deported to New Caledonia in 1872, she declared herself anarchist and set about organizing a school for the children of the deportees and, subsequently, the children of the indigenous people, the Kanaks. When the Kanaks rebelled in 1878, Michel backed them. Amnestied, she returned to Paris in 1880. Michel was jailed for leading a demonstration of the unemployed in 1883. Pardoned three years later, she took active part in the demonstrations to protest the execution of the Haymarket anarchists. After surviving an assassination attempt in 1888 she was imprisoned twice more before finding refuge in London. In the late 1890s, she set up a Free School in Fitzroy Square, working with Malatesta, Kropotkin and William Morris. She also embarked on a series of lecture tours across the UK, France, Belgium and Switzerland. In 1904, after completing a tour in Algeria, Michel contracted pneumonia. She died in Marseille in January 1905.[23]

JOHN MOST (1846–1906)

Most was born in Augsburg, Bavaria, and rebelled against school and Church authorities in his youth. After establishing contact with workers involved in the First International, Most spend the years 1869–1873 in and out of prison in Germany and Austria. In 1874 he was elected deputy to the Reichstag, an experience that encouraged his turn to anarchism. In 1879 he published the first issue of *Freiheit*, still then a member of the German Social Democratic Party (SPD). He was expelled in 1881 and imprisoned in London for writing an article applauding the assassination of Tsar Alexander II. In 1882 he left Britain for America to re-establish *Freiheit* in New York where he became a labour activist. He was imprisoned in 1886 for his defence of the Haymarket anarchists. Throughout the 1890s he used *Freiheit* to promote workers' causes. He was incarcerated in 1897 and again in 1901 after Leon Czolgocz's assassination of President McKinley. Released in 1903, Most resumed his propaganda work. He died in January 1906 in Cincinnati.[24]

OSCAR NEEBE (1850–1916)

Born in New York, Neebe was educated in Hesse-Cassel in Germany. He returned to New York when he was fourteen. Taking a series of low-paid jobs, he became a labour organizer. A brief spell in Philadelphia taught Neebe that racism had not been abolished with slavery and that enslavement, too, continued, albeit in different ways. In Chicago in 1877 he was discharged from his job and effectively blacklisted. He started to attend communist meetings, radicalized by a Commune celebration. In 1880 he became a manager of the *Arbeiter Zeitung*. The paper adopted the anarchist programme of the 1883 Pittsburgh Convention which launched the International Working People's Association. Arrested in 1886 and put on trial for conspiracy in the Haymarket bombing, Neebe was sentenced to fifteen years. He was pardoned in 1893. Neebe attended the 1907 Industrial Workers of the World (IWW) Convention. He became a follower of Daniel De Leon, who formed the Workers' International Industrial Union in 1908, when the IWW committed the Union to struggle by means of direct action.[25]

ALBERT PARSONS (1848–1887)

Parsons was born in Montgomery, Alabama, moved to the Texas frontier in the mid-1850s and in 1859 started an apprenticeship at the *Galveston Daily News*. In 1861 he joined a local volunteer force formed to support the slave-holders' rebellion. At fifteen he joined a cavalry brigade posted on the Mississippi. At the end of the war he bought land and hired ex-slaves to work it with him. In Waco in 1868 he founded and edited the *Spectator*. He joined the Republican Party, drawing the ire of local Ku Klux Klan and the admiration of former slaves. Appointed travelling correspondent for the *Houston Daily Telegraph*, Parsons left Waco in 1870 to work for the Internal Revenue in Austin, Texas. He went to Chicago after resigning this position and joined the Typographical Union. Now interested in labour politics he began to campaign for workers' rights. In 1876 he joined the Knights of Labor and became editor of an English-language labour paper, the *Socialist*. In 1877, when rail workers went on strike, he was identified as a leading labour agitator, dismissed from his job and told by police to quit Chicago. Parsons continued his activities, calling for the formation of a working man's party. In 1878 he organized the Trades Assembly of Chicago and, elected as its president, campaigned for the eight-hour day. Systematic corruption of the electoral system and an attempt by employers to disarm workers led Parsons to anarchism. In 1881 he joined the International Working People's Association, and in 1884 he became editor of the International's Chicago paper, the *Alarm*. On 4 May 1886, Parsons accepted an eleventh-hour request to address the crowd in Haymarket Square, leaving the event before the bomb went off. He left Chicago the next day, escaping the initial police haul. Parsons turned himself in June to stand trial. He was convicted and executed with George Engel, Adolph Fischer and August Spies.[26]

LUCY PARSONS (1851–1942)

Born in Virginia and raised in Texas, Lucy Parsons (née Gonzalez) was a labour organizer and agitator. She met Albert Parsons in 1870 and moved with him to Chicago in 1873, where she ran a dress shop to provide an income for the family. A member of the Knights of Labor, she also began to host meetings of the International Ladies' Garment Workers' Union. In 1883 she helped found the International Working People's Association. In the years leading up to the Haymarket bombing she wrote regularly for the anarchist press. After Albert's arrest, Lucy embarked on a fund-raising tour for the Haymarket anarchists. After the executions, she continued to agitate for anarchism, promoting values of solidarity and organization and calling for women's liberation and anti-racist activism. In 1905 she joined the Industrial Workers of the World (IWW). As editor of the IWW paper, the *Liberator*, she promoted a range of labour and women's causes. In 1925 she joined forces with the Communist Party group, International Labor Defence, to campaign for Sacco and Vanzetti and the African-American 'Scottsboro Eight', who had been sentenced to death, falsely accused of raping two white women in Memphis. She continued to campaign until she was killed in a house fire.[27]

PIERRE-JOSEPH PROUDHON (1809–1865)

Born and educated in Besançon, Proudhon distinguished himself as a Latinist and Greek scholar and worked as proof-reader and learner-compositor at a local printing house. Unemployed after the July Revolution in 1830, he taught at a school before going to Paris and embarking on a walking tour of France. Awarded a bursary from the Academy of Besançon in 1838, he published *What is Property?* in 1840. This was followed in 1846 by *System of Economic Contradictions or the Philosophy of Poverty*, a book that caused Marx to revise his positive assessment of Proudhon's critique of property and to publish the scornful *Poverty of Philosophy* (1847). After the 1848 Revolution, Proudhon built his reputation as a journalist and government critic. He called for workers to finance their own operations through co-operation and a system of reciprocal exchange. In 1849 he established a people's bank, which attracted a large number of subscribers but failed. Proudhon stood for election to the Constituent Assembly in 1848 and was elected in June. Against the Jacobins, Proudhon advanced an idea of social revolution and rejected the concept of political change. He also campaigned against universal suffrage. He was arrested and imprisoned in 1849 for insulting Louis Napoleon, producing *The General Idea of the Revolution in the Nineteenth Century* (1851) during his incarceration. He spent ten years in exile in Belgium from 1852, returning to France just before his death.[28]

ÉLISÉE RECLUS (1830–1905)

Born in Sainte-Foy, in the Savoie, Reclus studied theology at Montauban in southern France before moving to Berlin in 1851 to attend the courses run by the geographer Carl Ritter.

Escaping arrest for publicly denouncing Napoleon III, he left France at the end of 1851 and spent nearly a year working as a tutor in London and farmhand in Dublin. After Ireland he crossed the Atlantic and travelled in New Orleans, Chicago and Niagara Falls. He spent some time in Colombia in 1856 before returning to Paris in the same year. There, he signed a contract with the publisher Hachette in 1858 to publish his multi-volume *Universal Geography*. He met Bakunin in 1864 and in 1868 attended the meeting of the League of Peace and Freedom in Berne, speaking on the subject of federalism. Reclus fought with the Communards in 1871, and was subsequently jailed and sentenced to deportation. Escaping to Switzerland, he met up with Bakunin and joined the anarchist Jura Federation. In 1875 he declared his anarchism publicly at a lecture in Lausanne. He met Kropotkin in 1877, while working on the newspaper *Le Travailleur*. In the 1880s he published the essay *Evolution and Revolution* and Bakunin's *God and the State*, co-writing a prologue to the latter with Carlo Cafiero. He joined the editorial board of *Le Révolté* in 1884 and, while Kropotkin was in prison, prepared Kropotkin's first book, *Paroles d'un Révolté*, published in 1885. In 1889 Reclus made another trip to America, travelling widely. Appointed professor at the Free University in Brussels in 1892, he was barred from delivering his course on comparative geography. Finding that the university was not so free, he delivered his classes at the New University, which he helped to establish in 1894. In the same period he published the final volume of *Universal Geography* and the essay *Anarchy* (1896) and in 1903 he completed the manuscript of *L'Homme et la Terre* (1905). He died in 1905 shortly after finishing the prologue.[29]

RUDOLF ROCKER (1873–1958)

An anarcho-syndicalist, organizer and theorist, Rocker was born in Mainz and apprenticed to a bookbinder. He was expelled from the German Social Democratic Party in 1891 and gravitated towards anarchism, impressed by Ferdinand Domela Nieuwenhuis's critique of the authoritarianism of social democracy. He left Germany in 1892 and in 1895 settled in London's East End, where he made contact with Jewish anarchists. Rocker learned Yiddish and in 1898 was offered the editorship of the libertarian paper *Arbeter Fraint*. He took a leading role in establishing the Jubilee Street anarchist club, which functioned as a centre for adult education. In 1912 he led the East End tailors' strike, a solidarity action to support the West End tailors and end piece work. He was interned as an enemy alien in 1914 and the Jubilee Club and *Arbeter Fraint* were shut down the following year. At the end of the war, he returned to Berlin and devoted himself to the syndicalist movement. He left Germany in 1933, escaping arrest by the Gestapo. Making a short stop in London, he went to New York and embarked on a coast-to-coast lecture tour of the United States and Canada. He published *Nationalism and Culture* in 1938 and *Anarcho-Syndicalism* the following year.[30]

NICOLA SACCO (1891–1927)

One of two anarchists executed for murder after a notorious legal case failed to prove their guilt, Sacco was born in Italy, emigrated to America in 1908 and found work making shoes in Massachusetts. From 1912 to 1917 he was involved in anarchist fundraising and labour activism. He went to

Mexico in 1917 to avoid being drafted but returned to the United States soon after and resumed his anarchist activities. He was arrested in 1920 on the same day that a botched robbery had taken place in Massachusetts. He was charged with killing the guard and paymaster shot during the raid. The injustice of the trial and manipulation of the evidence against Sacco prompted worldwide protests, but he was electrocuted in 1927.[31]

MICHAEL SCHWAB (1853-1898)

Schwab was imprisoned for his involvement in the Haymarket Square bombing in Chicago in 1886. He was born in Franconia, southern Germany, apprenticed to a bookbinder and introduced to socialism in 1872. He joined the Social Democratic Labour Party and in the mid-1870s travelled across Germany promoting socialism. Having decided to emigrate to escape harsh working conditions in 1879, he went to Chicago in 1881 and began to work as a reporter and assistant editor for the *Arbeiter Zeitung*. He became a member of the autonomous German section of the Socialistic Labor Party (established after the dissolution of the First International) and began to organize socialist clubs, joining the International Working People's Association in 1883. Schwab attended the meeting in Haymarket Square, leaving before the bombing. He was arrested with August Spies the following day, but successfully appealed his death sentence and served six years of a life sentence before being pardoned. He resumed work with the *Arbeiter Zeitung* and sold labour literature in his shoe shop until his death.[32]

HENRY SEYMOUR (1860–1938)

A publisher, editor and campaigner born in Hayes, Kent, Seymour moved to Tunbridge Wells, worked as a painter and decorator and became a secularist, freethinker and radical. He founded the Tunbridge Wells Science Library, the first UK outlet for Benjamin Tucker's *Liberty*, and served as secretary to the Tunbridge Wells affiliate of the National Secular Society. He was an advocate for free love and joined the Legitimation League, an organization that campaigned against the designation of illegitimacy. Seymour was editor the League's paper the *Adult*. Having been convicted for blasphemy in 1882, he founded the Free Press Defence Committee in order to protest the prosecution of the League's secretary, George Bedborough, for selling Havelock Ellis's book *Sexual Inversion* (1896). Although he co-operated with his local branch of the nominally Marxist Social Democratic Federation, Seymour rejected Marx's theory of surplus value and was drawn to Tucker's anarchism. In the course of his life he supported a range of libertarian causes: he was against restrictive Sunday shop-opening hours, he sympathized with the anti-vivisection movement which opposed medical experimentation on hospital patients. He wrote pamphlets supporting direct action to protest the trial of the Haymarket anarchists and a warm biographical sketch of Bakunin. He is best remembered in anarchist circles for setting up the first British anarchist paper, *The Anarchist*, with Charlotte Wilson and Kropotkin in 1885 and spearheading the formation of the English Anarchist Circle. After parting company with his co-founders, he established the *Revolutionary Review* and took up the cause of free currency, collaborating with the campaigning group Free Currency Propaganda. He subsequently started a successful gramophone company, and ended up editing *Baconiana*, the magazine of the Bacon Society. Shortly before he died he wrote to Joseph Ishill, the anarchist printer and founder of Oriole Press, of his desire to resume political activity, convinced that currency monopoly was responsible for the world's enslavement.[33]

AUGUST SPIES (1855–1887)

One of the defendants in the Haymarket trial, Spies was born in Landeck in central Germany. He was educated by private tutors and attended the Polytechnic in Cassel. He decided to go to America when his father died in 1872 and worked for a while in New York before moving to Chicago. He became a socialist in 1875, joining the Socialistic Labor Party in 1877 and the Lehr-und-Wehr Verein, an organization of working men established to equip workers to defend themselves against employer violence. Spies stood for election but withdrew from electoral politics after witnessing wholesale political corruption. He also joined the Knights of Labor but dropped his membership on account of its ceremony and secrecy. In 1880 he campaigned as a revolutionary socialist and member of the International Working People's Association. He embarked on lecture tours, speaking in most industrial cities and gaining a reputation as an effective orator. He spoke at the Haymarket meeting on 4 May 1886 in favour of the eight-hour movement, a cause he did not regard as anarchist.[34]

MAX STIRNER (1806-1856)

Born Johann Kaspar Schmidt in Bayreuth, Stirner studied at the university in Berlin until 1834. He worked in a private school, preferring this to a position in the official school system. In 1840 Stirner joined the circle of the Young Hegelians, a libertarian philosophy group which for a while also attracted Marx and Engels. In 1842 Marx published two of Stirner's essays: *The False Principle of Our Education* and *Art and Religion* and in 1844 *The Ego and Its Own* was published. The book attracted trenchant critiques from leading Hegelians and was banned by government censors in 1845. Stirner worked for a while as a translator but struggled to make a living. In 1852 he was imprisoned as a debtor. He died in Berlin.[35]

LEO TOLSTOY (1828-1910)

Tolstoy studied Oriental languages and law in Moscow and Kazan. He inherited the family estate at Yasnaya Polyana in 1847, together with the title count, an honour bestowed on his ancestor Peter Tolstoy by Peter the Great in 1718. In 1852 he joined the army and took part in actions against Chechen fighters. In 1853 he became an antimilitarist. Refused discharge in 1855, Tolstoy was transferred to the Crimea garrison and took part in the battle of Sevastopol in 1856. After being discharged, Tolstoy went to Paris and read Proudhon's *What is Property?* He met Proudhon there in 1862, at the tail-end of a short European tour which he had spent learning about modern educational methods. When he returned to Russia he began publishing some of these ideas. In 1872, after the publication of *War and Peace*, he set up a free school on his estate. In 1881 he defended Sophia Perovskaya, one of the assassins of Tsar Alexander II. In 1884 he renounced his title and in 1885 he refused jury service. In 1890 he renounced the rights to his published works. Between 1893 and 1901 he published *The Kingdom of God is Within You* (1894), *Patriotism or Peace* (1896), *What is Art?* (1898) and *The Slavery of Our Times* (1900). He was excommunicated from the Russian Orthodox Church at the end of this period. He died in 1910, by which time he had given his name to an international movement.[36]

BENJAMIN TUCKER (1854–1939)

Editor of *Liberty*, Tucker was born in New Bedford, Massachusetts, and studied at the Massachusetts Institute of Technology (MIT). In 1874 he began to translate Proudhon's works and edit a short-lived journal, the *Radical Review*. Having worked on the *Boston Globe* from 1878 to 1889, he established *Liberty* in 1881. A German-language version was published in 1888. The paper ran until 1908. Tucker also ran two bookshops, the first in Boston and the second in New York. In 1893 he published *Instead of a Book*. Tucker left America in 1908 after a fire destroyed his Unique Book Store and printing press. Unable to establish a new venture in Europe, he withdrew from front-line anarchist politics. A Francophile, he adopted a strongly anti-German position during the First World War. In the 1920s he was involved in an acrimonious exchange with Victor Yarros, a one-time associate in the Boston anarchist club, who renounced anarchism. He lived in France, first near Paris and then near Nice before moving to Monaco, where he died.[37]

BARTOLOMEO VANZETTI (1888–1927)

Executed for murder after a notorious legal case failed to prove his guilt, Vanzetti was born in Piedmont, Italy, and went to America in 1908, the same year as Nicola Sacco, with whom he was tried. Like Sacco, Vanzetti became an anarchist activist in the years 1912–17 and went to Mexico in 1917 to avoid the draft. He was arrested in May 1920 on the same day that a botched payroll robbery took place in Massachusetts. The evidence linking him to the crime was weak and he was initially charged for involvement in a separate shoe-factory robbery that had taken place on Christmas Eve 1919. Vanzetti received a twelve-to-fifteen year sentence when the alibis of twenty Italians were discounted as unreliable. Charged with the killing of the guard and paymaster shot during the payroll hold-up Vanzetti was electrocuted in 1927.[38]

Chapter 2: Cultures

ALEXANDER BERKMAN (1870–1936)

Berkman was an activist and writer, companion of Emma Goldman and leading voice in the US anarchist movement. Born in Lithuania, he was the nephew of Mark Natanson, a member of the revolutionary Tchaikovsky Circle to which Kropotkin belonged. In 1888 he went to New York, meeting Goldman shortly after his arrival. Moved by the violence meted out to strikers in Pennsylvania, he attempted to assassinate Henry Frick, chair of the Board of Carnegie Steel in 1892. He served fourteen years and wrote the celebrated *Prison Memoirs of an Anarchist* (1912). After his release he co-edited *Mother Earth* with Goldman. He also helped set up the Ferrer Modern School in New York and offered classes there. In 1916 he established the journal *Blast*. With Goldman he took a leading role in anti-war no-conscription campaigns and was imprisoned for two years for his activities. He was then deported to Russia. Enthusiastic about the revolution, Berkman was deeply disillusioned by the dictatorship. He published his critique in *The Bolshevik Myth* (1925). He left Russia and settled in the South of France. Diagnosed with cancer, he committed suicide after completing *What is Communist Anarchism* (1929) and co-editing Goldman's autobiography, *Living My Life* (1931).[1]

ANANDA COOMARASWAMY (1877–1947)

Born in Colombo, Sri Lanka (then Ceylon), Coomaraswamy was taken to England at the age two by his mother, Elizabeth Beeby. His father, a distinguished barrister, scholar and politician, died on the day of their departure. Coomaraswamy studied mineralogy and botany at University College London, graduating in 1900. He became director of the mineralogical survey of Ceylon from 1903 to 1906. On his retirement, he initiated the Ceylon Social Reform Society, a movement for national education, promoting the teaching of vernacular languages in school and the revival of Indian culture. Coomaraswamy was attracted to the work of William Morris and the arts and crafts movement, which pioneered the decorative arts as a socially transformative politics. In 1910 he helped found the India Society to promote Indian art and knowledge of its long traditions. Members included Jawaharlal Nehru and Rabindranath Tagore, a leading light in the 'Swadeshi' movement which appealed to educated elites to reinvigorate Indian village life, working with rural populations. In 1917 he took up a post at the Boston Museum of Fine Arts. Coomaraswamy remained in Boston until his death, writing extensively on the arts and crafts of India and Ceylon and on literature, philosophy, Buddhism and comparative religion.[2]

SIGMUND ENGLÄNDER (1828–1902)

A writer and journalist, Engländer was born in Moravia into a middle-class Jewish family. Awarded a doctorate by the University of Vienna, in 1847 he became editor of the Viennese monthly *Der Salon: Mittheilungen aus den Kreisen der Literatur, Kunst und des Lebens*. Engländer discontinued its publication after falling foul of Austrian censors. In 1848 he supported the Vienna uprising and when the city was retaken by government forces he was one of twelve prisoners demanded by the military commander, General Windischgrätz, for execution. Engländer escaped to Frankfurt and then to Paris. He mixed with Heinrich Heine and Marx, who later accused him of being a spy. Working as a translator in the news agency of Charles Havas, he met Paul Julius Reuter, with whose help he produced a lithographed 'Correspondence'. This contained extracts of Parisian newspapers, original articles and news of events and it was offered by subscription to the external press. Engländer was arrested for his revolutionary activities and imprisoned in Mazas prison, Paris, before being expelled. He moved to England and became correspondent for several Continental papers and editor of the *Londoner Deutsches Zeitung*, founded by revolutionary and poet Gottfried Kinckel. He met up again with Reuter and took up the post of chief editor for the Reuter news agency. In 1871 Engländer's support for the Commune embarrassed

Reuter. Reuter introduced a policy of strict impartiality and Engländer promised to cease his political activity, but in 1873 he published *The Abolition of the State*. Compromised by this, Reuter sent him to Turkey, where Engländer remained until 1888. He continued to work for Reuter up to his retirement in 1894. Engländer published a number of books and pamphlets, including an account of prison life in Mazas and various novels. He died in Turin, three years after Reuter. Wanting nothing more to do with him, the Reuter family chose to ignore his passing and write him out of the company's history.[3]

LAWRENCE FERLINGHETTI (b. 1919)

Ferlinghetti is a poet, painter, playwright and founder of the City Lights Bookstore. He was brought up in France and New York, attended the University of North Carolina from 1937, joined the US Navy in 1941 and took part in the D-Day landings in 1944. He took a master's degree at Columbia University in 1947 and was awarded a doctorate from the Sorbonne in 1950. From Paris he went to San Francisco and started to publish the magazine *City Lights*, named after the Charlie Chaplin film. To support the magazine he opened the City Lights Pocket Book Store, later City Lights Books. It became a magnet for Beat writers and artists. Arrested in 1956 for printing and selling Alan Ginsberg's *Howl and Other Poems*, Ferlinghetti called on the American Civil Liberties Union to defend his rights to free speech. He won the case in 1957. In 1998 he was named San Francisco's first poet laureate and held this title until 2000.[4]

PAUL GOODMAN (1911–1972)

Goodman was an educator, essayist, novelist, poet, social critic and advocate of communitarian anarchism. He was born in New York, attended City College, part of the City University (CUNY), and was awarded a doctorate from the University of Chicago. His open bisexuality led to his expulsion from the university and also from his next two teaching jobs. He worked for ten years as a therapist, pioneering gestalt therapy, and living in near poverty. In the 1940s and early 50s he wrote for the magazines *Politics*, *Why?* and *Retort* and published four novels, a range of stories, poems and essays and five books. *Communitas: Means of Livelihood and Ways of Life* (1947), illustrated by his brother Percival, gained some attention but Goodman otherwise remained in oblivion until he published *Growing Up Absurd* in 1960. In 1962 he published *Utopian Essays and Practical Proposals* and *Compulsory Miseducation*. In 1966 he delivered the Canadian Broadcasting Corporation annual Massey Lecture, publishing this as *The Moral Ambiguity of America*. A vocal critic of the Vietnam War, Goodman helped set up Support in Action, a body that functioned to provide support for draft resisters. With his son Matthew, he was also involved in draft-card burnings. Critical of the Leninist tendencies and guerrilla tactics promoted by groups within the student movements, he distanced himself from the New Left in the late 1960s. The publication of *New Reformation: Notes of a Neolithic Conservative* in 1970 marked his break. Goodman elaborated an anarchist position that he called Jeffersonian and sometimes conservative. He was strongly attracted to Kropotkinian and Tolstoyan ideas, but the influences on his work were diverse.[5]

ISHIKAWA SANSHIRŌ (1876–1956)

A journalist and activist, Ishikawa was a participant in Kōtoku Shūshi's socialist society the *Heiminsha*. Like Kōtoku he opposed the Russo-Japanese War. Having been imprisoned in 1907 and 1910, he left Japan in 1911 and spent the years 1913–1920 in Europe. He met Edward Carpenter, the socialist writer and pioneering campaigner for homosexual rights, and became friends with Élisée Reclus. On his return to Japan he became an advocate of anarcho-syndicalism. He translated Kropotkin's work, wrote a biography of Reclus and promoted anarchism through the Mutual Study Society, which he helped found in 1927, and the Anarchist League of Japan, established in 1946.[6]

STAUGHTON LYND (B. 1929)

Lynd is a civil disobedience and anti-war activist and campaigner, lawyer and author. Raised in New York and educated at Harvard, Columbia and Chicago, he taught American history at Spelman College, Atlanta, and Yale University before his anti-war activities made him unemployable. He became a Quaker in the 1960s, was active in civil rights voter registration initiatives and in 1965 chaired the first anti-Vietnam War march in Washington DC. From 1976 until his retirement in 1996 he worked as a lawyer at the Legal Services in Youngstown, Ohio, specializing in employment law. In the 1970s he campaigned against the closure of the Youngstown steel mills and subsequently served as lead counsel in a legal action designed to reopen the mills under worker-community ownership. With Alice Lynd he continues to campaign against the death penalty and for prison reform.[7]

NESTOR MAKHNO (1889–1934)

Born into a poor rural family and raised by his widowed mother in the Ukraine, Makhno started working as a shepherd aged seven. He later worked as a hired farmhand and in a foundry. A committed revolutionary by the age of seventeen, he joined an anarchist-communist group and took up armed struggle. He was arrested in 1908 and sentenced to life for taking part in an action that resulted in the killing of a police officer. Amnestied in 1917, Makhno returned to his village and set up a commune of farm workers, a farm workers' union and peasant council. Having instigated the expropriation of local landowners, he organized the Revolutionary Insurgent Army of the Ukraine or Makhnovists. At first operating with the support of the Bolsheviks, Makhno went into opposition after the 1918 Treaty of Brest-Litovsk, which ceded Ukrainian territory to Germany. He led a campaign against occupying German and Austrian forces and by turns engaged the Red Army and joined with it to drive out forces loyal to the Tsar. In 1920 the Bolsheviks launched a decisive offensive against Makhno's militias. The army was decimated but Makhno escaped wounded and went into exile in Paris, where he died.[8]

HERBERT READ (1893–1968)

A poet, art critic and educationalist, Read grew up on a farm on the North York Moors and was educated in Halifax. He spent two years at the University of Leeds, during which time he mixed with the radicals of the Leeds Art Club, founded by the Nietzschean Alfred Orage. Enlisting in 1914, he served on the Western Front before taking a job at the

Ministry of Labour. He published his first poetry during the war and established himself in modernist literary circles as founder editor of the periodical *Arts and Letters*. In 1922 he started work at the Victoria and Albert Museum in London. In the 1930s he emerged as a champion of avant-garde visual art; in the latter part of the decade he became closely associated with Surrealism. In 1946 he played an instrumental role in the establishment of the Institute of Contemporary Arts in London. Read claimed that had been introduced to anarchism in 1911 through reading Edward Carpenter, though Carpenter kept his distance from anarchism and was more strongly influenced by his friends William Morris and Rabindranath Tagore. In any event, Read declared himself an anarchist in 1937, prompted by the revolution in Spain. He wrote a series of books and pamphlets on anarchist philosophy and art, anarchism and education, contributed to *Spain and the World*, *War Commentary*, *Revolt!* and *Freedom*. He also chaired the Freedom Defence Committee established to support the editors of *War Commentary* charged with subversion. His acceptance of a knighthood in 1952 brought the relationship with the London anarchists to an end. Read remained politically active and continued to publish until his death.[9]

SHIFU/ LIU SHAOBIN (1884–1915)

Active in the last years of the Qing dynasty, Shifu was a revolutionary, sometime exponent of assassination and anarchist-communist. He was born in Guangdong. Excelling at school, he turned against the education system after failing to pass provincial examinations. He set up a reading group to disseminate 'new knowledge' and campaigned for the establishment of a girls' school, grounding his lifelong advocacy of women's liberation. He was introduced to range of European revolutionary ideas in 1904 during a trip to Japan. He advocated assassination as a means of change and joined the underground resistance movement Tongmenghui – associated with Sun Yat Sen – which was then offering lessons in how to make explosives. In 1906 he returned to China. He was jailed for three years when a bomb exploded unexpectedly, leaving him badly injured. Shifu returned to activism in 1910, organizing the China Assassination Corps, which was involved in a number of plots. His mature anarchist doctrines were articulated in 1912 through his participation in the Conscience Society, a group established to propagate anarchism by educational means. Members observed twelve prohibitions regulating the consumption of meat, alcohol and tobacco; the use of servants and travel in rickshaws; marriage and the use of family names; service in official positions, the military, political assemblies and political parties; and religious observance. In 1914 he published a paper, *Voice of the People,* and established the Society of Anarchist-Communist Comrades. Attracted to Kropotkin's anarchism, Shifu became a critic of Sun Yat Sen, of political revolution and of Marxism. Weakened by his blast injuries and suffering from tuberculosis he died in Shanghai.[10]

B. TRAVEN (DATES UNKNOWN)

Traven was an author of twelve books, best known for his novel *The Treasure of the Sierra Madre,* which was turned into a film by John Huston in 1948. His real identity remains a mystery but he is usually known as Ret Marut, Bavarian revolutionary (?1890–1969). His writing includes the Jungle

Novels, a set of six books originally published between 1930 and 1939: *The Carreta, Government, March to the Monteria, Trozas, The Rebellion of the Hanged* and *A General from the Jungle*. They describe the vicious exploitation and growing rebelliousness of southern Mexican Indians in the period before the Mexican Revolution.[11]

COLIN WARD (1924–2010)

Ward was born in Essex and left school at fifteen. Until he was conscripted in 1942 he worked as a draughtsman in an architect's office. He heard Emma Goldman speak in London in 1938 and attended a rally to support the International Brigades in 1939. He fell in with Glasgow anarchists when he was drafted and in 1945 started to subscribe to *War Commentary*. Ward was called to give evidence at the trial of the paper's editors – John Hewetson, Vernon Richards and Philip Sansom – for conspiracy. He testified that their subversive writing had made no impact on him. He became involved in the post-war squatters movement and editor of *Freedom* in 1947. In 1961 he took up the editorship of the new journal *Anarchy* and in 1973 he published *Anarchy in Action*. This was one of nearly thirty books he wrote on topics ranging from allotments, utopias, education and social policy to town planning and childhood development.[12]

JOHN ZERZAN (B. 1943)

Raised in Salem, Oregon, Zerzan studied political science at Stanford University, history at San Francisco State University and completed his postgraduate degree at the University of Southern California. He became active in labour and left-wing politics in the 1960s and was arrested in 1966 at an anti-Vietnam protest. In his writing, Zerzan first explored the emergence of trade unionism and industrialization. This led to a study of technology and civilization in the 1980s. He attracted international attention in the 1990s when he began a correspondence with Ted Kaczynski, the ecological activist better known as the Unabomber, and refused to condemn his bombing campaign. Having settled in Eugene, Oregon, in the 1980s, Zerzan also became strongly linked to the anarchist movements that mushroomed there which helped catalyze the anti-capitalist activism of the noughties. He is the author and editor of a number of books, including: *Elements of Refusal* (1988), *Future Primitive* (1994), *Against Civilization* (1999), *Running on Emptiness: The Pathology of Civilization* (2002), *Twilight of the Machines* (2008) and *Future Primitive Revisited* (2012).[13]

Chapter 3: Practices

ERNESTO AGUILAR (B.?)

Aguilar is a media worker and organizer. In the 1990s he co-founded Black Fist, an anarchist collective in Houston, Texas, which co-convened the Anti-Authoritarian Network of Community Organizers conference in Atlanta in 1994. Aguilar was also involved in the formation of the Anarchist Black Cross Network, Houston Cop-watch and in a web development for the anarchist paper *Onward*. In 2001 he set up the Anarchist People of Color listserv and the APOC website, illegalvoices.org. This catalysed the formation of a number of US collectives and supporters held a conference at Wayne State University, Detroit, in 2003. In 2004 he edited *Our*

Culture, Our Resistance and worked on the APOC publication *Wildfire*.[1]

ÉMILE ARMAND (1872–1963)

Émile Armand was born Ernest-Lucien Juin Armand in Paris, the son of a Communard. A talented linguist, he studied Arabic, Persian and Hebrew as well as several European languages. He turned to anarchism in the mid-1890s. In 1901 he founded *L'Ère Nouvelle* with his partner, the Tolstoyan anarchist Marie Kugel. An antimilitarist and libertarian communist, Armand was attracted by the practical application of anarchist principles. After Kugel's death in 1906, he read Stirner's *The Ego and Its Own* (1844) and became interested in free love and neo-Malthusianism. After publishing *What is an Anarchist?* in 1908 Armand turned towards individualism, though he continued to work with Jean Grave and Élisée Reclus, both communists. He adopted an anti-war position in 1914 and was imprisoned in 1918 for his antimilitarist activities. Released in 1922, he began to publish Zo d'Axa's *L'En-Dehors*, the publication for which he is best known. A series of influential pamphlets followed in the 1920s and 30s. In 1927 he collaborated with a range of leading social theorists, including Edward Carpenter, John Henry Mackay and Henry Seymour, to produce *Les Différents Visages de l'anarchisme*. *L'En-dehors* was closed down in 1939, on the outbreak of the war. Armand was imprisoned in 1940 for two years. After the end of the war he produced a monthly magazine, *L'Unique*. He continued to contribute to the journal until his death in Rouen.[2]

HAKIM BEY (b. 1945)

Bey is the pseudonym or alter ego of Peter Lamborn Wilson, a scholar, cultural theorist and artist. He was born in Baltimore and brought up in New Jersey: his father was professor of English at Rutgers University. He left America in 1968, developing an interest in Sufism while on the hippie trail. He spent several years in Iran before moving on to south-east Asia in 1980/81. He has since given classes at the Jack Kerouac School of Disembodied Poetics at the Naropa University in Boulder, Colorado. Writing under the name Wilson, he has published *Escape from the Nineteenth Century* (1998), a study of Fourier, Proudhon, Marx, Nietzsche and modern progress, and *Heresies: Anarchist Memoirs, Anarchist Art* (2016), which combines reminiscences of his own activism with commentaries on anarchist artists. He is probably better known in anarchist circles as Hakim Bey, author of *TAZ*, a series of texts originally published in zine form in the mid and late 1980s.[3]

BOB BLACK (B. 1951)

Born in Detroit, Michigan, Black has been involved with the anarchist movement, mainly in North America, since the late 60s. Black is best known for his 1985 essay 'The Abolition of Work'. He has published a number of books: *The Abolition of Work and Other Essays* (1986), *Friendly Fire* (1992), *Beneath the Underground* (1994), *Anarchy after Leftism* (1997), *Nightmares of Reason* (2010) and *Debunking Democracy* (2011). Black is thought to have coined the term post-left anarchism, a phrase that appears in *Anarchy after Leftism*.[4]

ALFREDO BONANNO (b. 1937)

Bonanno is a leading exponent of insurrectionary anarchism, theorist, strategist and activist. He was born in 1937 in Catania, Sicily. In the 1960s he developed a model of decentralized, networked organizing, publishing his ideas in a series of pamphlets in the 1970s. He took an active part in the Italian insurrectionary movements of the 1970s, and was imprisoned for subversion in October 1972, but he continued to propagate anarchism. In 1977 he published *Armed Joy*, for which he received an eighteen-month sentence. In March 1980 he was charged with being a member of Azione Rivoluzionaria, an anarchist situationist armed group active from 1976. Cleared in 1981, he published the essay 'And We Will Always be Ready to Storm the Heavens Once Again: Against Amnesty', a defiant statement of his refusal to compromise with the authorities, in 1984. In 1988 he was ejected from the Forli antimilitarist congress by the majority of the anarchist-syndicalist tendency of the Italian Anarchist Federation (FAI). The following year he was arrested in connection with a robbery of a jewellery shop in Bergamo. At the start of 1993 Bonanno went to Greece to attend an event organized by the Anarchist Initiative in Athens, Thessalonika and Patras. In 2003 he was sentenced to six years and fined 2,000 euros for an insurrectionary robbery. He served part of the sentence in Trieste prison and the rest under house arrest. In March 2009 Bonanno returned to Greece and in October the same year he was arrested with a comrade, Christos Stratigopoulos, accused of driving the getaway car at a bank robbery in Trikala. Bonanno denied the charges but was jailed with Stratigopoulos, who admitted them. He served a year of the four-year sentence.[5]

MURRAY BOOKCHIN (1921-2006)

Bookchin was a left-libertarian autodidact, advocate of decentralized federalism and communalist democracy. Born in New York, he joined the youth organization of the American Communist Party, the Young Communist League aged nine. Alienated by the adoption of the Popular Front policy, he broke with Stalinism in 1935 and was expelled in 1937 during the Spanish Revolution for anarchist-Trotskyist tendencies. He worked in New Jersey as a foundryman and union organizer for the Congress of Industrial Unions. After being demobbed from the US Army he became a car worker and participant in the General Motors strike of 1946. Writing under the pen-name Lewis Herber, he published *Our Synthetic Environment* in 1962 to promote social ecology. In the latter part of the decade he developed the concept of post-scarcity, finding a foothold in the countercultural movements that blossomed in the 60s. In 1971 he co-founded the Institute for Social Ecology in Plainfield, Vermont, and started teaching at the liberal arts Ramapo College of New Jersey, becoming a full professor in 1977. In the 1960s and 70s Bookchin lectured across the US and Canada and was active in number of anti-nuclear, civil rights and anti-Vietnam War campaigns. He wrote nearly thirty books, including the collection *Post-Scarcity Anarchism* (1971), *The Ecology of Freedom* (1982), *Urbanization without Cities* (1992) and *Social Anarchism or Lifestyle Anarchism: An Unbridgeable Chasm* (1995).[6]

TOM BROWN (1900-1974)

Brown was an anarchist syndicalist born in Newcastle-on-Tyne in the north-east of England. Apprenticed as an engineer, he became a union organizer and shop steward. He joined the Communist Party after the Bolshevik takeover and served as its industrial organizer in the north-east. Disillusioned with Bolshevism, he subsequently quit the party. In 1934 Brown was involved in foundation of the Anti-Fascist League, a direct-action organization established to counter the rise of the British Union of Fascists in the north-east. Moving from the West Midlands to London in the mid-1930s he joined the editorial board of *Revolt!* with Marie-Louise Berneri and Vernon Richards and helped set up the Anarchist Federation of Britain. When *Revolt!* folded, Brown participated in *War Commentary*. He published the pamphlets *Trade Unionism or Syndicalism* in 1942 and *The Social General Strike. Why 1926 Failed* in 1946. In 1945 he helped launch *Direct Action* for the Anarchist Federation and in 1946, when the Anarchist Federation became the Syndicalist Workers' Federation (SWF), he joined the Syndicalist International. He remained active in the SWF until his death.[7]

SANTE GERONIMO CASERIO (1873–1894)

Caserio achieved notoriety after killing President Carnot of France in 1894. Born in Lombardy, he was a fervent Catholic in his youth and planned to enter a seminary to train as a priest. Apprenticed at fourteen to a Milanese baker, he became an anarchist when he was sixteen or seventeen. He was imprisoned in Milan for distributing anarchist materials, travelling to Switzerland on his release. He worked as a baker until June 1894, when he decided to assassinate Carnot on account of his failure to commute the death sentence on August Vaillant, who had bombed the French Chamber of Deputies the year before. After fatally stabbing Carnot, Caserio attempted to escape, having determined to return to Italy to kill the Pope and King Umberto I. He was guillotined after being found guilty at a two-day trial.[8]

BART DE LIGT (1883–1938)

De Ligt was born near Utrecht. He studied theology at the University of Utrecht, where he discovered Kant, Fichte, and the socialism of William Morris and John Ruskin. In 1909 he joined the Union of Christian Socialists. The following year he became pastor of the Reformed Church at Nuenen near Eindhoven in the Netherlands. In 1914 he co-authored *The Guilt of the Churches*, a manifesto which accused the Churches of complicity in the imperialist system. During the war he campaigned for the rights of conscientious objectors. After delivering an antimilitarist sermon in 1915, de Ligt was expelled from the area by the local military commander. His writings were proscribed in the armed forces. In 1917 he was imprisoned and banned from two more areas. Soon after the end of the war he resigned from the Church and the Union of Christian Socialists, no longer regarding himself a Christian. In 1921 he was imprisoned again, for organizing a general strike to demand the release of a conscientious objector. The same year he founded the International Anti-Militarist Bureau, the successor to Ferdinand Domela Nieuwenhuis's International Anti-Militarist Union. He continued to campaign as an antimilitarist throughout the inter-war years, corresponding with Gandhi and taking up a position as his vocal, sympathetic critic. He was also an active member of the War Resisters International. In 1934 de Ligt presented an anti-fascist, anti-Nazi *Plan of a Campaign Against All Wars and Preparation for War*. This was later incorporated into *The Conquest of Violence*, published just before his death in Nantes.[9]

JAMES GUILLAUME (1844–1916)

Described by Max Nettlau as a Swiss collectivist and internationalist, Guillaume identified as a Proudhonist. A leading light in the Jura Federation of the International, Guillaume was a close associate of Bakunin's until 1874, but he was lukewarm about Bakunin's concept of revolution. In the late 1860s he declined to join the Alliance of Social Democracy. As an anti-authoritarian Guillaume took Bakunin's part against Marx when the First International collapsed but attempted to heal the divisions between the two wings of the movement. He later published a four-volume history drawing on documents published in the *Bulletin* of the Jura Federation, *L'International: Documents et souvenirs* (1864–1878). Guillaume developed his understanding of this collectivism in *Une Commune sociale*, published in 1870, and the essay *Ideas on Social Organization*, which followed six years later. Accepting that there was a distinction between the collectivist principle of distribution according to work and the communist ideal of distribution according to need, Guillaume remained unwilling to commit anarchists to any predetermined position. In 1877 he argued that workers themselves would decide how to distribute resources and that their decisions would likely be influenced by the abundance of supplies. In the 1880s and 90s Guillaume became friendly with Kropotkin, though the two later disagreed about the prospects of syndicalist organization. Guillaume was active in the

French militant syndicalist union the Confédération Géné-
rale du Travail from 1903 until the outbreak of war in 1914.
He died in Switzerland.[10]

ANN HANSEN (b. 1953)

Ann Hansen was born in Ontario. She became interested in
radical politics when still at school, instinctively drawn to the
urban guerrilla group Front de Libération du Québec, which
struggled for independence in the 1960s. She studied Marxism at the University of Waterloo but became disillusioned
with the Marxist-Leninist groups who valued interpretative
philosophy over practical politics. Taking an interest in the
European urban movements that appeared in the 1970s, she
left Canada to study in London. In Paris she made contact
with a group involved in support work for the Red Army Faction (RAF). Hansen's critique of RAF tactics dovetailed with
her increasing absorption with autonomist politics. Hansen
decided to return to Canada to initiate militant action there.
In the early 1980s she formed Direct Action in Vancouver
with Juliet Belmas, Gerry Hannah, Doug Stewart and Brent
Taylor. Later known as the Vancouver Five or the Squamish
Five, Direct Action's major activities occurred in 1982 and
included the bombing of the Cheekye-Dunsmuir BC Hydro
substation on Vancouver Island in May, and the bombing of
the Litton Industries factory in Toronto in October. Hansen
also participated in anti-porn actions directed against Red
Hot Video outlets in British Columbia, organized by the
Wimmin's Fire Brigade. In November 1982 three stores
were fire-bombed, two of them sustaining serious damage.
Hansen wrote the communiqués outlining the collective's

objections to violence against women and children. She was arrested with the other members of Direct Action in January 1983 somewhere near Squamish, British Columbia. 'Free the Five' rallies were organized in the group's support and to challenge mainstream media reporting of the trial. Direct Action members were sentenced to life in prison in June 1984. Their sentences now complete, all have been released. Hansen has since published *Direct Action: Memoirs of an Urban Guerrilla* (2001) and co-authored, with Juliet Belmas, *This Is Not a Love Story: Armed Struggle Against the Institutions of Patriarchy* (2002).[11]

HE-YIN ZHEN (1884–c.1920)

He-Yin Zhen was a feminist writer and thinker. She was born in Yizheng, in Jiangsu, the coastal province north of Shanghai. She went to Tokyo in 1907 and joined Chinese revolutionaries exiled there with her husband Liu Shipei. They established the Society for the Study of Socialism and promoted a form of Tolstoyan anarchism. She also formed the Society for the Restoration of Women's Rights and played a leading role in the anarchist-feminist journal *Natural Justice*. In 1907–8 she published 'On the Question of Women's Liberation', a critique of the manifesto *The Women's Bell*, sometimes regarded as the first Chinese statement of feminism. She was also the author of 'On the Question of Women's Labour', 'Economic Revolution and Women's Revolution' and 'On the Revenge of Women'. She is thought to have entered a Buddhist order after the death of Liu Shipei in 1919 and the time and circumstances of her death are not fully known.[12]

ÉMILE HENRY (1872–1894)

The son of a Communard, Henry was one of the most notorious of the anarchist propagandists by the deed and advocates of violence in the 1890s. He was born in Barcelona, where his father had fled to avoid a death sentence. After completing his school education he found a job with a construction engineer. He quit after nearly three months and went to Paris where he worked as a bookkeeper. In 1891 Charles Malato invited him to join an anarchist group where he established a reputation as an intellectual. He was arrested in 1892 in police raids that followed anarchist attacks in the city but was not detained. After another bombing in November 1892 and to avoid further arrest, Henry left Paris for London. He returned to Paris in 1893. In February that year a home-made bomb he planted at the offices of the Mining Company of Carmaux was discovered and removed to a Paris police station, where it exploded, killing six people, five of them police. In December the same year, he detonated a bomb in the Café Terminus, wounding seventeen. Henry attempted to escape but staff gave chase and captured him. After explaining the motives for his attack at his trial, Henry was guillotined.[13]

GORD HILL (b.?)

A member of the Kwakwaka'wakw nation, Hill is a writer, artist and militant involved in Indigenous resistance, anti-colonial and anti-capitalist movements. Exposed to anarchist literatures in Vancouver's punk scene, he was radicalized by the ways of living practised within the subculture. Hill describes his politics as anti-authoritarian rather than anarchist and advocates direct action through grass-roots organizing. He has been active in campaigns against the 2010 Vancouver Olympics and to prevent mining, fracking and pipelines in British Colombia.[14]

BELL HOOKS (b. 1952)

A feminist, writer and artist, Gloria Jean Watkins, known by her preferred name bell hooks, was born in Kentucky. Educated at Stanford, Wisconsin, and the University of California, Santa Cruz, she is best known as a sociologist, cultural critic and analyst of intersectionality, cultural difference, race and knowledge in feminism. Her work has had a profound influence in academia and on a wide range of justice movements and campaigns, including in anarchism. Having famously refused to allow her life and work to be pigeon-holed by others, hooks has responded positively to the anarchist embrace of her thinking about patriarchy and racism and has engaged with anarchists to explore the overlaps. Her books include *Ain't I a Woman: Black Women and Feminism* (1981), *Teaching to Transgress: Education as the Practice of Freedom* (1994) and *Where We Stand: Class Matters* (2000).[15]

GEORGE JACKSON (1941–1971)

A leading figure in the Black Panther Party, Jackson was raised in a Catholic family on the West Side of Chicago. In 1956 his father took a job in Los Angeles, troubled by the truancy and police conflicts in Chicago. Jackson was arrested soon after the move for 'suspicion of joyriding'. This marked the start of a cycle of arrests, detentions and escapes which came to an end in 1960 when he was jailed for taking part in an armed gas station robbery and stealing $70. Jackson was given an indeterminate sentence in 1961, spending time in Soledad and San Quentin prisons. In Soledad in 1968, he set up a Black Panther chapter with W. L. Nolen. The same year, after Nolen and two other black inmates were killed by prison guards, Jackson was accused of the revenge killing of a white guard, along with Fleeta Drumgo and John Cluchette. He was shot dead in the San Quentin prison yard in the course of an attempted prison break. His book *Soledad Brother: Letters from Prison* was published in 1970 and *Blood in My Eye* appeared after his death.[16]

KŌTOKU SHŪSUI (1871–1911)

Executed following the Great Treason trial, Kōtoku was an advocate of anarchist communism. He left Nakamura, the small village where he was born, in 1887 to study English in Tokyo but was expelled from the city on account of his association with his academic sponsor, a political undesirable. He became acquainted with socialist ideas in 1889. In 1893 he became a journalist and joined the Society for the Study of Socialism. With the onset of the 1904 Russo-Japanese War he broke with social democracy and adopted a militant anti-war position. He set up the group *Heiminsha*, or the Commoners' Society. This published its own paper and Kōtoku was imprisoned after publishing a translation of *The Communist Manifesto* in 1905. He spent his five-month sentence reading about anarchism and the idea of propaganda by the deed. On release he travelled to America and organized the revolutionary party *Shakai Kakumeito* with Japanese comrades in San Francisco and Oakland. On his return to Japan in 1906 he advocated direct action and called for the overthrow of the imperial government. He advanced a strategy that combined mass political education with covert revolutionary violence. Kōtoku was arrested when a conspiracy to assassinate the Emperor was uncovered in May 1910. He had not played a direct part in the plot, but as the leading advocate of anarchist communism he was hanged with eleven others. The authorities played fast and loose with the law in convicting the anarchists at the Great Treason trial, but appeals lodged in 1955 and 1961 by some of those imprisoned for their involvement in the conspiracy and by descendants of the condemned failed.[17]

GUSTAV LANDAUER (1870–1919)

Landauer was a political theorist, poet and novelist who studied philosophy, Shakespeare and German culture at the universities of Heidelberg and Berlin. He joined the Social Democratic Party (SPD) in 1888 but was attracted to Tolstoyan ideas and the principle of anarchism without adjectives. In 1891 he joined the Berlin Independent Socialists. The group was expelled from the SPD. The same year he edited the first issue of *Der Sozialist*. After the 1893 Zurich Congress of the Second International *Der Sozialist* declared for anarchism. Landauer published his novel, *The Pastor of Death*, the same year and was given a one-year prison sentence for inciting civil disobedience. After publishing a German-language translation of Kropotkin's *The Conquest of Bread* (1892), he went to London to attend the 1896 Congress of the Second International, meeting with Kropotkin, Louise Michel, Malatesta and Reclus. The following year he campaigned for the Monjuich anarchists and became a close friend of Fernando

Tárrida del Mármol. As well as translating Kropotkin's *Fields, Factories and Workshops* (1898), *Mutual Aid* (1902) and *The Great French Revolution* (1909), he also translated works by Oscar Wilde. He published *Volk and Land: Thirty Socialist Theses* in 1906 and *Revolution* the following year. In 1908 he founded the Socialist League, which had sections in Berlin and Switzerland, and in 1911 published *For Socialism*. Landauer also produced a widely circulated anti-war manifesto. *Der Sozialist* closed in 1915 but Landauer continued to agitate against the war. In 1918 he supported the Bavarian Council Republic. He was arrested in 1919 when central government and far-right paramilitary forces crushed it. Landauer was brutally beaten before being shot in May 1919.[18]

WOLFI LANDSTREICHER (b. ?1958)

Raised in the American Midwest in a fundamentalist Christian family, Landstreicher is an anarchist and egoist, translator, pamphleteer and publisher of the bulletin *My Own*. Inspired by the countercultural movements of the 1960s, he dropped out of college in 1975. Rejecting religion, he moved from Tolstoyan Christian anarchism to egoism. Landstreicher's egoism has been shaped by an engagement with Italian insurrectionism, particularly the work of Alfredo Bonanno. He is best known as the author of the book/zine collection *Willful Disobedience*. He is a contributor to the journals *Anarchy*, *A Journal of Desire Armed* and *Modern Slavery*.[19]

M. P. LECOMPTE (DATES UNKNOWN)

Marie Paula 'Minnie' LeCompte was secretary of the Manhattan branch of the Socialistic Labor Party. In 1879 she became associate editor of the group's paper, *Labor Standard*. She translated Bakunin's *God and the State* (1882) and Kropotkin's *Appeal to the Young* (1880) into English, the latter appearing in the San Francisco paper *The Truth*. In 1883 she was involved in a bread riot in Berne and in 1884 she went to Geneva and worked at the Imprimerie Jurassienne, sending funds to support Kropotkin's newspaper *Le Révolté*. Later that year she moved to Marseille and in 1885 she joined the editorial staff of the short-run paper *Le Droit Social* with J. Torrens, Ugo Parrini and Justin Mazade, a trio she had met in Geneva. In 1885–6 she was still involved in the movement and sent letters to Henry Seymour's London monthly the *Anarchist*. In 1888 she was living in Aix-en-Provence. She is thought to have dropped out of the anarchist movement thereafter.[20]

CINDY MILSTEIN (b.?)

Cindy Milstein is a community organizer and educator. She has been involved in numerous projects, including the Institute for Anarchist Studies, Station 40 (an anarchist(ic) home and social centre in San Francisco), the Interference Archive in Brooklyn, Occupy Philly and Black Sheep Books in Montpelier, Vermont. She also taught at the Institute for Social Ecology. She is the author of *Anarchism and Its Aspirations* (2010) and editor of *Taking Sides: Revolutionary Solidarity and the Poverty of Liberalism* (2015).[21]

DAVID NICOLL (1859–1919)

Part of the Commonweal Group of anarchists who gravitated to William Morris's Socialist League, Nicoll was born in Houndsditch in London's East End and was brought up in a relatively comfortable household. His mother died sometime between 1861 and 1871 and his father in 1878. Having squandered a substantial inheritance, Nicoll worked as a journalist. He joined the Socialist League in 1884 and was an active propagandist. In 1890 he took over the editorship of the League's paper, *Commonweal*. Imprisoned in 1892, he had a breakdown and remained incapacitated after his release. He spent his later life in penury as a street vendor, selling revolutionary literature, and died in St Pancras Hospital.[22]

FERDINAND DOMELA NIEUWENHUIS (1846–1919)

The outstanding figure in the Dutch labour movement, Nieuwenhuis was an anarchist anti-war activist. Brought up in a Lutheran household, he practised as a Lutheran preacher for nine years from 1870. His antimilitarism had its roots in his opposition to the Franco-Prussian War; his interest in labour movement politics and social justice grew gradually throughout the 1870s. He left the Church in 1879 to promote social democracy in the Netherlands. Bringing his socialist politics to bear on his antimilitarism, Nieuwenhuis promoted the organization of labour unions to prevent war through a general strike. The championing of this internationalist strategy of direct action put him at odds with the German Social Democratic Party in the Second International. He broke with the latter in 1896 and aligned himself with anarchism. He produced a report on antimilitarism for the 1900 Paris International Anarchist Congress and argued for the creation of a new International to advance the idea of a general strike against war and the mass refusal of conscription. In 1904 he became the general secretary of the newly formed

International Anti-Militarist Union, forerunner of the War Resisters' International. Nieuwenhuis pressed the case for antimilitarist politics in the anarchist movement, in the face of some resistance. In 1914 he argued strongly against the war and he campaigned as an antimilitarist until his death.[23]

ŌSUGI SAKAE (1885–1923)

Ōsugi Sakae was the foremost anarchist theoretician and publicist active in Japan in the early twentieth century. He attended one of Japan's seven Kadet Schools intent on pursuing a military career but became disaffected with this prospect and in 1902 went to Tokyo to study literature and languages. In 1903 he started to attend the *Heiminsha* ('Commoners' Society'), Kōtoku Shūsui's socialist society. Arrested in 1906 for participating in a popular protest against bus fare increases, Ōsugi was marked by the authorities as a radical. His response was actively to embrace socialism. Between 1906 and 1910 he spent two further terms in prison and read a wide range of European anarchist texts. After his release, just before Kōtoku's execution, Ōsugi set up the first of a series of journals. He continued to write until his death. At first positive about the Bolshevik Revolution, he broke with Bolshevism in 1922, translated sections of Alexander Berkman's critique and promoted the Makhnovists. In 1922 he was invited to attend the International Congress of Anarchists in Berlin scheduled to take place in 1923. He left Japan in December 1922, travelling first to Paris. He was arrested at a May Day demonstration and deported. Ōsugi arrived back in Japan in July 1923 and was arrested in September in military police round-ups ordered after the Great Kantō earthquake. Ōsugi was murdered in custody, together with Itō Noe, his partner, and his six-year-old nephew Munekazu. They had been beaten and strangled before their bodies were dumped in an abandoned well.[25]

LUIGI PARMEGGIANI (1858–1945)

Born in Reggio Emilia, Parmeggiani claimed to have been apprenticed in 1872 to a printer and then a jeweller. In 1880 he went to France, visiting Brussels in 1888 and settling in London in 1888. During this period he participated in a number of illegalist anarchist groups and practised revolutionary expropriation. In 1889, aggrieved by an accusation that he was a police spy, he travelled to Italy where he attempted to kill the editors of the papers he held responsible for the slur. Sentenced to thirty years, he returned to London where he headed up the anti-organizationalist group *L'Anonimato/La Libera Initiativa* in opposition to Malatesta and Merlino. The ensuing debate was bitter but Malatesta came to his aid when Parmeggiani was threatened in 1892 with extradition to serve the thirty year sentence. In the 1890s he ran a high-end antiques shop in London's Bedford Square. Using the name Louis Marcy he sold several dubious pieces of medieval art to the Victoria and Albert Museum and the British Museum. In 1903 he returned to Paris to take care of his antiques business. Arrested as an anarchist, he was sentenced to five months. The police found items valued at 2 million francs in his house but the provenance was uncertain. From 1907 to 1914 he edited an art journal in Paris. His contributions issued fierce attacks on capitalist art collectors, dealers and forgers. Parmeggiani left Paris in 1918 and settled in Reggio Emilia in 1924, selling his entire collection of antiquities to the municipality.[24]

ASSATA SHAKUR (b. 1947)

Assata Shakur was listed on the FBI's most wanted list in 2013 with a $2 million bounty on her head. Given the name Jo Anne Deborah Byron, Shakur spent her early life in Queens, New York, and moved to Wilmington, North Carolina, in 1950. In 1970 she joined the Harlem branch of the Black Panther Party. The following year she joined the Black Liberation Army, branded anarchist by the FBI. A warrant was issued for her arrest in 1972. In 1973, following a shoot-out which left her wounded and her friend Zayd Shakur dead, she was charged with the killing of Werner Forester, a New Jersey state trooper. She was given a life term in 1977. She described the trial as a 'legal lynching' in an open letter to Pope John Paul II. Shakur escaped in 1979 and has been living as a political exile in Cuba since 1984. She made a tape of 'To My People' while in prison in 1973. Her autobiography was dramatized by debbie tucker green and broadcast by the BBC in 2017.[26]

VALERIE SOLANAS (1936–1988)

Author of the *SCUM Manifesto*, Solanas was born in Ventor, New Jersey, and moved to Washington DC with her mother after her parents' divorce. In 1951 she left the family home. Graduating from high school in 1954 she attended the University of Maryland at College Park and the University of Minnesota, where she enrolled on a postgraduate course in psychology. After attending classes at Berkeley she dropped out of university. In Greenwich Village in 1966 she wrote a play *Up Your Ass*. She approached Andy Warhol with a view to financing its production and gave him a copy of the script. She wrote the *SCUM Manifesto* in 1967 and distributed mimeographed copies, securing an advance from the publisher Maurice Girodias to write a novel based upon it. She appeared in two Warhol films, *I, a Man* and *Bikeboy*, but relations with Warhol soured after he informed her that he had lost the script to *Up Your Ass*. Believing that the deal she had struck with Girodias was exploitative and negotiated for Warhol's benefit, Solanas bought a pistol, prepared to shoot Girodias. In 1968, finding that Girodias was away, she waited at the Factory for Warhol to arrive and fired three times. Warhol was badly wounded with the third shot. Solanas turned herself in the same day. Initially found incompetent to stand trial, she was sent to a psychiatric hospital later that year. The following year she received a three-year sentence for reckless assault. After her release in 1971 she was rearrested for issuing threats and readmitted to hospital for psychiatric treatment. She died in San Francisco of pneumonia and emphysema.[27]

FLORA TRISTAN (1803–1844)

Feminist and advocate of international labour organizing, Tristan was a writer and activist. She left her abusive husband, father of her three children, in her early twenties. Having journeyed around Europe, she travelled to Peru in 1833 to make a bid for her father's inheritance. This proved unsuccessful: her parents' marriage had not been legitimized by French Church authorities and she was technically illegitimate. Tristan began to write about women's oppression during her stay. Returning to Paris in 1834, she published a series of pamphlets: *On the Necessity of Welcoming Foreign Women*, *Petition for the Reinstatement of Divorce* and *Petition for the Abolition of Capital Punishment*. After a stay in Britain in 1839 she published a critique of bourgeois privilege and social deprivation, *Promenades dans Londres* (1840). She wrote her proposals for reform in 1843 in Paris, publishing her ideas as *The Workers' Union*.[28]

UCHIYAMA GUDŌ (1874–1911)

Uchiyama was a Sōtō Zen priest and anarchist activist. Ordained in 1897, he became interested in socialism in 1903, influenced by Kōtoku. He began to play an active role in the movement in 1905 and took Kōtoku's part in 1907 when he advocated direct action as a means to confront severe state repression. In 1908 Uchiyama set up a clandestine press in his temple and produced anarchist-communist pamphlets. The rejection of the divinity of the Emperor, rural emancipation and the abolition of military conscription were the three main tenets of his anarchist programme and he set these ideas in a framework inspired by Buddhist traditions of communitarian social engagement, autonomy, independence and self-rule. His pamphlet *Museifu kyōsan kakumei* ('Anarchist Communist Revolution') inspired Miyashita Takichi (1875–1911), one of the plotters involved in the High Treason Incident. Arrested in 1910, Uchiyama was sentenced to death and hanged on 24 January 1911. He was the only one of the priests tried for conspiracy to be executed. His arrest triggered his expulsion from the Sōtō sect but he was restored to the order in 1993 when the unfairness of the trial, the injustice of his execution and the repressive character of the Imperial order were recognized.[29]

CHARLOTTE WILSON (1854–1944)

Associated with Peter Kropotkin and the London Freedom group in the late nineteenth century, Wilson was educated at the exclusive Cheltenham Ladies' College and at Merton Hall (later Newnham College) at Cambridge University. In the 1870s she moved to London. She joined the Society of the Friends of Russian Freedom, a group that brought together liberals and progressives with anti-Tsarist nihilists and anarchists and the Men and Women's Club, which explored questions of marriage, prostitution and heterosexual relationships. She advocated anarchism from 1884, after the well-publicized jailing of Kropotkin in France. She began writing articles for *Justice*, the paper of the revolutionary socialist Social Democratic Federation, and joined the Fabian Society. Elected to its executive in 1885, Wilson was also a member of the Hampstead reading group which met to discuss the work of Marx, Proudhon and other continental socialists. With Henry Seymour, she helped establish *The Anarchist*. When Kropotkin settled in London, she set up the newspaper *Freedom* with him. The first issue appeared in 1886. She contributed her own work to *Freedom* and edited and translated other writings. She withdrew from Freedom in 1895 and gravitated back towards the Fabians where she campaigned for a range of women's causes. Awarded an OBE in recognition of the work she did to support prisoners of war, she left Britain for the United States in the inter-war period. She died in Westchester County, New York.[30]

Chapter 4: Conditions

DAVID ANDRADE (1859–1928)

David Andrade was born in Collingwood, Victoria. His parents had come to Australia from Middlesex, England. He joined the Australasian Secular Association as a freethinker but in 1886 became a founder member of the Melbourne Anarchist Club (MAC), the first anarchist organization in Australia, and the Melbourne Co-operative. Andrade was the MAC's secretary, lead organizer and main theoretician. Introduced to Proudhon's work through Benjamin Tucker's *Liberty*, Andrade was the author of *Money: A Study of the Currency Question* (1887), *Our Social System* (n.d.) and *An Anarchist Plan of Campaign* (1888). He also wrote a utopian novel, *The Melbourne Riots and How Harry Holdfast and his Friends Emancipated the Workers* (1892).[1]

MARIE-LOUISE BERNERI (1918–1949)

Marie-Louise Berneri spent her youth in Paris, having been forced to flee fascist Italy in 1926 with her parents Camillio and Giovanna Berneri, both well-known anarchists. She studied child psychology at the Sorbonne before travelling to London in 1937. She made two trips to Spain during the Revolution, where her father was killed, and participated in relief efforts for Spanish war orphans and refugees. Having acquired British citizenship through her marriage to Vernon Richards, Berneri was joint editor of the journals *Spain and the World* (1937–9) and *War Commentary* (1939–45), both published by Freedom Press. She took a leading role in the relief effort for Spanish refugees and in the Freedom group's propaganda work. She also used her multilingual skills to maintain contacts with European anarchists. Arrested in 1945 with other members of the *War Commentary* group, she was charged with conspiracy and the dissemination of seditious material. Berneri was acquitted on the grounds that she could not legally conspire with her husband, Vernon Richards, and so became responsible for *Freedom* during for that period. She published *Workers in Stalin's Russia* in 1944. *Journey Through Utopia* was first published posthumously in 1950. A selection of her writings for *War Commentary* and *Freedom* was published under the title *Neither East nor West* in 1988.[3]

LOUISA SARAH BEVINGTON (1845–1895)

Louisa Bevington was an anarchist-communist essayist, philosopher and poet active in London. Born in Battersea to Quaker parents, she began writing poetry in 1871. Some of her early work was published by the philosopher Herbert Spencer, whose writings on evolution had exercised a strong influence upon her. She published her first two volumes, *Key-Notes* and *Poems, Lyrics and Sonnets* in 1876 and 1882 respectively. In 1882 Bevington left London for Germany. She married the following year. The marriage lasted eight years. Bevington took her husband's name, Guggenberger, but her work was published under the names Arbor Leigh and L. S. Bevington. Back in London she entered into anarchist circles, becoming well established as an anarchist poet. On friendly terms with Louise Michel, Kropotkin and other leading figures on the London anarchist scene, she contributed to the anarchist-communist journals *Liberty* and *The Torch*. Her essays include 'Why I am an Expropriationist' (1894), 'Dynamitism' (1895) and 'Anarchism and Violence' (1896) and in 1895 she wrote the Manifesto for the Anarchist Communist Alliance with James Tochatti, editor of *Liberty*. The same year, suffering from mitral valve disease, she published *Liberty Lyrics*, a collection of poems previously published in the anarchist press.[2]

NOAM CHOMSKY (b. 1928)

Academic, public intellectual and activist, Chomsky has an international reputation as a theorist of linguistics and relentless critic of US foreign policy. Born in Philadelphia, he studied at the universities of Pennsylvania and Harvard before taking up a post at Massachusetts Institute of Technology. His work explores the nefarious effects of corporate power in US public life, the violent assertion of US hegemony across the world and the newspeak that normalizes systematic state-capitalist terrorism, exploitation and adventurism. Orwell's *Homage to Catalonia*, which he read as a child when Franco declared victory in Spain in 1939, was a formative influence. He has since identified as an anarchist in the tradition of Bakunin and Kropotkin, developing their perspectives on power and the state to advance his own critical politics. Chomsky is also well known for his rejection of Leninism and vanguardism and advocacy of anarchist-syndicalist organization.[4]

GUY DEBORD (1931–1994)

A film-maker and writer, Debord is remembered for his collaboration with Raoul Vaneigem, philosopher and author of *The Revolution of Everyday Life* (1967), and for his enormously influential book *The Society of the Spectacle* (1967). Its opening line contained the fundamental thesis: 'The whole life of those societies in which modern conditions of production prevail presents itself as an immense accumulation of spectacles. All that once was directly lived has become mere representation.' Splitting with the anti-art, Dada-inspired Letterist Isidore Isou, Debord set up the Letterist International (LI) in the early 1950s before founding the Situationist International (SI) in 1957. The SI was dissolved in 1972. In 1989 Debord published *Comments on the Society of the Spectacle*. He committed suicide five years later.[5]

DAVID GRAEBER (b. 1961)

The anthropologist and activist Graeber was born on the West Side of Manhattan, studied at the State University of New York (Purchase College) and the University of Chicago. He is professor of anthropology at the London School of Economics. In the early 2000s he participated in actions in Quebec City and Genoa, at the Republican National Conventions in Philadelphia and New York and the New York meeting of the World Economic Forum. He also took part in the 2010 London student tuition fee protests. Graeber has become best known for the leading role he played in the planning and enactment of the occupation of Zuccotti Park in 2011 and his high-profile analysis of the Occupy movement that this action sparked. His books include *Fragments of an Anarchist Anthropology* (2004), *Direct Action: An Ethnography* (2009), *Debt: The First 5,000 Years* (2011) and *The Democracy Project: A History, a Crisis, a Movement* (2013).[6]

MOSES HARMAN (1830–1910)

Born in western Virginia and raised in southern Missouri, Harman trained as a teacher. He became an abolitionist and was run out of pro-slavery territory for promoting the cause. Harman was also a leading campaigner for free speech and promoted open discussion of birth control and sex. As an advocate of free love, he entered into a free union with his partner Susan Scheuck. They had three children; two survived and the third died with Susan in childbirth. In 1879 Harman moved with the surviving children, George and Lillian, to Valley Falls, Kansas, where he worked as a teacher. He joined the Valley Falls Liberal League, which campaigned for the separation of Church from State and in 1880 became editor of the group's periodical, *Valley Falls Liberal*. In 1881 the paper took the name the *Kansas Liberal*. Between 1883 and 1907 it ran under the name *Lucifer, the Lightbearer*. In 1886 he published 'the Markland letter', which described forced marital sex as rape. Harman was prosecuted for obscenity under the terms of the Comstock Act of 1873. He was served with an arrest warrant in 1887 and spent the next eight years meeting bonds to secure his freedom. In 1888, when *Lucifer* was already under indictment, he republished the Markland Letter. In 1890 he published 'the O'Neill letter'. Written by a physician, this described the harm caused to women subject to rape in marriage. New charges were served and in 1891 Harman received a one-year term for its publication. He received another sentence in 1895. On his release in 1896 he moved *Lucifer* to Chicago. In 1905 Harman was tried for publishing two more articles, 'The Fatherhood Question' and 'More Thoughts on Sexology'. He was sentenced to a year's hard labour. He was seventy-five years old. After this transfer to Joliet, Illinois, Harman was spared further rock-breaking when his health failed. On his release *Lucifer* changed its name again to the American *Journal of Eugenics*. Harman died in Los Angeles and the journal disappeared with him.[7]

MAX NETTLAU (1865–1944)

Nettlau was an anarchist writer and historian. Born in Vienna, he defined himself as a libertarian socialist by 1880. He read Bakunin's *God and the State* in 1882, the same year he finished school and started to study European linguistics, specializing in Celtic languages. In 1885 he arrived in London to study manuscripts in the British Library and met William Morris. He met Kropotkin in 1888 and Malatesta in 1889. In 1890 Nettlau's first essays on anarchism appeared in Most's *Freiheit*. In the early 1890s he started to travel in order to gather material for his historical research, meeting Reclus in Switzerland. Preliminary work on Bakunin was published in 1895 and a biography followed in 1896, but Nettlau continued to work on the project and published four further volumes in 1903. Encouraged and funded by Reclus, Nettlau started to work on a definitive bibliography of anarchism. This was published in 1897, with a prologue by Reclus. Later that year Nettlau met Voltairine de Cleyre, during her stay in London. In 1914 Nettlau was in Vienna and he remained there for the duration of the war. Having amassed a collection of 40,000 books and pamphlets, he was ruined financially by the post-war currency devaluation. The collection was dispersed across Europe. In the 1920s Nettlau published more work on Bakunin, an essay on Kropotkin and a study of Malatesta. Studies of Reclus and the revolutionary syndicalist Ferdinand Pelloutier, the International and the Bakuninists in Spain followed. Living in Barcelona in 1935, Nettlau set up a historical archive before leaving Spain the following year. In 1937 he supervised the installation of his collection in the Institute of Social History in Amsterdam. The remains of the collection in Vienna were recovered after the *Anschluss* in 1938 but the entire library was removed to Germany after the Nazi invasion of the Netherlands. He died in Amsterdam two years before his collection was returned to the city.[8]

SAUL NEWMAN (b. 1972)

Newman is a political theorist based at Goldsmiths, University of London, best known for his articulation of post-anarchist theory. He came to anarchism from Trotskyism, critical of Marxism's authoritarianism and inability to address problems of state power. His identification of Stirner as a key figure for poststructuralist theory and as a conduit from modern/humanist to postmodern/posthumanist is distinctive. Newman's recent statements of his approach include *The Politics of Postanarchism* (2010) and *Postanarchism* (2016).[9]

FERNANDO PESSOA (1888–1935)

A critic, philosopher and writer, Pessoa is a leading figure of the early twentieth century European Modernist movement and regarded as one of the greatest poets in the Portuguese language. Born in Lisbon, he spent his childhood in South Africa before returning to Lisbon to study literature. Dropping out of formal education he began to publish in the

1910s. Pessoa adopted a number of different personas or 'heteronyms' during the course of his life, writing in Portuguese as Alberto Caeiro, Ricardo Reis and Álvaro de Campos, in English as Alexander Search and Charles Robert Anon and in French as Jean Seul. He adopted a multitude of other alter egos. Much of his work, which he deposited in a trunk in his rented apartment, remains unpublished. His best-known prose work is *The Book of Disquiet*, published in 1913.[10]

PAUL SIGNAC (1863–1935)

The son of a wealthy Paris saddle-maker, the artist Signac is credited with Georges Seurat with the development of pointillism. He studied architecture before taking up painting when he was eighteen. In 1884 he helped establish the Salon des Indépendants with Seurat and Odilon Redon. This ran un-juried exhibitions, showing the work of anyone who wished to exhibit. Signac and Seurat both identified as anarchist and Signac wrote anonymously for Jean Grave's *La Révolte*. After the death of Seurat in 1891, he sailed to St Tropez, eventually setting up a studio there. He painted *In the Time of Harmony* in 1893–5, taking his subtitle ('the Golden Age is not in the Past, it is in the Future'), from a text by Charles Malato. The painting is often taken as a statement of a politics that centred on principles of individual self-expression and collective harmony. His painting *The Wrecker* (1897–9), which depicts a male worker swinging a pickaxe in the foreground and another crow-barring stones from a monumental building behind, indicates that his anarchism had a creatively destructive edge, too.[11]

REBECCA SOLNIT (b. 1961)

Solnit is an independent writer, historian and activist, born in Connecticut and brought up in California. Her parents were active in civil rights and anti-Vietnam War movements. She became involved in anti-nuclear activism in the late 1980s. After spending a year at the American University in Paris she studied English and journalism at Berkeley. She has written widely on feminism, western and indigenous history, popular power, social change and insurrection. Her books include *Hope in the Dark* (2004) and *Men Explain Things to Me* (2014).[12]

FERNANDO TÁRRIDA DEL MÁRMOL (1861–1915)

An advocate of anarchism without adjectives, Tárrida del Mármol became Engineer-Director and distinguished professor of mathematics at the Polytechnic Academy of Barcelona. Born in Cuba, he arrived in Spain during the 1868 revolution and moved to anarchism from republicanism inspired by the Proudhonist and federalist ideas of Pi y Margall, President of the First Spanish Republic of 1873, and Anselmo Lorenzo, the key promoter of anarchism in Spain. In 1889 he advocated anarchism without adjectives, contributing to a debate with anarchist communists in *La Révolte*. He was imprisoned in the Monjuich fortress following the 1896 bombing of the annual Corpus Christi parade in Barcelona. Released after two months, he went to Paris, wrote an account of his incarceration and, armed with papers and letters from fellow prisoners, published accounts of the atrocities committed against anarchists. Writing in the journal *La Revue Blanche*, he initiated a campaign against Cánovas del

ANARCHIST BIOGRAPHIES

Castillo, the prime minister who had ordered the tortures. As well as drawing attention to repression in Spain, Tárrida discussed the violence meted out by the Spanish authorities in Cuba, Puerto Rico and the Philippines. After being expelled from France he moved to London where he became a leading figure in émigré anarchist circles and a friend of Malatesta, Rocker and Nettlau. He is buried in the Brockley and Ladywell cemeteries in South London.[13]

HANS WIDMER AKA P.M. (b. 1947)

Widmer is a Zurich-based anarchist, retired teacher and philologist and advocate of degrowth and urban redesign. A member of the Midnight Notes collective he describes himself as an anti-68er and is best known as the author of *bolo'bolo* (1983). Widmer has published over fifteen books, including *Die Andere Stadt/The Other City* in 2017.[14]

GEORGE WOODCOCK (1912–1995)

A writer, poet, anarchist and historian of anarchism, Woodcock wrote or edited an estimated 150 books, including the highly influential *Anarchism: A History of Libertarian Ideas and Movements* (1962) and *The Anarchist Reader* (1977). Born in Winnipeg, he spent his youth in England. He began to write in his early teens, entering into London's literary circles in the late 1930s. On the outbreak of the war, he registered as a conscientious objector and performed civilian service in the War Agricultural Committee. He started the magazine *NOW* in 1940 and after inviting him to contribute to it he met the anarchist educator and art critic Herbert Read. Read suggested he make contact with the London Freedom group. Woodcock worked on *War Commentary* and wrote a series of anarchist pamphlets, including *Anarchy or Chaos* (1944). When the editors of *War Commentary* were arrested in 1945, he helped set up the Freedom Defence Committee. Woodcock returned to Canada in 1949 and established his reputation as Canada's leading literary light. He founded the journal *Canadian Literature* in 1959 and remained its editor until 1976.[15]

VICTOR YARROS (1865–1956)

A radical journalist and lawyer, Yarros was an émigré from the Ukraine. Born in Kiev, he was drawn into revolutionary activity when he was seventeen, attracted to the socialism of Fourier and Marx. He read Bakunin, Kropotkin, Most and Reclus after his arrival in America in the mid-1880s and became an anarchist-communist. Under the influence of John Stuart Mill and Herbert Spencer he subsequently moved towards individualism. Drawn to the non-violent, philosophical anarchism of the Boston anarchists, Yarros struck up a friendship with Benjamin Tucker after meeting him at a lecture in New Haven. Tucker invited him to work on the paper *Liberty* and he began to write for the journal in late 1885, becoming its leading contributor and Tucker's associate editor. Yarros followed Tucker from Boston to New York in the early 1890s but philosophical differences eventually caused a rift: having briefly flirted with Stirnerism, Yarros considered Tucker's turn to egoism a rejection of the individualist and philosophical doctrines they had initially promoted. After marrying Rachelle Slobodinsky, a notable clinical obstetrician and radical, Yarros moved to Chicago in 1895. He took an editorial post on the *Chicago Daily News*.

In 1914, having lost his job at the paper, he became law partner to Clarence Darrow for eleven years. Later in life he rejected anarchism and embraced social democracy, publishing his critique 'Philosophical Anarchism: Its Rise, Decline and Eclipse' in the *American Journal of Sociology* in 1936.[16]

Chapter 5: Prospects

STUART CHRISTIE (b. 1946)

Stuart Christie is a leading exponent of class-struggle anarchism, and an author and publisher. He is probably best known for his attempt to assassinate General Franco and for his fierce opposition to the Edward Heath government (1970–74). However, apart from his association with members of the Angry Brigade – for which he was arrested, tried and acquitted in 1971 – he was also involved with the Glasgow Committee of 100 and with Spies for Peace (groups critical of the passive, strictly legal and symbolic campaigning of the anti-nuclear movement) and in the revival of the Anarchist Black Cross, the prisoner support organization. All these activities are documented in his 2004 three-part autobiography *The Christie File* (comprising *Granny Made Me an Anarchist*, *General Franco Made Me a 'Terrorist'* and *Edward Heath Made Me Angry*). His imprints include Refract Publications, Cienfuegos Press, Meltzer Press and now Christie Books, but he has sponsored a number of other publishing projects, including, in the 1980s, the *Anarchist Encyclopedia*. Christie is a historian of anarchism, particularly Spanish anarchism, and of anarchist ideas – the co-author with Albert Meltzer of *The Floodgates of Anarchy* (1970) and editor of the three-volume *¡Pistoleros!* (2010–13).[1]

DANIEL COHN-BENDIT (b. 1945)

Member of the European Parliament and co-founder of the Greens/Free European Alliance Group, Cohn-Bendit emerged as a leader of the student movement in May 1968. Expelled from France after the Paris events, he went to Frankfurt and promoted anarcho-leftist squatting. He published *Obsolete Communism: The Left-Wing Alternative*, co-authored with his brother Gabriel, in 1968. The book title was intended as a response to Lenin's *Left-Wing Communism, an Infantile Disorder* (1920) and it advanced a libertarian anti-capitalist critique of Soviet communism.[2]

SCOTT CROW (b. 1967?)

crow is an anarchist community organizer, writer, strategist and public speaker. He is the co-founder of the Common Ground Collective and Treasure City Thrift, an anti-waste, ecological not-for-profit store and community space in Austin, Texas. He took part in a 2003 Greenpeace storming of the ExxonMobile HQ in Irving, Texas, dressed in a tiger suit, toured in a rock band and ran Century Modern, a co-operative antiques business in Dallas, before participating in the community relief effort in New Orleans. He is the author of *Black Flags and Windmills* (2011).[3]

ZO D'AXA (1864–1930)

A pamphleteer and antimilitarist, founder of the journal *L'En-dehors*, d'Axa came from a bourgeois background and spent his youth adventurously, hunting in Africa and mixing in bohemian circles in Belgium. He entered the anarchist scene after returning to Paris in 1889. Briefly imprisoned for conspiracy in Mazas prison, Paris, he left Paris for London, making contact with Charles Malato, Louise Michel and the artists Lucien and Camille Pissaro. From there he travelled to Holland and across Germany to Italy, Greece, Constantinople and Jaffa. He sailed back to London, from where he was extradited to France. He was imprisoned once more. Following his release in 1894 he published *De Mazas à Jerusalem*. The book, illustrated by Lucien Pissaro and Félix Vallotton, was widely acclaimed. D'Axa became an outspoken antimilitarist during the Dreyfus Affair. In 1900 he resumed his travels, this time going to America. He committed suicide after he returned to France.[4]

CAROL ERHLICH (b.?)

An anarchist and feminist, Erhlich entered into activism in the 1960s and was co-founder member of the journal *Social Anarchism* and member of three Baltimore collectives: The Great Atlantic Radio Conspiracy, Research Group One and the alternative non-credit Baltimore School. In 1971 she joined the American Studies Department at the University of Maryland, teaching courses on feminism and social change. She subsequently worked as an editor at the Johns Hopkins University Press. She was co-editor of *Reinventing Anarchy* (1979).[5]

MARIAN LEIGHTON (b. 1948)

Marian Leighton grew up in Cherryfield, Washington County, and attended Northeastern and Clark universities. She came to anarchism under the influence of Ayn Rand and as an ex-supporter of Barry Goldwater, the Republican candidate who in 1964 ran against Lyndon B. Johnson for US

President. Her involvement in the women's movement led her to socialist anarchism. In 1971 Leighton worked with the Black Rose anarcho-feminist group and was a participant in a seminar on forms of female expression at the Massachusetts Goddard Cambridge Feminist Studies programme. She co-founded the Rounder Records Collective in Boston in 1970 with the aim of promoting American roots music. The label moved to Nashville in 2014. She is the author of *Anarcho-feminism* and *Louise Michel* (1974) and *Voltairine de Cleyre: An Introduction* (1975).[6]

CATHY LEVINE (b. 1950?)

Feminist anarchist and member of the Boston area Black Rose Collective for a brief period in the 1970s, Levine grew up in an affluent neighbourhood in the north-east of America. She withdrew from anarchist politics shortly after writing *The Tyranny of Tyranny* (1979) and worked for many years as a public servant. She remains active in community politics.[7]

ALBERT MELTZER (1920–1996)

Meltzer was a London-born class-struggle anarchist. He attended his first anarchist meeting in 1935. A year later he took part in arms smuggling to support Spanish anarcho-syndicalists in their revolutionary struggles. Having left school in 1937, he was involved in setting up the paper *Revolt!* and in efforts to establish a UK-wide anarchist federation. He was later part of the London group that organized around the paper *War Commentary* and the Anarchist Federation. Registered as a conscientious objector, Meltzer agitated against the war and worked with Tom Brown to spread anti-war propaganda. He was imprisoned for desertion. In the 1960s Meltzer was involved in the publication of the one-page broadsheet *Ludd* and the satirical magazine *Cuddon's Cosmopolitan Review*. In 1967 he collaborated with Stuart Christie to re-establish the Anarchist Black Cross (ABC) to support jailed anarchists and political prisoners. In 1968 Meltzer and Christie started to publish a monthly *Bulletin* of the ABC. This became *Black Flag* in 1970. The same year Meltzer and Christie published *The Floodgates of Anarchy*. In the late 1970s Meltzer took a leading role establishing the Kate Sharpley Library, storing the early collection in Brixton, South London.[8]

ABDULLAH ÖCALAN (b. 1948)

Symbolic leader of the Kurdish movement, Öcalan grew up in south-east Turkey, studied politics at Ankara University and was a founder member of the Kurdistan Workers' Party (PKK). Established to secure independence and rights for Kurds in Turkey in 1978, the PKK entered into a period of armed struggle in 1984 and orchestrated a series of bombings, kidnappings and assassinations. The PKK has been designated terrorist by the international community ever since. Öcalan left his operational base in Syria in 1998 when the Turkish government demanded that he be handed over for trial. On the run, he was seized by Turkish Special Forces in Kenya in 1999. After a trial that the European Court of Human Rights deemed unfair, he was sentenced to death for high treason. Reforms set in train by Turkey's EU accession talks resulted in a commutation of the sentence, but no re-trial. Öcalan has been imprisoned since 1999, the sole inmate in a prison on an island in the Sea of Marmara. After reading Murray Bookchin's work in prison, Öcalan revised some of his earlier commitments to Kurdish national independence and Marxism-Leninism. He has outlined his ideas in the multi-volume *Civilization: The Age of Masked Gods and Disguised Kings* (Norway: New Compass, 2015).[9]

SOPHIA PEROVSKAYA (1853–1881)

A revolutionary executed for her part in the assassination of Tsar Alexander II in 1881, Perovskaya was born into a noble St Petersburg household, where her father served as governor-general. In 1866 she settled in the Crimea with her mother. When she returned to St Petersburg in 1869 she entered nihilist circles and attended lectures in maths and sciences at the Alarchinksy University for Women. She joined the Tchaikovsky Circle in 1871 and profoundly influenced its ethics. She spent a year teaching in a rural school in Stavropol in the Samara in 1872, returned to the capital the following year and was arrested for her propaganda work in 1874. She joined *Zemlya i Volya* in 1878 and went underground after a subsequent arrest. Having embraced terrorism, she was involved in one unsuccessful assassination plot before she joined *Narodnaya Volya*. She participated in two further conspiracies before the Tsar was finally killed. She was hanged with four of her comrades on 3 April 1881.[10]

MALIK RAHIM (b. 1948)

Community organizer, co-founder the Louisiana chapter of the Black Panther Party, Common Ground and the Louisiana Green Party, Rahim was born Donald Guyton. He joined the Black Panthers on returning from Vietnam. In 1970 he was involved in a thirty-minute shoot-out when police attacked the house in New Orleans that served as a centre for operations. He was acquitted of attempted murder along with the thirteen other Panthers. He left New Orleans for San Francisco, served a five-year sentence for armed robbery, converted to Islam in 1989 and returned to New Orleans before Hurricane Katrina struck. He has spent forty years participating in anti-poverty projects. On 23 November 2008 he published an essay, 'This is Criminal', in the *San Francisco Bay View*. This set out his analysis of racism and explained that 'people are dying for no other reason than lack of organization'.[11]

MURRAY ROTHBARD (1926–1995)

Attracted as a student at Columbia University to Austrian economics, Rothbard was an advocate of laissez-faire and individualist anarchy. Having studied with Ludwig von Mises, he became Academic Vice-President of the Mises Institute, worked at the Brooklyn Polytechnic Institute and was appointed S. J. Hall Distinguished Professor of Economics at the University of Nevada. He described his views as libertarian, not anarchist, and advocated limited government to defend property and person.[12]

JERRY RUBIN (1938–1994)

Founder of the counter-cultural Youth International or Yippies, Rubin described himself as the P. T. Barnum of the revolution. He attended Oberlin College, Ohio, and the University of Cincinnati before working as a sports reporter for the *Cincinnati Post* and attending Berkeley. He became Project Director of the 1967 100,000-strong anti-Vietnam March on the Pentagon. In 1968 he was ejected from the US House of Representatives Un-American Activities Committee and stood trial as one of the Chicago seven after disrupting the 1968 Democratic Convention. He was acquitted of conspiracy and charges of incitement were quashed on appeal. *Do It! Scenarios of the Revolution* was published in 1970. Rubin popularized the mantra 'Don't trust anyone over 30' and described himself as a perpetual adolescent. On reaching thirty he revised the cut-off to forty to correct the misapprehension that age rather than outlook was decisive for 'hippie longhair culture'. Rubin subsequently aged, moved away from countercultural politics and renounced anti-capitalism. He died in Los Angeles.[13]

YEKATERINA SAMUTSEVICH (b. 1982)

Trained at the Moscow Power Engineering Institute, Samutsevich worked as a software developer before enrolling in the first graduating class at Moscow's Rodchenko Art School, an international photography and art school inspired by the Russian avant-garde. She was radicalized as a feminist and joined the street-art Voina group. She adopted an anti-government position having been caught up in the harsh police response to demonstrations. She was one of five women to set up Pussy Riot in 2011. The group produced four videos and performed at tube stations and in Red Square before targeting Moscow's Christ the Saviour Cathedral, a site chosen because of the Church's support for President Putin and to highlight the sexism of Russian Orthodox practice. Arrested after this performance she was convicted for 'hooliganism motivated by religious hatred'. Samutsevich stirred controversy when her sentence was suspended, leaving two other participants in jail. She has campaigned for LGBT rights in Russia.[14]

Notes

ABBREVIATIONS

IISH: International Institute of Social History
Muñoz, *Anarchists*: Vladimiro Muñoz, *Anarchists: A Biographical Encyclopedia*, trans. Scott Johnson (New York: Gordon Press, 1981)

INTRODUCTION: ANARCHISM – MYTHS AND REALITIES

1. Sir Frederic Kenyon, *War Graves: How the Cemeteries Abroad Will Be Designed*, Report to the Imperial War Graves Commission (London: HMSO, 1918), p. 7.
2. Kenyon, *War Graves*, p. 8.
3. Eric Gill to the *Burlington Magazine*, April 1919, in Walter Shewring (ed.), *Letters of Eric Gill* (London: Jonathan Cape, 1947), p. 129.
4. Gill to the *Burlington Magazine*, p. 131.
5. Gill to the *Burlington Magazine*, p. 129.
6. Gill to the *Burlington Magazine*, p. 130.
7. Eric Gill, *Autobiography* (London: Jonathan Cape, 1940), p. 194.
8. See Benjamin Franks, Nathan Jun and Leonard Williams (eds), *Anarchism: A Conceptual Approach* (Abingdon: Routledge, 2018), pp. 1–12.
9. See especially Michael Schmidt and Lucien van der Walt, *Black Flame: The Revolutionary Class Politics of Anarchism and Syndicalism* (Edinburgh and Oakland: AK Press, 2009), part 1.
10. See Centre for a Stateless Society, online at https://c4ss.org/.
11. See the Ludwig von Mises Institute, online at https://mises.org/.

NOTES

12. For a discussion, see Spencer Sunshine, 'Rebranding Fascism: National Anarchists' (2008), online at https://libcom.org/library/rebranding-fascism-national-anarchists-spencer-sunshine.
13. Muñoz, *Anarchists*.

CHAPTER 1: TRADITIONS

1. Tom Goyens, *Beer and Revolution: The German Anarchist Movement in New York City, 1880–1914* (Urbana and Chicago: University of Illinois Press, 2007), p. 76.
2. Richard T. Ely, *French and German Socialism in Modern Times* (New York: Harper & Brothers, 1883), p. 185.
3. Association Internationale des Travailleurs, Fédération Jurassienne, Section de Propagande de Genève, Rapport de la Section sur les diverses questions mises à l'ordre du jour du Congrès Fédéral jurassien du 5 Août 1877, IISH Jura Federation papers.
4. Muñoz, *Anarchists*, ch. 17, p. 2.
5. John P. Altgeld, *Reasons for Pardoning Fielden, Neebe and Schwab* (Chicago, 1893), p. 63.
6. Louise Michel, 'Speeches and Journalism, November 1880–January 1882', in *The Red Virgin: Memoirs of Louise Michel*, ed. and trans. Bullitt Lowry and Elizabeth Ellington Gunter (Tuscaloosa: University of Alabama Press, 1981), p. 123.
7. Goyens, *Beer and Revolution*, p. 107.
8. 'The Chicago Anniversary', *Freedom*, December 1888.
9. Peter Kropotkin, 'The Commune of Paris Address', *Freedom*, April 1893.
10. Michael Bakunin, *The Paris Commune and the Idea of the State* (London: Centre International de Recherches sur l'Anarchisme, 1971), p. 2.
11. Karl Marx, 'The Paris Commune', *The Civil War in France* [1871], online at https://www.marxists.org/archive/marx/works/1871/civil-war-france/ch05.htm [last access 7 June 2018].
12. Peter Kropotkin, manuscript of the article 'Bakunin' published in *Freedom*, 1905, IISH, Nettlau Collection, 2672.
13. Haymarket Statements of the Accused: Address of Louis Lingg, online at https://www.marxists.org/subject/mayday/articles/speeches.html#LINGG.
14. G. P. English was a reporter for the *Chicago Tribune* instructed to report only the most inflammatory remarks made at the Haymarket meeting.

See Paul Avrich, *The Haymarket Tragedy* (Princeton: Princeton University Press, 1984), p. 203.

15 Haymarket Statements of the Accused: Address of Samuel Fielden, online at https://www.marxists.org/subject/mayday/articles/speeches. html#FIELDEN.

16 Harriet Jacobs, *Incidents in the Life of a Slave Girl*, ed. L. Maria Child, in *Narrative of the Life of Frederick Douglass, an American Slave and Incidents in the Life of a Slave Girl*, Introduction by Kwame Anthony Appiah (New York: The Modern Library, 2000), p. 306.

17 Haymarket Statements of the Accused: Address of Albert Parsons, online at https://www.marxists.org/subject/mayday/articles/speeches. html#PARSONS

18 Haymarket Statements of the Accused: Address of Albert Parsons, online at https://www.marxists.org/subject/mayday/articles/speeches. html#PARSONS

19 Frederick Lohr, *Anarchism: A Philosophy of Freedom* (London: Frederick Lohr, n.d [1941/42]), p. 46.

20 Ezra H. Heywood, *Uncivil Liberty* (Colorado Springs: Ralph Myles, 1978), pp. 9–10.

21 Lucy Parsons, 'Speech to the Industrial Workers of the World, 1905', online at the Lucy Parsons Project http://flag.blackened.net/lpp/writings/speech_to_iww.html.

22 Louise Michel, 'The Kanaks were seeking the same liberty we had sought in the Commune', in Nic Maclellan (ed.), *Louise Michel* (Melbourne and New York: Ocean Books, 2004), p. 96.

23 Peter Kropotkin, 'Chicago Martyrs Commemoration', *Freedom*, December 1896.

24 Staughton Lynd and Andrej Grubacic, *Wobblies and Zapatistas: Conversations on Anarchism, Marxism and Radical History* (Oakland: PM Press, 2008), pp. 12–15.

25 Muñoz, *Anarchists*, ch. 17, p. 9.

26 *Le Procès des Anarchistes de Chicago* (Paris: La Révolte, 1892), pp. 30–31.

27 Telegrams received for the Chicago Martyrs Meeting, 11 November 1892, Holborn Town Hall, Presburg Papers, IISH.

28 John Merriman, *Massacre: The Life and Death of the Paris Commune of 1871* (New Haven and London: Yale University Press, 2014), p. 207.

29 Michael J. Schaack, *Anarchy and Anarchists: A History of the Red Terror and the Social Revolution in America and Europe* (Chicago: F. J. Schulte & Company, 1889), pp. 682–3.

30 Cesare Lombroso, 'Illustrative Studies in Criminal Anthropology III: The Physiognomy of the Anarchists', *Monist*, 1 (3), 1891, pp. 336–43; Michael Schwab, 'A Convicted Anarchist's Reply to Professor Lombroso', *Monist* 1 (4), 1891, pp. 520–24.

31 J. Hayes-Sadler to the Earl of Iddesleigh, 23 August 1886, in Ruth Kinna (ed.), *Early Writings on Terrorism* (London: Routledge, 2006), vol. 1.

32 Rosemary O'Kane, *Terrorism* (Cheltenham: Edward Elgar, 2005), vol. 1, p. x.

33 Paul Wilkinson, *Terrorism and the Liberal State*, 2nd edn (London: Macmillan, 1986), p. 98.

34 Michael Kronenwetter, *Terrorism: A Guide to Events and Documents* (London: Greenwood Press, 2004), pp. 26–7.

35 E. V. Zenker, *Anarchism: A Criticism and History of the Anarchist Theory* (New York and London: Knickerbocker Press, 1897), p. 318.

36 Ely, *French and German Socialism in Modern Times,* p. 187.

37 Zenker, pp. 160, 162.

38 Henry Seymour, *Michael Bakounine: A Biographical Sketch* (London: H. Seymour, 1888), p. 4.

39 'Chief of Anarchists', *Grey River Argus* (New Zealand), 4 September 1912 [18 June 2013].

40 A list is available at Lidiap: http://www.bibliothekderfreien.de/lidiap/eng/.

41 Work by Kropotkin, Bakunin, Goldman, Tolstoy, Reclus, Malatesta and Jean Grave appeared alongside writings of Chinese anarchists in Chinese journals. See Arif Dirlik, *Anarchism in the Chinese Revolution* (Berkeley: University of California Press, 1991), pp. 154–5.

42 Dirlik, *Anarchism in the Chinese Revolution*, p. 155.

43 Paul Avrich, 'Prison Letters of Ricardo Flores Magón to Lilly Sarnoff', *International Review of Social History*, 22 (3), 1977, p. 379 [379–422].

44 Steven Hirsch and Lucien van der Walt, 'Rethinking Anarchism and Syndicalism: The Colonial and Postcolonial Experience, 1870–1940', in Hirsch and van der Walt (eds), *Anarchism and Syndicalism in the Colonial and Postcolonial World, 1870–1940*, p. xl.

45 See Adi H. Doctor, *Anarchist Thought in India* (Bombay: Asia Publishing House, 1964), p. 108; Nitis Das Gupta, 'Indian Anarchists', *Indian Journal of Political Science* 59 (1/4), 1998, pp. 106–14; Hayrettin Yücesoy, 'Political Anarchism, Dissent, and Marginal Groups in the Early Ninth Century: The ṣūfīs of the Muʿtazila Revisited', in Paul M. Cobb (ed.), *The Lineaments of Islam: Studies in Honor of Fred McGraw Donner* (Leiden: Brill, 2012), pp. 61–84; Sam Mbah and I. E. Igariwey, *African Anarchism: A History of a Movement* (Tucson: See Sharp Press, 1997).

46 Charles Malato, 'Some Anarchist Portraits', *Fortnightly Review*, 1 September 1894, http://libertarian-library.blogspot.co.uk/2012/12/charles-malato-some-anarchist-portraits.html [31 January 2017].

CHAPTER 2: CULTURES

1 William Shakespeare, *King Lear*, IV.6.154–162.
2 Rudolf Rocker, *Nationalism and Culture*, trans. Ray E. Chase (St Paul, Minnesota: Michael E. Coughlin, 1978 [1937]).
3 Rocker, *Nationalism and Culture*, p. 343.
4 Charlotte Brontë, *Jane Eyre*, ch. 31, para. 4, online at Project Gutenberg https://www.gutenberg.org/files/1260/1260-h/1260-h.htm
5 John Locke, *The Second Treatise of Government*, ch. XVIII, § 202, p. 448, in Peter Laslett (ed.), *John Locke: Two Treatises of Government* (Cambridge: Cambridge University Press, 1963).
6 Sigmund Engländer, *The Abolition of the State: An Historical and Critical Sketch of the Parties Advocating Direct Government, a Federal Republic or Individualism* (London: Forgotten Books, 2015 [1873]), p. 42.
7 Engländer, *The Abolition of the State*, p. 43.
8 Engländer, *The Abolition of the State*, p. 43.
9 Engländer, *The Abolition of the State*, p. 42.
10 Engländer, *The Abolition of the State*, pp. 40, 42.
11 Engländer, *The Abolition of the State*, pp. 42–3.
12 Engländer, *The Abolition of the State*, p. 44.
13 Engländer, *The Abolition of the State*, pp. 47–8.
14 Albert Parsons, https://www.marxists.org/subject/mayday/articles/speeches.html#PARSONS
15 Engländer, *The Abolition of the State*, p. 73.
16 Engländer, *The Abolition of the State*, p. 44.
17 Engländer, *The Abolition of the State*, p. 48.
18 Engländer, *The Abolition of the State*, p. 46.
19 Engländer, *The Abolition of the State*, pp. 102, 107.
20 Engländer, *The Abolition of the State*, p. 48.
21 Michael Bakunin, *God and the State* (London Anarchist Groups, 1893/[1870–71]), pp. 9, 16. Emphasis in original. Text (1882), online at https://theanarchistlibrary.org/library/michail-bakunin-god-and-the-state.pdf

22 Michael Bakunin, *The Political Theology of Mazzini and the International*, trans. Sarah E. Holmes, online at http://wiki.libertarian-labyrinth.org/index.php?title=The_Political_Theology_of_Mazzini_and_the_International [last access 25 March 2017].

23 Bakunin, *God and the State*, p. 14.

24 Bakunin, *God and the State*, p. 9.

25 Leo Tolstoy, 'Master and Man', in *Master and Man and Other Stories*, trans. Paul Foote (Harmondsworth: Penguin, 1979), pp. 67–126.

26 Tolstoy, 'Master and Man', p. 93.

27 Tolstoy, 'Master and Man', p. 96.

28 Tolstoy, 'Master and Man', p. 113.

29 Bakunin, *God and the State*, p. 7.

30 Bakunin, *God and the State*, p. 19.

31 *John Locke*, Laslett (ed.), n. on ch. IV, § 24, p. 326.

32 Peter Kropotkin, 'Les Droits Politiques', in Élisée Reclus (ed.), *Paroles d'un d'un Révolté*, new edition (Paris: Marpon et Flammarion, n.d.), p. 39.

33 Simone Weil, *The Need for Roots* (London and New York: Routledge, 2003 [1949]), p. 99.

34 Weil, *The Need for Roots*, p. 108.

35 Weil, *The Need for Roots*, p. 47.

36 Élisée Reclus, 'Hégémonie de l'Europe', *Société Nouvelle*, April 1894, p. 28.

37 Ananda Coomaraswamy, 'What Has India Contributed to Human Welfare?', in *The Dance of Śiva: Fourteen Indian Essays* (New York: The Sunwise Turn, 1918), pp. 15–17 [1–17].

38 Reclus, 'Hégémonie de l'Europe', p. 28.

39 Élisée Reclus, 'Culture and Property' [1905], in John Clark and Camille Martin (eds and trans.), *Anarchy, Geography, Modernity: Selected Writings of Elisée Reclus* (Oakland: PM Press, 2013), p. 202 [202–7].

40 Federico Ferretti, 'Élisée Reclus in Louisiana (1853–1855): Encounters with Racism and Slavery', *American Association of Geographers Newsletter*, 1 February 2018, online at http://news.aag.org/2018/02/elisee-reclus-in-louisiana-1853–1855-encounters-with-racism-and-slavery/ [last access 11 June 2018].

41 Élisée Reclus, 'War', *Freedom*, May 1898.

42 Voltairine de Cleyre, 'The Mexican Revolution', in Alexander Berkman (ed.), *Selected Works of Voltairine de Cleyre* (New York: Mother Earth, 1914), p. 257 [253–75].

43 De Cleyre, 'The Mexican Revolution', p. 255.

44 De Cleyre, 'The Mexican Revolution', p. 258.

45 De Cleyre, 'The Mexican Revolution', p. 260.

46 De Cleyre, 'The Mexican Revolution', pp. 258–9. Emphasis in original.

47 De Cleyre, 'The Mexican Revolution', pp. 262–3.

48 De Cleyre, 'The Mexican Revolution', p. 267.

49 De Cleyre, 'The Mexican Revolution', p. 254.

50 The 1828 Webster-Merriam dictionary defines education as: '[t]o bring up, as a child; to instruct; to inform and enlighten the understanding; to instill into the mind principles of arts, science, morals, religion and behavior.' The 1798 and 1835 dictionaries of the French Academy adopt the following definition: 'Action to raise, train a child, a young man, a young girl, develop his intellectual and moral faculties' and 'knowledge and practice of the usages of society, with regard to manners, respect, and politeness'. Webster's dictionary of 1828 at http://webstersdictionary1828. com/Dictionary/educate; *Le Dictionnaire de l'Académie française*, http:// artfl-project.uchicago.edu/content/artfl-reference-collection.

51 Lucy Parsons, 'The Principles of Anarchism' [1905–1910], *Black Anarchism: A Reader* (Black Rose Anarchist Federation/Federación Anarquista Rosa Negra, n.d.), p. 3, online at http://blackrosefed.org/black-anarchism-a-reader/ [last access 13 June 2017].

52 Dirlik, *Anarchism in the Chinese Revolution*, p. 162.

53 Shifu quoted in Edward S. Krebs, *Shifu, Soul of Chinese Anarchism* (Lanham: Rowman & Littlefield, 1998), pp. 106, 119.

54 Alexander Berkman, *ABC of Anarchism* (London: Freedom Press, 1980 [1929]), p. 42.

55 Oscar Neebe, *Autobiographies of the Haymarket Martyrs*, online at https:// libcom.org/library/neebe-oscar-autobiography [last access 14 June 2018].

56 Adolph Fischer, *Autobiographies of the Haymarket Martyrs*, online at https:// libcom.org/library/fischer-adolph-autobiography [last access 14 June 2018].

57 Max Stirner, *The False Principle of Our Education*, trans. Robert H. Beebe, ed. James J. Martin (Colorado Springs: Ralph Myles, 1967 [1842]), pp. 12–13.

58 Michael Young, *The Rise of the Meritocracy* (Harmondsworth: Penguin, 1958). Colin Ward comments on Michael Young in Colin Ward and David Goodway, *Talking Anarchy* (Nottingham: Five Leaves, 2003), pp. 91–2.

59 Colin Ward, *Talking Schools* (London: Freedom Press, 1995), online at https://libcom.org/library/talking-schools-colin-ward.

60 Peter Kropotkin, *Fields, Factories and Workshops* (London: Thomas Nelson, 1912 [1898]), p. 378, online at https://theanarchistlibrary.org/library/petr-kropotkin-fields-factories-and-workshops-or-industry-combined-with-agriculture-and-brain-w#toc5 [last access 17 November 2017].

61 Leonard Ayres, 'Military Drill in High Schools', *The School Review*, 25 (3), March 1917, p. 157 [157–60].

62 Ward, *Talking Schools*, p. 68.

63 Herbert Read, *The Education of Free Men* (London: Freedom Press, 1944), pp. 4–5.

64 Paul Goodman, *The Moral Ambiguity of America: The Massy Lectures for 1966* (Toronto: CBC Publications, 1966), p. 15.

65 Goodman, *The Moral Ambiguity of America*, p. 9.

66 Paul Goodman, *Compulsory Miseducation* (Harmondsworth: Penguin, 1971 [1962]).

67 Goodman, *The Moral Ambiguity of America*, p. 40.

68 Goodman, *The Moral Ambiguity of America*, p. 78.

69 Goodman, *The Moral Ambiguity of America*, p. 76.

70 Paul and Percival Goodman, *Communitas: Means of Livelihood and Ways of Life*, 2nd edn (New York: Vintage, 1960 [1947]).

71 Goodman, *The Moral Ambiguity of America*, p. 86.

72 Stirner, *The False Principle of Our Education*.

73 Frederick Lohr, *Anarchism: A Philosophy of Freedom* (London: Frederick Lohr, n.d. [1941/42]), p. 53.

74 Michael Bakunin, 'All-Round Education' [1869], in Robert M. Cutler (ed. and trans.), *The Basic Bakunin: Writings 1869–71* (New York: Prometheus Books, 1992). Emphasis in original.

75 Francisco Ferrer, *The Origin and Ideals of the Modern School* (London: Watts and Co., 1913), pp. 15, 21.

76 Justin Mueller, 'Anarchism, the State, and the Role of Education', in Robert H. Haworth (ed.), *Anarchist Pedagogies: Collective Actions, Theories and Critical Reflections on Education* (Oakland: PM Press, 2012), pp. 23–4.

77 *Advertising Shits in Your Head: Strategies for Resistance* (London: Dog Section Press, 2017), pp. 12–14.

78 Webster's 1913 dictionary, online at http://www.websters1913.com/words/Propagandism.

79 Errico Malatesta and Carlo Cafiero, letter to the *Bulletin de la Fédération Jurassienne*, repr. in Ruth Kinna (ed.), *Early Writings on Terrorism*, vol. 1.

80 CrimethInc. Ex-Workers Collective, 'Gord Hill, Indigenous Artist and Anarchist: An Interview', 1 August 2017, online at https://crimethinc.com/2017/08/01/an-interview-with-gord-hill [last access 21 November 2017].

81 Voline [pseudo. Vsevolod Mikhailovich Eichenbaum], *The Unknown Revolution* (Montreal: Black Rose, 1975 [1947]), p. 630.

82 Voline, *The Unknown Revolution*, p. 197.

83 Emma Goldman, 'Intellectual Proletarians', in Alix Kates Shulman (ed.), *Red Emma Speaks* (London: Wildwood House, 1979 [1914]), p. 176 [176–85].

84 Krebs, *Shifu, Soul of Chinese Anarchism*, p. 194.

85 Dirlik, *Anarchism in the Chinese Revolution*, p. 162.

86 Goodman, *The Moral Ambiguity of America*, p. 45.

87 John Zerzan, 'Running on Emptiness: The Failure of Symbolic Thought', in *Running on Emptiness: The Pathology of Civilization* (Los Angeles: Feral House, 2002), pp. 1–16.

88 Nadine Willems, 'Transnational Anarchism, Japanese Revolutionary Connections, and the Personal Politics of Exile', *Historical Journal*, 61 (3), 2017 pp. 719–41.

89 Sho Konishi, *Anarchist Modernity: Cooperatism and Japanese-Russian Intellectual Relations in Modern Japan* (Cambridge, Mass. and London: Harvard University Press, 2013), p. 98.

90 Kropotkin, 'Finland: A Rising Nationality', in *The Nineteenth Century*, March 1885, p. 14, online at https://archive.org/details/al_Petr_Kropotkin_Finland_A_Rising_Nationality_a4/page/n13 [last access 23 February 2019].

91 Simon Springer, *The Anarchist Roots of Geography: Toward Spatial Emancipation* (Minneapolis: University of Minnesota Press, 2016), p. 129.

92 Kropotkin, *An Appeal to the Young* [1880], available online at https://theanarchistlibrary.org/library/petr-kropotkin-an-appeal-to-the-young.

93 Staughton Lynd and Andrej Grubacic, *Wobblies and Zapatistas: Conversations on Anarchism, Marxism and Radical History* (Oakland: PM Press, 2008), pp. 51, 138, 174.

94 A. J. Withers for the Ontario Coalition Against Poverty (OCAP), 'Fighting to Win: Radical Anti-Poverty Organising', in Uri Gordon and Ruth Kinna (eds), *Routledge Handbook of Radical Politics*, forthcoming.

CHAPTER 3: PRACTICES

1 Andrew X, 'Give Up Activism', *Do Or Die*, 9 (2009), online at https://theanarchistlibrary.org/library/andrew-x-give-up-activism [last access 21 November 2017].

2 Lucy Parsons, 'The Principles of Anarchism' [1905–1910], *Black Anarchism: A Reader* (Black Rose, Anarchist Federation/Federación Anarquista Rosa Negra, n.d.), pp. 3–4, online at http://blackrosefed.org/black-anarchism-a-reader/ [last access 13 June 2017].

3   *Reality Now*, 7 (1987), in Allan Antliff (ed.), *Only a Beginning: An Anarchist Anthology* (Vancouver: Arsenal Pulp Press, 2004), p. 71.

4   David Nicoll, 'The Walsall Anarchists Condemned to Penal Servitude', in *Life in English Prisons (100 years ago), Mysteries of Scotland Yard – Startling Revelations* (London: Kate Sharpley Library, n.d.), p. 10.

5   Ira L. Plotkin, *Anarchism in Japan: A Study of the Great Treason Affair 1910–1911* (Lewiston: Edwin Mellen Press, 1990), p. 105.

6   Louise Michel, *The Red Virgin: Memoirs of Louise Michel*, ed. and trans. Bullitt Lowry and Elizabeth Ellington Gunter (Alabama: University of Alabama Press, 1981), pp. 122, 128.

7   Charlotte Wilson, *Anarchism and Outrage* (London: Freedom, 1893), pp. 3–4.

8   Spanish Atrocities Committee, *Revival of the Inquisition,* repr. from *Freedom* (London: J. Perry, 1897), pp. 3, 6.

9   Charles Malato, 'About Caserio', *Torch* (London), August 1894, p. 4.

10 Peter Kropotkin to Max Nettlau, 9 October 1895, Nettlau Collection, IISH.

11 Peter Kropotkin, letter to the editor of *Nation*, 31 May 1912, p. 367.

12 Bakunin, 'The Policy of the International' [1869], in Sam Dolgoff (ed.), *Bakunin on Anarchism* (Montreal: Black Rose, 1980), p. 167.

13 Organizational Platform of the General Union of Anarchists (Draft), online at http://www.nestormakhno.info/english/newplatform/organizational.htm [last access 2 July 2017].

14 Tom Brown, *Tom Brown's Syndicalism* (London: Phoenix Press, 1990), p. 60.

15 John Henry Mackay, *The Anarchists: A Picture of Civilization at the Close of the Nineteenth Century*, trans. George Schumm (Boston, Mass.: Benj. R. Tucker, 1891), p. 290.

16 Rudolf Rocker, *Anarcho-Syndicalism* (London: Phoenix Press, n.d. [1938]), p. 44.

17 Emma Goldman, *Living My Life* (New York: Dover, 1970 [1931]), vol. II, pp. 755, 770.

18 Alexander Berkman, *The ABC of Anarchism* (London: Freedom Press, 1980 [1929]), p. 83.

19 Emma Goldman to Cassius Cook, 2 August 1937, in David Porter (ed.), *Vision on Fire: Emma Goldman on the Spanish Revolution* (Edinburgh, Oakland and West Virginia: AK Press, 2nd edn. 2006), p. 223.

20 Emma Goldman to Harry Kelly, 29 June 1937, in Porter (ed.), *Vision on Fire*, p. 45.

21 *You Can't Blow Up a Social Relationship: The Anarchist Case against Terrorism* (1978–9), reproduced by the Anarchist Communist Federation (San Francisco: Acrata Press, 1981; repr. 1985 with an introduction by Chaz Bufe), p. 21.

22 *You Can't Blow Up*, p. 7.

23 Francis Dupuis-Déri, *Who's Afraid of the Black Blocs: Anarchy in Action around the World*, trans. Lazer Lederhendler (Toronto: Between the Lines, 2013), p. 71.

24 Vancouver Media Co-op, 'People's Movement vs. "Some Peoples" Movement? Tactical Diversity in Successful Social Movements', online at http://vancouver.mediacoop.ca/blog/bineshii/15604 [accessed 17 June 2017].

25 George Jackson, prison letter 21 June 1971, reprinted in *Fascism: Its Most Advanced Form is Here in America* (Baltimore: Firestarter Press, n.d.).

26 Anon., *The Incomprehensible Black Anarchist Position*, 3 November 2012, online at https://theanarchistlibrary.org/library/anonymous-the-incomprehensible-black-anarchist-position.a4.pdf [last access 8 July 2017]. Assata Shakur's 'To My People' is online at http://www.thetalkingdrum.com/tmp.html.

27 Anna Feigenbaum, 'Death of a Dichotomy: Tactical Diversity and the Politics of Post-Violence', *Upping the Anti*, 5, online at http://uppingtheanti.org/journal/article/05-death-of-a-dichotomy/ [17 June 2017].

28 Francis Dupuis-Déri and Thomas Déri, *Anarchy Explained to My Father*, trans. John Gilmore (Vancouver: New Star Books, 2017), p. 79.

29 Uri Gordon, *Anarchy Alive! Anti-Authoritarian Politics from Practice to Theory* (London: Pluto, 2008), ch. 1.

30 Quoted in Michael Loadenthal, *The Politics of Attack: Communiqués and Insurrectionary Violence* (Manchester: Manchester University Press, 2017), p. 145.

31 CrimethInc., podcast #9, *No Time to Wait*, online at https://crimethinc.com/podcast/9 [last access 8 October 2018].

32 Loadenthal, *The Politics of Attack*, p. 141.

33 Alfredo Bonanno, *Errico Malatesta and Revolutionary Violence* (London: Elephant Editions, 2011 [2007]), p. 10.

34 Loadenthal, *The Politics of Attack*, p. 52.

35 Wolfi Landstreicher, 'A Violent Proposition: Against the Weighted Chain of Morality', in *Willful Disobedience* (Ardent Press, 2009), p. 32.

36 Wolfi Landstreicher, 'The Question of Organization', in *Willful Disobedience*, p. 33.

37 Chicago Anarcho-Feminists, 'An Anarcho-Feminist Manifesto' [1971], *Anarcho-Feminism: Two Statements* (London: Black Bear, 1974), n.p.

38 Anarkismo.net established May Day 2005, online at https://anarkismo.net/about_us.

39 IAF Principles, online at http://i-f-a.org/index.php/principles [last access 5 July 2017].

40 Zabalaza, online at https://zabalaza.net/home/ [last access 8 October 2018].

41 About the IWW, online at https://iww.org/content/about-iww [last access 5 July 2017].

42 The Statutes of Revolutionary Unionism (IWA), IV Goals and Objectives of the IWA, online at http://www.iwa-ait.org/content/statutes [last access 5 July 2017].

43 For a discussion see Peter Gelderloos, 'Insurrection v. Organization: Reflections on a Pointless Schism', online at https://theanarchistlibrary.org/library/peter-gelderloos-insurrection-vs-organization [13 June 2017].

44 Bob Black, *Anarchy After Leftism* (New York: CAL Press, 1997), pp. 144, 149.

45 Bob Black, 'The Marginals Marco Polo', *Beneath the Underground* (Portland, OR: Feral House, 1994), p. 107.

46 Black, 'The Marginals Marco Polo', pp. 106–7.

47 Hakim Bey, TAZ: *The Temporary Autonomous Zone: Ontological Anarchy, Poetic Terrorism*, online at https://theanarchistlibrary.org/library/hakim-bey-t-a-z-the-temporary-autonomous-zone-ontological-anarchy-poetic-terrorism#toc4 [last access 5 July 2017].

48 Nadia C. ,'Your Politics Are Boring As Fuck', *Days of War, Nights of Love* (CrimethInc. 11 August 2000), online at https://crimethinc.com/2000/09/11/your-politics-are-boring-as-fuck [last access 5 July 2017].

49 Robert Wringham, 'An Invitation to New Escapology', *New Escapologist or: Goodbye to All That*, 1 (2008), p. 12.

50 Cindy Milstein, *Anarchism and Its Aspirations* (Edinburgh and Oakland: AK Press/Institute for Anarchist Studies, 2010), p. 56.

51 Murray Bookchin, *Social Anarchism or Lifestyle Anarchism: An Unbridgeable Chasm* (Edinburgh and Oakland: AK Press, 1995), p. 16.

52 Murray Bookchin, 'The Left that Was', in *Social Anarchism or Lifestyle Anarchism*, p. 66.

53 Bookchin, *Social Anarchism or Lifestyle Anarchism*, p. 59.

54 Matthew Wilson, *Biting the Hand that Feeds Us: In Defence of Lifestyle Politics*, Dysophia open letter #2 (Leeds: Dysophia, n.d.), p. 4.

55 Takurō Higuchi, 'Global Anarchism and the Will of the Earth – Implications of Eastern Resonances', in Kikaru Tanaka, Masaya Hiyazaki and Chihaur Yamanaka (eds), *Global Anarchism: Past, Present and Future – New Anarchism in Japan* (Tokyo: Association for Anarchism Studies/Kansai, 2014), p. 140.

56 Wilson, *Biting the Hand that Feeds Us*, p. 5.

57 Marianne Maeckelbergh, 'Horizontal Decision-Making across Time and Place', *Cultural Anthropology*, 27 July 2012, online at https://culanth. org/fieldsights/64-horizontal-decision-making-across-time-and-place [16 June 2017].

58 Alix Kates Shulman, 'Dances with Feminists' [1991], Emma Goldman Papers, online at http://www.lib.berkeley.edu/goldman/Features/ danceswithfeminists.html [24 June 2017].

59 Kirwin R. Shaffer, *Anarchism and Countercultural Politics in Early Twentieth-Century Cuba* (Florida: University Press of Florida, 2005), p. 11.

60 Gabriel Kuhn and Sebastian Kalicha interview Allan Antliff, Richard Day and Taiaiake Alfred, excerpt from *Anarchismus weltweit: Von Jakarta bis Johannesburg* (Berlin: Verlag Unrast, 2010; Victoria: Black Raven editions, n.d.), p. 10.

61 Ricardo Flores Magón, *Manifesto of the Mexican Liberal Party*, 1911, online at https://theanarchistlibrary.org/library/ricardo-flores-magon-manifesto-of-the-mexican-liberal-party [last access 14 November 2017].

62 Karl Marx and Friedrich Engels, *The Communist Manifesto* [1848], ch. 1, online at https://www.marxists.org/archive/marx/works/1848/communist-manifesto/ch01.htm.

63 Gustave Brocher Papers, IISH, f. 79, online at https://search.socialhistory. org/Record/ARCH00115/ArchiveContentList#Acb04e901b6.

64 Gustave Brocher Papers, IISH, f. 70, online at https://search.socialhistory. org/Record/ARCH00115/ArchiveContentList#21.

65 Marx and Engels, *The Communist Manifesto* [1848], ch. 1, online at https:// www.marxists.org/archive/marx/works/1848/communist-manifesto/ ch01.htm.

66 Alexander Berkman, *ABC of Anarchism* (London: Freedom Press, 1980 [1929]), pp. 44–5.

67 Gustav Landauer, *For Socialism*, trans. David J. Parent (St Louis: Telos Press, 1978 [1911]), p. 48.

68 Landauer, *For Socialism*, p. 78.

69 Landauer, *For Socialism*, pp. 77–8.

70 Landauer, *For Socialism*, p. 125.

71 Errico Malatesta, *Fra Contadini: A Dialogue on Anarchy*, trans. Jean Weir (Catania: Bratach Dubh Editions, 1981 [1884]), pp. 14–15.

72 Sean Reilly, 'The Middle Class', *The Heavy Stuff*, 3 (London: Class War Federation, n.d.), pp. 2–9.

73 The Combahee River Collective Statement, Combahee River Collective/ Zillah Eisenstein, April 1977, online at http://combaheerivercollective.

weebly.com/the-combahee-river-collective-statement.html [last access 7 July 2017].

74 Audre Lorde, 'Learning from the 60s' [1982], excerpt reproduced in *Dysophia, Anarchist Debates on Privilege*, *Dysophia* 4, November 2013, online at http://www.blackpast.org/1982-audre-lorde-learning-60s [last access 17 July 2017].

75 Wayne Price, 'What is Class Struggle Anarchism?', 2007 online at https://theanarchistlibrary.org/library/wayne-price-what-is-class-struggle-anarchism#toc4 [last access 7 July 2017].

76 'Normalization and its Discontents: An Interview with Ladelle McWhorter', *Upping the Anti: A Journal of Theory and Action*, 11 (2010), p. 61.

77 Afed, 'A Class Struggle Analysis of Privilege Theory from the Women's Caucus', 24 October 2012, online at https://afed.org.uk/a-class-struggle-anarchist-analysis-of-privilege-theory-from-the-womens-caucus/ [last access 7 July 2017].

78 R. Lowens, 'How Do You Practice Intersectionalism? An Interview with bell hooks', online at http://nefac.net/bellhooks [last access 7 July 2017].

79 'Normalization and its Discontents', p. 71.

80 'Interview with Ernesto Aguilar of the Anarchist People of Color (APOC)', Colours of Resistance Archive, online at http://www.coloursofresistance.org/596/interview-with-ernesto-aguilar-of-the-anarchist-people-of-color-apoc/ [last access 7 July 2017].

81 'Interview with Taiaiake Alfred', Gabriel Kuhn and Sebastian Kalicha, in an excerpt from *Anarchismus weltweit*, p. 24.

82 Gustav Landauer, 'Weak Statesmen, Weaker People', in Gabriel Kuhn (ed. and trans.), *Gustav Landauer, Revolution and Other Writings: A Political Reader* (Oakland: PM Press, 2010 [1910]), p. 214.

83 Colin Ward, *Anarchy in Action* (London: Freedom Press, 1983 [1973]), p. 11.

84 Abby Martin, 'The Unheard of Story of Hurricane Katrina: Blackwater, White Militas, and Community Empowerment', in *Emergency Hearts/Molotov Dreams: A scott crow Reader* (Cleveland, OH: GTK Press, 2015), p. 41.

85 Quoted in Marie M. Collins and Sylvie Weil-Sayre, 'Flora Tristan: Forgotten Feminist and Socialist', *Nineteenth-Century French Studies*, 1 (4) (Summer 1973), p. 229 [229–34].

86 A reference to Milton, *Paradise Lost*. See George W. Whiting and Ann Gossman, 'Siloa's Brook, the Pool of Siloam, and Milton's Muse', *Studies in Philology*, 58 (2) (1961), pp. 193–205.

87 Voltairine de Cleyre, 'Direct Action', in Alexander Berkman (ed.), *Selected Works of Voltairine de Cleyre* (New York: Mother Earth Publishing, 1914), p. 223 [220–242].

88 De Cleyre, 'Direct Action', p. 222.

89 Voltairine de Cleyre, 'The Gates of Freedom' [1891], in Eugenia C. DeLamotte, *Gates of Freedom: Voltairine de Cleyre and the Revolution of the Mind* (Ann Arbor: University of Michigan Press, 2007), p. 249 [235–50].

90 He-Yin Zhen, 'On the Question of Women's Liberation' [1907], in Lydia H. Liu, Rebecca E. Karl and Dorothy Ko (eds), *The Birth of Chinese Feminism: Essential Texts in Transnational Theory* (New York: Columbia University Press, 2013), pp. 53–71.

91 Valerie Solanas, *SCUM Manifesto* (Edinburgh and San Francisco: AK Press, 1997), pp. 42–3.

92 Saul D. Alinksy, *Rules for Radicals: A Pragmatic Primer for Realistic Radicals* (New York: Vintage Books, 1989 [1971]), p. 25.

93 Michel, *The Red Virgin*, p. 142.

94 Black, *Anarchy after Leftism*, p. 141.

95 Emma Dixon, 'Women, Love and Anarchism: The Rise of British Second Wave Feminism', *Perspectives*, 2011, Institute for Anarchist Studies, online at http://anarchiststudies.mayfirst.org/node/512 [last access 11 July 2017].

96 Ann Hansen, *Direct Action: Memoirs of an Urban Guerrilla* (Toronto and Edinburgh/Oakland: Between the Lines/AK Press, 2002), p. 24.

97 *Anarchy* magazine, 113 (July 1970), online at https://libcom.org/files/Anarchy%20No113.compressed.pdf [last access 11 July 2017].

98 'Anarcha-Feminism and Anarcho-Machismo in Spain', interview with the Valeries by Jeremy Kay, December 2013, online at http://anarchalibrary.blogspot.co.uk/2013/06/anarcha-feminism-and-anarcho-machismo.html [last access 18 July 2017].

99 Ōsugi Sakae quoted in Masaya Hiyazaki, 'Between Revolution and War – From the Perspective of Ōsugi's Theory of "The Expansion of Life"', in *Global Anarchism*, p. 114.

100 'Anarcha-Feminism and Anarcho-Machismo in Spain'.

CHAPTER 4: CONDITIONS

1 Max Nettlau, 'Panarchy: A Forgotten Idea of 1860', trans. John Zube, in Aviezer Tucker and Gian Piero de Bellis (eds), *Panarchy: Political Theories of Non-Territorial States* (Abingdon: Routledge, 2016 [1909]), pp. 36–42.

2 Émile Armand, 'Live as Experiment', in *Individualist Anarchism, Revolutionary Sexualism* (Austin, TX: Pallaksch Press, 2012), pp. 55–6.

3   Émile Armand, 'Future Society', in *Individualist Anarchism, Revolutionary Sexualism*, p. 40.

4   Bob James, *Anarchism and State Violence in Sydney and Melbourne, 1886–1896*, ch. 4, online at Radical Tradition, http://www.takver.com/history/aasv/aasvo4.htm [last access 13 November 2017].

5   D. A. Andrade, *An Anarchist Plan of Campaign* (1888), online at http://www.takver.com/history/raa/raao8.htm [last access 13 November 2017].

6   Victor Yarros, 'Property in Ideas and Equal Liberty', *Liberty*, 7 February 1891, online at http://fair-use.org/liberty/1891/02/07/property-in-ideas-and-equal-liberty [last access 30 November 2017].

7   Victor Yarros, *Anarchism: Its Aims and Methods* (Boston: Benj. R. Tucker, 1887), p. 3.

8   Yarros, *Anarchism*, pp. 27–30.

9   Yarros, *Anarchism*, pp. 11–12.

10 Yarros, *Anarchism*, p. 19.

11 Yarros, *Anarchism*, p. 15.

12 Yarros, *Anarchism*, pp. 23–4.

13 Alexander Skirda, *Facing the Enemy: A History of Anarchist Organization from Proudhon to May 1968*, trans. Paul Sharkey (Edinburgh and Oakland/London and Berkeley: AK Press/Kate Sharpley Library, 2002), pp. 124–5.

14 The Group of Russian Anarchists Abroad, *The Organizational Platform of the General Union of Anarchists (Draft)*, 20 June 1926, reproduced in Skirda, pp. 192, 194 [192–213].

15 *Organizational Platform*, p. 197.

16 *Organizational Platform*, p. 203.

17 *Organizational Platform*, pp. 206–7.

18 *Organizational Platform*, p. 212.

19 *Organizational Platform*, pp. 210–11.

20 *Organizational Platform*, p. 194.

21 Ronald Fraser, *Blood of Spain: The Experience of Civil War, 1936–1939* (London: Allen Lane, 1979), pp. 348–51.

22 Gaston Leval, *Collectives in the Spanish Revolution* (London: Freedom Press, 1975), p. 131.

23 Leval, *Collectives in the Spanish Revolution*, p. 133.

24 James Guillaume, *Ideas on Social Organization* [1876], Section D, online at http://theanarchistlibrary.org/library/james-guillaume-ideas-on-social-organization#toc8 [last access 17 November 2017].

25 Leval, *Collectives in the Spanish Revolution*, p. 135.

26 Yarros, *Anarchism*, p. 14.

27 Fernando Pessoa, *The Anarchist Banker*, trans. Margaret Jull Costa, in Eugénio Lisboa (ed.), *The Anarchist Banker and Other Portuguese Stories*, vol. 1 (Manchester: Carcanet, 1997), pp. 88–114.

28 Franz Oppenheimer, 'Reminiscences of Peter Kropotkin', in *Centennial Expressions on Peter Kropotkin, 1842–1942, by Pertinent Thinkers* (Los Angeles: Rocker Publications Committee, 1962), pp. 6–8.

29 Anon., *Anarchy Against Utopia!*, online at https://theanarchistlibrary.org/library/anonymous-anarchy-against-utopia [last access 14 November 2017].

30 Marie-Louise Berneri, *Journey Through Utopia* (London: Freedom Books, 1982), p. 8.

31 Colin Ward, *Utopia* (Harmondsworth: Penguin, 1974), p. 8.

32 L. S. Bevington, *Common-sense Country* [1896], online at http://webapp1.dlib.indiana.edu/vwwp/view?docId=VAB7040&doc.view=print [last access 16 November 2017].

33 Robyn Roslak, *Neo-Impressionism and Anarchism in Fin-de-Siècle France: Painting, Politics and Landscape* (Aldershot: Ashgate, 2007), p. 143.

34 Yarros, *Anarchism*, p. 6.

35 Martin Buber, *Paths in Utopia*, trans. R. F. C. Hull (Boston: Beacon Press, 1958), p. 7.

36 L. S. Bevington, *An Anarchist Manifesto* (London, 1895), online at http://webapp1.dlib.indiana.edu/vwwp/view?docId=VAB7013&doc.view=print [last access 16 November 2017].

37 See Judith Skhlar, 'The Political Theory of Utopia: From Melancholy to Nostalgia', *Daedalus*, 94 (2) (1965), p. 370 [367–81].

38 Buber, *Paths in Utopia*, p. 14.

39 *Organizational Platform*, p. 193.

40 Buber, *Paths in Utopia*, p. 16.

41 Unusually in agreement with Marx, Kropotkin also questioned the wisdom of setting up intentional communities; not only were they exclusive and often dysfunctional, but they were essentially escape routes rather than instruments of social transformation. Kropotkin modernized socialist utopianism by proposing to use communalization as a means of struggle as well as an end in itself. Matthew Adams, 'Rejecting the American Model: Peter Kropotkin's Radical Communalism', *History of Political Thought*, 25 (1), pp. 147–73.

42 Peter Kropotkin, *The Conquest of Bread* [1892] (London: Elephant Editions, 1985), p. 192.

43 George Woodcock, *New Life to the Land* (London: Freedom Press, 1942), p. 3.

44 Harold Bolce, *The New Internationalism* (New York: D. Appleton and Company, 1907), pp. 1, 308.

45 Peter Kropotkin, *Fields, Factories and Workshops* (London: Thomas Nelson, 1912 [1898]), ch. 2, online at https://theanarchistlibrary.org/library/petr-kropotkin-fields-factories-and-workshops-or-industry-combined-with-agriculture-and-brain-w#toc5 [last access 17 November 2017].

46 Kropotkin, *Fields, Factories and Workshops*, ch. 2.

47 Kropotkin, *Fields, Factories and Workshops*, ch. 5.

48 Kropotkin, *Fields, Factories and Workshops*, ch. 5.

49 Deric Shannon, 'The End of the World as We Know It?: Toward a Critical Understanding of the Future', in Deric Shannon (ed.), *The End of the World as We Know It? Crisis, Resistance and the Age of Austerity* (Edinburgh and Oakland: AK Press, 2014), p. 493.

50 Takis Fotopoulos, *The Multidimensional Crisis and Inclusive Democracy*, ch. 4, online at https://ww.inclusivedemocracy.org/journals/ss/ch4 [last access 17 November 2017].

51 P.M. [Hans Widmer], *bolo'bolo* (1983), p. 5.

52 P.M., *bolo'bolo*, p. 6.

53 P.M., *bolo'bolo*, p. 16.

54 P.M., *bolo'bolo*, p. 4.

55 P.M., *bolo'bolo*, p. 19.

56 P.M., *bolo'bolo*, p. 26.

57 P.M., *bolo'bolo*, p. 30.

58 P.M., *bolo'bolo*, p. 50.

59 P.M., *bolo'bolo*, p. 48.

60 P.M., *bolo'bolo*, pp. 38–42.

61 P.M., *bolo'bolo*, p. 76.

62 P.M., *bolo'bolo*, p. 33.

63 Hakim Bey [Peter Lamborn Wilson], *Temporary Autonomous Zone* ('Ratholes in the Babylon of Information'), online at https://hermetic.com/bey/taz3#labeltaz [last access 21 November 2017].

64 Bey, *Temporary Autonomous Zone* ('The Dinner Party').

65 Bey, *Temporary Autonomous Zone* ('Music as an Organizational Principle').

66 Tom Goyens, *Beer and Revolution: The German Anarchist Movement in New York City, 1880–1914* (Urbana and Chicago: University of Illinois Press, 2007), p. 7.

67 *Organizational Platform*, p. 198.

68 George Woodcock, *Anarchism: A History of Libertarian Ideas and Movements* (Cleveland and New York: Meridian, 1962), p. 33.

69 Saul Newman, *Postanarchism* (Cambridge: Polity, 2016), pp. 120–23.

70 Noam Chomsky, *Deterring Democracy* (London: Verso, 1991); Edward S. Herman and Noam Chomsky, *Manufacturing Consent* (New York: Pantheon Books, 1988).

71 Rebecca Solnit, 'Worlds Collide in a Luxury Suite: Some Thoughts on the IMF, Global Injustice, and a Stranger on a Train', *Huffington Post*, 22 May 2011, updated 22 July 2011, online at https://www.huffingtonpost.com/rebecca-solnit/worlds-collide-in-a-luxur_b_865307.html [last access 27 November 2011].

72 Rebecca Solnit, 'Democracy Should Be Exercised Regularly, On Foot', *Guardian*, 6 July 2006, online at https://www.theguardian.com/commentisfree/2006/jul/06/comment.politics [last access 27 November 2011].

73 Murray Bookchin, 'Listen, Marxist!', in *Post-Scarcity Anarchism* (Edinburgh and Oakland: AK Press, 2004 [1970]), p. 135 [108–43].

74 Murray Bookchin, 'What is Social Ecology?', in *Social Ecology and Communalism* (Edinburgh and Oakland: AK Press, 2007), p. 45 [19–52].

75 Murray Bookchin, *The Next Revolution: Popular Assemblies and the Promise of Direct Democracy* (London: Verso, 2015), p. 71.

76 Bookchin, *The Next Revolution*, p. 70.

77 Murray Bookchin, Preface to *Urbanization Without Cities: The Rise and Decline of Citizenship* (Montreal: Black Rose, 1992), p. x.

78 Guy-Ernest Debord, *The Society of the Spectacle*, ch. 7: 'The Organization of Territory', para. 174, online at http://library.nothingness.org/articles/SI/en/display/24 [last access 4 June 2018].

79 Bookchin, *Urbanization Without Cities*, p. 3.

80 Bookchin, Preface to *Urbanization Without Cities*, p. x.

81 Bookchin, *The Next Revolution*, p. 66.

82 Bookchin, 'Radical Politics', in *Social Ecology and Communalism*, p. 66.

83 Bookchin, *The Limits of the City* (New York: Harper Torchbooks, 1974), p. 137.

84 Bookchin, 'Radical Politics', p. 61.

85 Bookchin, *The Next Revolution*, p. 87.

86 David Graeber, 'Enacting the Impossible (On Consensus Decision Making)', Occupy Wall Street, 29 October 2011, online at http://occupywallst.org/article/enacting-the-impossible/ [last access 2 December 2017].

87 Murray Bookchin, 'What is Communalism? The Democratic Dimension of Anarchism', *Democracy & Nature: The International Journal of Politics and Ecology*, 3 (2) (1995), pp. 1–17, online at https://www.democracynature.org/vol3/bookchin_communalism.htm [last access 5 May 2017].

88 Émilie Breton, Sandra Jeppesen, Anna Kruzynski and Rachel Sarrasin (Research Group on Collective Autonomy), 'Prefigurative Self-Governance and Self-Organization: The Influence of Antiauthoritarian (Pro)Feminist, Radical Queer, and Antiracist Networks in Quebec', in Aziz Choudry, Jill Hanley and Eric Shragge (eds), *Organize! Building from the Local for Global Justice* (Oakland: PM Press, 2012), pp. 158–9 [156–173].

89 David Graeber, *The Democracy Project: A History, a Crisis, a Movement* (London: Allen Lane, 2013), p. 155.

90 Graeber, *The Democracy Project*, p. 160.

91 A. J. Bauer, 'This is What Democracy Feels Like: Tea Parties, Occupations and the Crisis of State Legitimacy', in Cristina Beltrán, Rana Jaleel and Andrew Ross (eds), *Is This What Democracy Looks Like?*, online at https://what-democracy-looks-like.org/its-the-democracy-stupid/.

92 P.-J. Proudhon, *What is Property? An Inquiry into the Principle of Right and of Government* [1840], trans. Benj. R. Tucker (London: William Reeves, 1969 [1898]), p. 264.

93 Midnight Notes, vol. 1, *Strange Victories: The Anti-Nuclear Movement in the US and Europe* (Brooklyn, NY and Jamaica Plain, MA, 1979), online at http://www.midnightnotes.org/mnpublic.html [last access 5 May 2018].

CHAPTER 5: PROSPECTS

1 See the lists maintained on the Anarchist Portal, online at https://en.wikipedia.org/wiki/Portal:Anarchism.

2 David Porter, 'Revolutionary Realization: The Motivational Energy', in Howard J. Ehrlich et al., *Reinventing Anarchy* (London: Routledge and Kegan Paul, 1979), pp. 214, 217.

3 Emma Goldman, 'Was My Life Worth Living?', *Harper's Monthly Magazine*, vol. CLXX (December 1934), online at http://www.lib.berkeley.edu/goldman/pdfs/PublishedEssaysandPamphlets_WasMyLifeWorthLiving.pdf [last access 2 June 2018].

4 Chicago Anarcho-Feminists, 'An Anarcho-Feminist Manifesto', in Dark Star Collective (ed.), *Quiet Rumors*, 3rd edition (Oakland, CA: AK Press, 2012), pp. 15–17.

5 Abdullah Öcalan, *Manifesto for a Democratic Civilization* (Norway: New Compass, 2015), p. 62.

6   The Project of a Democratic Syria, https://peaceinkurdistancampaign.com/
     resources/rojava/the-project-of-a-democratic-syria/ [last access 17 May
     2018].

7   James C. Scott, *Two Cheers for Anarchism* (New Jersey: Princeton
     University Press, 2012), p. xvi.

8   Abby Martin, 'The Unheard Story of Hurricane Katrina: Blackwater, White
     Militias, and Community Empowerment', in *Emergency Hearts/Molotov
     Dreams: A scott crow Reader* (Cleveland, OH: GTK Press, 2015), p. 42.

9   Noam Chomsky, 'Noam Chomsky on American Foreign Policy and US
     Politics', interview with Cenk Uygur, *The Young Turks*, 26 October 2010,
     online at https://chomsky.info/20101026/ [last access 19 May 2018].

10   Noam Chomsky, 'Talking Policy: Noam Chomsky on Academia and U.S.
     Foreign Policy', interview with *World Policy*, 22 July 2016, online at https://
     worldpolicy.org/2016/07/22/talking-policy-noam-chomsky-on-academia-
     and-u-s-foreign-policy/ [last access 19 May 2018].

11   George Woodcock, *Homes or Hovels: The Housing Problem and Its Solution*
     (London: Freedom Press, 1944), p. 27.

12   Chomsky, 'Noam Chomsky on American Foreign Policy and US Politics'.

13   Paul and Percival Goodman, *Communitas: Means of Livelihood and Ways of
     Life*, 2nd edn (New York: Vintage, 1960 [1947]), p. 223.

14   Goodman, *Communitas*, p. 221.

15   Goodman, *Communitas*, p. 224.

16   *Manifeste de l'En-dehors*, 15 November 1926, in É. Armand (trans. and ed.),
     Les Différents Visages de l'anarchisme (Paris: Édition de l'En-dehors, 1927),
     pp. 56–65.

17   Errico Malatesta, *Fra Contadini: A Dialogue on Anarchy*, trans. Jean Weir
     (Catania: Bratach Dubh Editions, 1981 [1884]), p. 3.

18   Francis Dupuis-Déri and Thomas Déri, *Anarchy Explained to My Father*,
     trans. John Gilmore (Vancouver: New Star Books, 2017), pp. 199–200.

19   bell hooks, 'How Do You Practice Intersectionalism?', an interview with
     bell hooks, Randy Lowens, June 2009, Common Struggle/Lucha Común,
     online at http://nefac.net/bellhooks [last access 4 June 2018].

20   Andrew Stevens, 'Looking Back at Anger', an interview with Stuart
     Christie, *3am Magazine*, 2004, online at http://www.3ammagazine.com/
     politica/2004/apr/interview_stuart_christie.html [last access 15 June
     2018].

21   Steven Pinker, 'The Moral Instinct', *The New York Times Magazine*, 13
     January 2008, online at https://www.nytimes.com/2008/01/13/magazine/
     13Psychology-t.html [last access 4 June 2018].

22 Peter Kropotkin, 'Letter to French and British Trade Union Delegates' [1901], in I. McKay (ed.), *Direct Struggle Against Capital: A Peter Kropotkin Anthology* (Edinburgh, Oakland, and Baltimore: AK Press, 2014), p. 360. [359–61].

23 Holly Devon, 'Defending the Collective: an Interview with Malik Rahim', *Iron Lattice*, 11 April 2017, online at http://theironlattice.com/index. php/2017/04/11/defending-the-collective-an-interview-with-malik-rahim/ [last access 4 June 2018].

24 Holly Devon, 'Defending the Collective: an Interview with Malik Rahim'.

25 Tim Shorrock, 'The Street Samaritans', *Mother Jones*, March/April 2006, online at https://www.motherjones.com/politics/2006/03/street-samaritans-2/ [last access 4 June 2018].

26 Neille Ilel, 'A Healthy Dose of Anarchy', *Reason*, December 2006, online at https://reason.com/archives/2006/12/11/a-healthy-dose-of-anarchy [last access 4 June 2018].

27 Murray Rothbard, 'The Political Thought of Étienne de la Boétie', introduction to *The Politics of Obedience: The Discourse of Voluntary Servitude by Etienne de la Boétie*, trans. Harry Kurz (New York: Free Life, 1975), p. 13.

28 Rothbard, 'The Political Thought of Étienne de la Boétie', pp. 28–29.

29 Saul Newman, *Postanarchism* (Oxford: Polity, 2016), p. 128.

30 Rothbard, 'The Political Thought of Étienne de la Boétie', p. 29.

31 Emma Goldman, 'The Tragedy of Woman's Emancipation', in Alix Kates Shulman (ed.), *Red Emma Speaks* (London: Wildwood House, 1979 [1914]), p. 141.

32 Angry Brigade communiqués, online at http://www.spunk.org/texts/groups/agb/sp000539.txt [last access 5 June 2018].

33 The Invisible Committee, 'Let's Destitute the World', *Now*, trans. Robert Hurley (Ill Will Editions, November 2017), p. 45.

34 Liberate Tate, online at http://www.liberatetate.org.uk/performances/ [last access 5 June 2018].

35 Dorian Lynskey, 'Deft Punk/Pussy Riot's Yekaterina Samutsevich speaks out', *Guardian G2*, 21 December 2012, pp. 6–9.

36 John Henry Mackay, *The Anarchists: A Picture of Civilization at the Close of the Nineteenth Century*, trans. George Schumm (Boston: Benj. R. Tucker, 1891), p. 105.

37 Mackay, *The Anarchists*, pp. 47–8.

38 Mackay, *The Anarchists*, p. 23.

39 Uchiyama Gudō, 'Prison Fragment', in Fabio Rambelli (ed.), *Zen Anarchism: The Egalitarian Dharma of Uchiyama Gudō* (Berkeley: Institute of Buddhist Studies and BDK America, 2013), p. 69.

40 Anon., *Malevolent Europe: Regarding Refugee Oppression and Resistance at the Borders* (Ill Will Editions, 2015).

ANARCHIST BIOGRAPHIES

Introduction: Anarchism: Myths and Realities

1 Fiona MacCarthy, *Eric Gill* (London: Faber and Faber, 2011).

2 Paul Sharkey, 'Vladimiro Muñoz 1920–2004', *Bulletin of the Kate Sharpley Library*, 61 (February/March 2010), online at https://www.katesharpleylibrary.net/dnckro [last access 23 February 2018].

Chapter 1: Traditions

1 Peter Lamborn Wilson, 'Stephen Pearl Andrews (22 March 1812–21 May 1886)', in Kent P. Ljungquist (ed.), *Antebellum Writers in New York: Second Series* (Farmington Hills, MI: Gale, 2002), pp. 3–15, see *Dictionary of Literary Biography Complete Online*, http://link.galegroup.com/apps/doc/NCPTFV664682651/DLBC?u=loughuni&sid=DLBC [last access 17 February 2018].

2 Muñoz, *Anarchists*.

3 Nunzio Pernicone, *Italian Anarchism 1864–1892* (Edinburgh and Oakland: AK Press, 2009); Pietro Di Paola, *The Knights Errant of Anarchy: London and the Italian Anarchist Diaspora (1880–1917)* (Liverpool: Liverpool University Press, 2013).

4 Allan Antliff, *Anarchy and Art: From the Paris Commune to the Fall of the Berlin Wall* (Vancouver: Arsenal Pulp Press, 2007); 'Gustave Courbet: A Biography', Musée d'Orsay, Paris, online at http://www.musee-orsay.fr/en/collections/courbet-dossier/biography.html#c19275 [last access 5 March 2018].

5 Muñoz, *Anarchists*.

6 George Engel, 'Autobiography', online at https://libcom.org/library/engel-george-autobiography [last access 25 February 2018].

7 Paul Avrich, *The Modern School Movement: Anarchism and Education in the United States* (Edinburgh and Oakland: AK Press, 2006 [1980]).

8   Samuel Fielden, 'Autobiography', online at https://libcom.org/library/
    fielden-samuel-autobiography [last access 25 February 2018]; Blaine
    McKinley, 'Samuel Fielden', in Dave Roediger and Franklin Rosemont (eds),
    Haymarket Scrapbook (Chicago: Charles Kerr & Co., 1986).

9   Adolph Fischer, 'Autobiography', online at https://libcom.org/library/
    fischer-adolphe-autobiography [last access 25 February 2018].

10 Muñoz, *Anarchists*.

11 Shulman (ed.), *Red Emma Speaks*.

12 Louis Patsouras, *The Anarchism of Jean Grave: Editor, Journalist and
    Militant* (Montreal: Black Rose, 2003); Constance Bantman, *The French
    Anarchists in London, 1880–1914: Exile and Transnationalism in the First
    Globalization* (Liverpool: Liverpool University Press, 2013).

13 Martin Henry Blatt, *Free Love and Anarchism: The Biography of Ezra
    Heywood* (Urbana: University of Illinois Press, 1989).

14 Philip S. Foner, *The Case of Joe Hill* (New York: International Publishers,
    1970 [1965]).

15 Muñoz, *Anarchists*.

16 Louis Lingg, 'Autobiography', online at https://libcom.org/library/lingg-
    louis-autobiography [last access 25 February 2018]; Paul Avrich 'The Bomb-
    Thrower: A New Candidate', in Roediger and Rosemont (eds), *Haymarket
    Scrapbook*.

17 J. B. Pick, *A Nest of Anarchists*, online at http://winamop.com/nest.htm [last
    access 18 March 2018].

18 Thomas A. Riley, *Germany's Poet-Anarchist: John Henry Mackay* (New York:
    The Revisionist Press, 1972); Hubert Kennedy, 'Afterword', *The Hustler: The
    Story of a Nameless Love from Friedrichstrasse* (Xlibris, 2002).

19 Muñoz, *Anarchists*.

20 Max Nettlau, 'Errico Malatesta: Rough Outlines of His Life Up Till 1920',
    online at the Libertarian Labyrinth http://www.library.libertarian-labyrinth.
    org/items/show/2473 [last access 23 February 201]; Pernicone, *Italian
    Anarchism 1864–1892*; Di Paola, *The Knights Errant of Anarchy*.

21 Constance Bantman, 'Charles Malato', in Immanuel Ness (ed.),
    International Encyclopedia of Revolution and Protest: 1500 to the Present, vol.
    4 (Chichester: Wiley-Blackwell, 2009), pp. 2171–2.

22 'F. S. Merlino', biography, Centro Studi Francesco Saverio Merlino, online
    at http://www.centrostudifsmerlino.org/ [last access 23 February 2018]; Di
    Paola, *The Knights Errant of Anarchy*.

23 Muñoz, *Anarchists*.

24 Muñoz, *Anarchists*.

25 Oscar Neebe, 'Autobiography', online at https://libcom.org/library/neebe-oscar-autobiography [last access 25 February 2018]; Franklin Rosemont, 'Oscar Neebe', in Roediger and Rosemont, *Haymarket Scrapbook*.

26 Albert Parsons, 'Autobiography', online at https://libcom.org/library/autobiography-parsons [last access 26 February 2018].

27 Gale Ahrens, 'Lucy Parsons: Mystery Revolutionist, More Dangerous than a Thousand Rioters', in Lucy Parsons, *Freedom, Equality and Solidarity: Writings and Speeches 1878–1937* ed., Gale Ahrens (Chicago: Charles H. Kerr, 2004), pp. 1–26; 'Lucy Parsons: Woman of Will', Industrial Workers of the World, online at https://www.iww.org/history/biography/LucyParsons/1 [last access 26 February 2018].

28 K. Steven Vincent, 'Proudhon, Pierre-Joseph', online at https://libcom.org/library/proudhon-pierre-joseph [last access 16 March 2018].

29 Muñoz, *Anarchists*.

30 William J. Fishman, 'Rocker, Rudolf', *Oxford Dictionary of National Biography* (September 2004).

31 Nunzio Pernicone, 'Sacco, Nicola', *American National Biography Online*, February 2000, online at http://www.english.illinois.edu/maps/poets/m_r/millay/sacco.htm [last access 5 March 2018].

32 Michael Schwab, 'Autobiography', online at https://libcom.org/library/schwab-michael-autobiography [last access 26 February 2018]; David Roediger, 'Michael Schwab', in Roediger and Rosemont (eds), *Haymarket Scrapbook*.

33 Peter Ryley, *Making Another World Possible: Anarchism, Anti-capitalism and Ecology in Late 19th and Early 20th Century Britain* (London: Bloomsbury, 2013).

34 August Spies, 'Autobiography', online at https://libcom.org/library/spies-august-autobiography [last access 26 February 2018].

35 Muñoz, *Anarchists*.

36 Muñoz, *Anarchists*.

37 Riley, *Germany's Poet-Anarchist*; Paul Avrich, 'An Interview with Oriole Tucker', online at http://uncletaz.com/liberty/oriole.html [last access 6 March 2018]; Wendy McElroy, 'Benjamin Tucker, *Liberty* and Individualist Anarchism', online at https://web.archive.org/web/20051024160827/http://www.zetetics.com/mac/tir1.htm [last access 6 March 2018].

38 Nunzio Pernicone, 'Vanzetti, Bartolomeo', *American National Biography Online*, February 2000, reproduced at http://www.english.illinois.edu/maps/poets/m_r/millay/sacco.htm [last access 5 March 2018].

Chapter 2: Cultures

1   Kathlyn Gay and Martin K. Gay, *Encyclopedia of Political Anarchy* (Santa Barbara CA: ABC-CLIO, 1999).

2   G. R. Seaman, 'Coomaraswamy, Ananda Kentish', *Oxford Dictionary of National Biography* (2004).

3   John Entwisle, 'Reuters' First Editor – Scoundrel, Womaniser and Journalist of Flair', *Baron*, online at http://www.thebaron.info/archives/reuters-first-editor-scoundrel-womaniser-and-journalist-of-flair [last access 26 February 2018]; 'Dr. Sigmund Engländer', Obituary, *Jewish Chronicle*, 19 December 1902, pp. 10–11; Christine Lattek, *Revolutionary Refugees: German Socialism in Britain 1840–1860* (London: Routledge, 2006).

4   'Lawrence Ferlinghetti', *Dictionary of World Biography*, online at http://www.notablebiographies.com/supp/Supplement-Ca-Fi/Ferlinghetti-Lawrence.html [last access 28 February 2018]; 'Lawrence Ferlinghetti', The Poetry Foundation online at https://www.poetryfoundation.org/poets/lawrence-ferlinghetti [last access 28 February 2018].

5   Paul Goodman, *Drawing the Line: Political Essays*, ed. Taylor Stoehr (New York: Free Life, 1977); Taylor Stoehr (ed.), *The Paul Goodman Reader* (Oakland: PM Press, 2011).

6   David G. Nelson, 'Ishikawa Sanshirō', in Immanuel Ness (ed.), *International Encyclopedia of Revolution and Protest: 1500 to the Present*, vol. 5 (Chichester: Wiley-Blackwell, 2009), pp. 1807–8.

7   Staughton Lynd, author biography, at PM Press, online at http://www.pmpress.org/content/article.php/staughtonlynd [last access 6 March 2018]; Tiffany L. Stanley, 'Sharing Life, and a Lifetime of Causes', *Harvard Magazine*, 2010, online at https://harvardmagazine.com/2010/05/sharing-life-and-a-lifetime-of-causes [last access 6 March 2018].

8   Gay and Gay, *Encyclopedia of Political Anarchy*.

9   Matthew S. Adams, *Kropotkin, Read and the Intellectual History of British Anarchism* (Basingstoke: Palgrave Macmillan, 2015); Carissa Honeywell, *A British Anarchist Tradition: Herbert Read, Alex Comfort and Colin Ward* (New York: Continuum, 2011).

10 Edward S. Krebs, *Shifu, Soul of Chinese Anarchism* (Lanham: Rowman and Littlefield, 1998).

11 Tapio Helen, 'B. Traven's Identity Revisited', University of Helsinki, *Historiallisia Papereita*, 12 (2001), online at http://historiallinenyhdistys.fi/muinaiset_sivut/julk/traven01/traven.html [last access 17 March 2018].

12 S. Mills, 'Colin Ward: The "Gentle" Anarchist and Informal Education', *The Encyclopaedia of Informal Education*: http://infed.org/mobi/

colin-ward-the-gentle-anarchist-and-informal-education/ [last access
22 February 2018]; Ken Worpole, 'Colin Ward Obituary', *Guardian*, 22
February 2010.

13 Ruth Kinna and Matthew Wilson, 'Key Terms', in Ruth Kinna (ed.),
Bloomsbury Companion to Anarchism (London: Bloomsbury, 2012);
'Anarchy in the USA', *The Guardian*, 18 April 2001, https://www.theguardian.
com/world/2001/apr/18/mayday.features11 [last access 23 February
2019].

Chapter 3: Practices

1 'Interview with Ernesto Aguilar of the Anarchist People of Color (APOC)',
Female Species, archived at Colours of Resistance, online at http://www.
coloursofresistance.org/596/interview-with-ernesto-aguilar-of-the-
anarchist-people-of-color-apoc/ [last access 17 February 2018]; Deric
Shannon, Anthony J. Nocella, II, and John Asimakopoulos (eds), *The
Accumulation of Freedom: Writings on Anarchist Economics* (Oakland and
Edinburgh: AK Press, 2012).

2 Muñoz, *Anarchists*.

3 Peter Lamborn Wilson, 'Roses and Nightingales: Looking for Traditional
Anarchism in Iran', *Fifth Estate*, 363; Hans Ulrich Obrist, 'In Conversation
with Hakim Bey', online at http://www.e-flux.com/journal/21/67669/in-
conversation-with-hakim-bey/ [last access 6 March 2018].

4 Kinna and Wilson, 'Key Terms'.

5 'Some Biographical notes from the Solidarity Initiative, Athens, March
2010', *Actforfreedomnow!*, online at https://actforfreedomnow.wordpress.
com/2010/05/19/some-biographical-notes-from-the-solidarity-initiative-
in-athens-march-2010 [last access 22 February 2018]; Michael Loadenthal,
The Politics of Attack: Communiqués and Insurrectionary Violence
(Manchester: Manchester University Press, 2017).

6 Janet Biehl, 'Introduction', *The Murray Bookchin Reader* (Montreal:
Black Rose, 1999); Andy Price, 'Murray Bookchin', *Independent*,
18 August 2006.

7 Anon., 'About Tom Brown', in *Tom Brown's Anarchism* (London:
Phoenix Press, 1990); Tom Brown and Albert Meltzer, 'Newcastle
Fights the Fascists', Kate Sharpley Library, online at https://www.
katesharpleylibrary.net/z613pb [last access 5 March 2018]; Tom Brown,
'Story of the Syndicalist Workers' Federation: Born in Struggle', Kate
Sharpley Library, online at https://www.katesharpleylibrary.net/wdbt17
[last access 5 March 2018].

8 'Caserio at the Guillotine', *The New York Times,* 16 August 1894; Roderick Kedward, *The Anarchists: The Men Who Shocked an Era* (London: Macdonald: 1971).

9 Peter van den Dungen, 'Bart de Ligt: Non-Violent Anarcho-Pacifist' (2003), Satyagraha Foundation for Nonviolence Studies, online at http://www. satyagrahafoundation.org/bart-de-ligt-1883-1938-non-violent-anarcho-pacifist/ [last access 17 February 2018].

10 Max Nettlau, *A Short History of Anarchism* (London: Freedom Press, 1996).

11 Ann Hansen, *Direct Action: Memoirs of an Urban Guerrilla* (Between the Lines/AK Press: Toronto/Edinburgh and Oakland: 2002); 'Hansen, Ann', University of Victoria Archives, online at https://www.memorybc.ca/ann-hansen-fonds [last access 23 February 2018]; Megan Ellis, 'The Anti-Porn Movement in B.C.', *Canadian Woman Studies/Les Cahiers de la Femme,* online at https://rancom.files.wordpress.com/2011/10/12709.pdf [last access 23 February 2018].

12 Lydia H. Liu, Rebecca E. Karl and Dorothy Ko (eds), *The Birth of Chinese Feminism: Essential Texts in Transnational Theory* (New York: Columbia University Press, 2013); Arif Dirlik, *Anarchism in the Chinese Revolution* (Berkeley: University of California Press, 1991).

13 Jean Maitron, *Ravachol et les Anarchistes* (Paris: Gallimard, 1992); Charles Malato, 'Some Anarchist Portraits', *Fortnightly Review,* CCCXXXIII (1894).

14 'Never Idle: Gord Hill on Indigenous Resistance in Canada', *Portland Radicle,* 18 March 2013, online at https://portlandradicle.wordpress. com/2013/03/18/never-idle-gord-hill-on-indigenous-resistance-in-canada/ [last access 23 February 2018]; Comrade Black, 'Drawing (A) Militant Resistance: Interview with Indigenous Artist and Author Gord Hill', 15 September 2012, online at https://fernwoodpublishing.ca/authors/view/gord-hill [last access 23 February 2018].

15 bell hooks Institute, online at http://www.bellhooksinstitute.com/#/about/ [last access 16 April 2018].

16 Earl Caldwell, 'Jackson an Enigma in Life and Death', *The New York Times,* 20 September 1971.

17 Ira L. Plotkin, *Anarchism in Japan: A Study of the Great Treason Affair 1910–1911* (Lewiston: Edwin Mellen Press, 1990).

18 Muñoz, *Anarchists.*

19 Wolfi Landstreicher, 'Feral Faun talks with Void Network', online at https://www.youtube.com/watch?v=1TQ6Xe1yr4E [last access 16 April 2018].

20 Paul Avrich, *The Haymarket Tragedy* (Princeton, NJ: Princeton University Press, 1984); Marianne Enckell, 'Le Compte, Marie Paula "Minnie"',

Dictionnaire des militants anarchistes, online at http://militants-anarchistes. info/spip.php?article10730 [last access 22 February 2018].

21 Cindy Milstein, 'About Cindy Milstein', *Outside the Circle*, online at https:// cbmilstein.wordpress.com/about/ [last access 22 February 2018].

22 Hermia Oliver, *The International Anarchist Movement in Late Victorian England* (London: Croom Helm, 1983).

23 Bert Altena, '"No man and no penny": Ferdinand Domela Nieuwenhuis, anti-militarism and the opportunities of the First World War', in Matthew Adams and Ruth Kinna (eds), *Anarchism 1914–1918: Internationalism, Anti-Militarism and War* (Manchester: Manchester University Press, 2017).

24 'The Anarchist and Forger Louis Marcy', in Mark Jones, Paul T. Craddock and Nicholas Barker (ed.), *Fake? The Art of Deception* (Berkeley: University of California Press, 1990); Pietro Di Paola, *The Knights Errant of Anarchy: London and the Italian Anarchist Diaspora (1880–1917)* (Liverpool: Liverpool University Press, 2013).

25 Thomas A. Stanley, *Ōsugi Sakae, Anarchist in Taishō Japan: The Creativity of the Ego* (Cambridge, Mass.: Harvard University Press, 1982).

26 Assata (Shakur), *An Autobiography,* digitized by RevSocialist for Socialist Stories, online at https://libcom.org/files/assataauto.pdf [last access 28 February 2018]; 'Assata Shakur, Former Black Panther in Cuba', *Democracy Now!*, online at https://www.democracynow.org/1998/1/22/assata_shakur_former_black_panther_in [last access 28 February 2018].

27 Freddie Baer, *About Valerie Solanas*, online at http://www.womynkind.org/valbio.htm [last access 26 February 2018].

28 Beverly Livingston, *Flora Tristan: The Workers' Union* (Urbana: University of Illinois Press, 1983).

29 Fabio Rambelli (ed.), *Zen Anarchism: The Egalitarian Dharma of Uchiyama Gudō* (Berkeley, CA: Institute of Buddhist Studies and BDK America, Inc. 2013).

30 Nicholas Walter, Introduction to *Charlotte Wilson: Anarchist Essays* (London: Freedom Press, 2000).

Chapter 4: Conditions

1 Andrew Reeves, *Australian Dictionary of Biography*, National Centre of Biography, Australian National University, online at http://adb.anu.edu.au/biography/andrade-david-alfred-5024/text8359, published first in hardcopy 1979, [last access 14 October 2018].

2 Eijun Senaha, 'A Life of Louisa Sarah Bevington', Hokkaido University, 2000, online at https://eprints.lib.hokudai.ac.jp/dspace/bitstream/2115/33979/1/101_PL131-149.pdf [last access 27 April 2018].

3   Vernon Richards, 'Biographical Note', in *Journey Through Utopia* (London: Freedom Press, 1982); International Institute of Social History, 'Anarchists in Court, England, April 1945', online at http://www.iisg.nl/collections/war-commentary/war-commentary.php [last access 5 March 2018].

4   Chomsky discusses his relationship to anarchist and radical movements in interviews including 'The New Radicalism' (1971), 'Anarchism' (1974), 'The Relevance of Anarcho-Syndicalism' (1976), 'On Anarchy, Civilization and Technology' (1991), 'Anarchism, Marxism and Hope for the Future' (1995), 'On Anarchism' (1996), 'Activism, Anarchism and Power' (2002) and 'Students Should Become Anarchists' (2011): www.chomsky.info [last access 16 May 2018].

5   'Guy Debord Obituary', *Independent*, 2 January 1995.

6   Drake Bennett, 'Who's Behind the Mast', *Bloomberg Businessweek*, 27 October 2011; 'David Graeber: Career Biography', *Anthropology of Contemporary Issues*, online at http://web.colby.edu/contemporary-issues/occupy-wall-street-career-biography/.

7   Wendy McElroy, 'Moses Harman: The Paradigm of a Male Feminist', in Wendy McElroy (ed.), *Individualist Feminism of the Nineteenth Century: Collected Writings and Biographical Profiles* (Jefferson, NC: McFarland & Co., 2001).

8   Vladimiro Muñoz, *Max Nettlau: Historian of Anarchism*, trans. Lucy Ross (New York: Revisionist Press, 1978).

9   Süreyyya Evren, Kursad Kiziltug and Erden Kosova, 'Interview with Saul Newman', *Siyahi Interlocal: Journal of Postanarchist Theory, Culture and Politics*, April 2005.

10   Richard Zenith, 'Fernando Pessoa: The Poet of Many Masks', *Casa Fernando Pessoa*, online at http://casafernandopessoa.cm-lisboa.pt/index.php?id=2252&L=4 [last access 16 March 2018].

11   Richard Thomson, 'Ruins, Rhetoric and Revolution: Paul Signac's *Le Démolisseur* and Anarchism in the Late 1890s', *Art History*, 36 (2), 2013.

12   Rebecca Solnit, 'Biography', online at http://rebeccasolnit.net/biography/ [last access 17 March 2018]; Susanna Rustin, 'Rebecca Solnit: A Life in Writing', *Guardian*, 29 June 2013.

13   George Esenwein, *Anarchist Ideology and the Working-class Movement in Spain 1868–1898* (Berkeley: University of California Press, 1989); Benedict Anderson, *Under Three Flags: Anarchism and the Anti-Colonial Imagination* (London: Verso, 2005).

14   Anon, *Anarchism in Switzerland* (Memphis TN: Books LCC, 2010), pp. 19–23; Daniel Fritzsche, 'Linker Kult-Autor P.M.: "Wir müssen in

Viersternehotels wohnen, um die Welt zu retten"', *Neue Zürcher Zeitung*, 10 November 2018, online at https://www.nzz.ch/zuerich/wir-muessen-in-viersternehotels-wohnen-um-die-welt-zu-retten-ld.1435356 [last access 23 February 2019].

15 Douglas Fetherling, *The Gentle Anarchist: A Life of George Woodcock* (Vancouver: Douglas and McIntyre, 1998).

16 Victor S. Yarros, *Adventures in the Realm of Ideas* (1947,) online at the Molinari Institute: http://praxeology.net/VY-ARI-1.htm [last access 17 March 2018]; Victor S. Yarros, *My 11 Years with Clarence Darrow* (Kansas: Haleman-Julius Publications, 1950); James J. Martin, *Men Against the State: The Expositors of Individualist Anarchism in America 1827–1908* (Colorado: Ralph Myers, 1970 [1953]).

Chapter 5: Prospects

1 Ruth Kinna and Matthew Wilson, 'Key Terms', in Ruth Kinna (ed.), *Bloomsbury Companion to Anarchism* (London: Bloomsbury, 2012).

2 'Dany', biography, online at http://www.cohn-bendit.eu/en/dany/lebenslauf/index [last access 15 June 2018]; Daniel Cohn-Bendit and Claus Leggewie, '1968: Power to the Imagination', *New York Review of Books*, 10 May 2018.

3 scott crow, *Witness to Betrayal: scott crow on the Exploits and Misadventures of FBI Informant Brandon Darby* (Oakland: Emergency Hearts Publishing, 2014); Colin Moynihan and Scott Shane, 'For Anarchist, Details of Life as F.B.I. Target', *The New York Times*, 28 May 2011.

4 'Notice biographique', Béatrice Arnac d'Axa, IISH, online at http://www.iisg.nl/collections/zodaxa/zodaxa.php.

5 *Reinventing Anarchy*, ed. Howard J. Ehrlich, Carol Ehrlich, David DeLeon and Glenda Morris (London: Routledge and Kegan Paul, 1979).

6 *Black Rose*, 1, 1975, available at http://dwardmac.pitzer.edu/Anarchist_Archives/journals/blackrose/blackrose.html [last access 2 June 2018]; Michael F. Scully, *The Never-Ending Revival: Rounder Records and the Folk Alliance* (Urbana and Chicago: University of Illinois Press, 2008); Rounder Records Story, http://www.rounder.com/history/ [last access 2 June 2018].

7 Private correspondence.

8 Stuart Christie, 'Albert Meltzer: Anarchy's Torchbearer', *Guardian*, 8 May 1996; Albert Meltzer, *I Couldn't Paint Golden Angels*, online at http://libcom.org/history/i-couldnt-paint-golden-angels-sixty-years-commonplace-life-anarchist-agitation [last access 22 February 2018].

9 The Kurdish Project, online at https://thekurdishproject.org/history-and-culture/famous-kurds/abdullah-ocalan/; 'Profile: Abdullah Öcalan', *Al Jazeera*, 21 March, 2013, online at https://www.aljazeera.com/news/europe/2013/03/201332114565201776.html [last access 17 May, 2018].

10 Cathy Porter, *Fathers and Daughters: Russian Women in Revolution* (London: Virago, 1976).

11 Micelle Garcia, 'For a Former Panther, Solidarity after the Storm', *Washington Post*, 4 December 2005; Malik Rahim, 'This is Criminal', *San Francisco Bay View*, 23 November 2008, online at http://sfbayview.com/2008/11/%E2%80%98this-is-criminal%E2%80%99/ [last access 4 June 2018].

12 David Gordon, 'Murray Newton Rothbard', Mises Institute, online at https://mises.org/profile/murray-n-rothbard [last access 15 June 2018]; Murray N. Rothbard, 'Are Libertarians Anarchists? "Mises Institute" https://mises.org/library/are-libertarians-anarchists [last access 15 June 2018].

13 Jerry Rubin, *Do It! Scenarios of the Revolution* (London: Jonathan Cape, 1970); Eric Page, 'Jerry Rubin, 56, Flashy 60's Radical Dies; "Yippies" Founder and Chicago 7 Defendant', *The New York Times*, 30 November 1994.

14 Miriam Elder, 'Pussy Riot profile: Yekaterina Samutsevich', *Guardian*, 8 August 2012; Matthew Bannister 'Yekaterina Samutsevich: "Why I joined Pussy Riot"', *Outlook*, BBC World Service, 10 December 2012.

Further Reading

CHAPTER 1: TRADITIONS

First International

Anarchy Archives, History of the International Workingmen's Association, online at http://dwardmac.pitzer.edu/Anarchist_Archives/firstinternationalhist.html.

Paris Commune

Mitchell Abidor (ed. and trans.), *Voices of the Paris Commune* (Oakland: PM Press, 2015)

Élie Reclus, *La Commune de Paris, au jour le jour, 1871, 19 mars–28 mai* (Paris: Librairie C. Reinwald, 1908), online at https://archive.org/details/lacommunedeparis00recluoft.

Robert Tombs, *The War Against Paris, 1871* (Cambridge: Cambridge University Press, 1981),

Haymarket

The Haymarket Affair Digital Collection, online at http://www.chicagohistoryresources.org/hadc/

Paul Avrich, *The Haymarket Tragedy* (Princeton, NJ: Princeton University Press, 1984)

Dave Roediger and Franklin Rosemont (eds), *Haymarket Scrapbook* (Chicago: Charles Kerr Publishing, 1986/Edinburgh and Oakland: AK Press, 2011)

Anarchist Canon, Global and Transnational Histories

Major works of historical anarchists can be accessed at Anarchy
    Archives: http://dwardmac.pitzer.edu/
Paul Avrich, *Anarchist Voices: An Oral History of Anarchism
    in America* (Edinburgh and Oakland: AK Press, 2005)
Constance Bantman and Bert Altena (eds), *Reassessing the
    Transnational Turn: Scales of Analysis in Anarchist and
    Syndicalist Studies* (Oakland: PM Press, 2017)
Robert Graham (ed.), *Anarchism: A Documentary History of
    Libertarian Ideas* (3 vols), vol. 1: *From Anarchy to Anarchism
    300 CE to 1939* (Montreal: Black Rose, 2005); vol. 2: *The
    Emergence of the New Anarchism (1939–1977)* (Montreal: Black
    Rose, 2009); vol. 3: *The New Anarchism (1974–2012)* (Montreal:
    Black Rose, 2012)
Daniel Guérin (ed.), *No Gods, No Masters*, trans. Paul Sharkey
    (Oakland and Edinburgh: AK Press, 1998)
Ruth Kinna and Süreyyya Evren, 'Introduction: Blasting the
    Canon', *Anarchist Developments in Cultural Studies*, 1 (2013),
    online at https://journals.uvic.ca/index.php/adcs/article/view/
    17135
Ilham Khuri-Makdisi, *The Eastern Mediterranean and the Making
    of Global Radicalism, 1860–1914* (Berkeley: University of
    California Press, 2013)
Geoffroy de Laforcade and Kirwin Shaffer (eds), *In Defiance of
    Boundaries: Anarchism in Latin American History* (Gainesville:
    University Press of Florida, 2015)
Barry Maxwell and Raymond Craib (eds), *No Gods, No Masters, No
    Peripheries: Global Anarchisms* (Oakland: PM Press, 2015)

Anarchism, Marxism and libertarianism

Wendy McElroy, *Individualist Feminism of the Nineteenth Century:
    Collected Writings and Biographical Profiles* (Jefferson, NC:
    McFarland & Co., 2001)

James J. Martin, *Men Against the State: The Expositors of Individualist Anarchism in America, 1827–1908* (Colorado Springs: Ralph Myles, 1970)

Alex Prichard, Ruth Kinna, Saku Pinta and David Berry (eds), *Libertarian Socialism: Politics in Black and Red* (Oakland: PM Press, 2017)

Peter Ryley, *Making Another World Possible: Anarchism, Anti-capitalism and Ecology in Late 19th and Early 20th Century Britain* (New York and London: Bloomsbury, 2013)

Lucien van der Walt and Michael Schmidt, *Black Flame: The Revolutionary Class Politics of Anarchism and Syndicalism* (Edinburgh and Oakland: AK Press, 2009)

Paul Thomas, *Karl Marx and the Anarchists* (London: Routledge & Kegan Paul, 1980)

Anarchist periodicals

Lidiap list of digitized anarchist periodicals: http://www.bibliothekderfreien.de/lidiap/eng/index.html

CHAPTER 2: CULTURES

Education, Free Skools and Pedagogy

Paul Avrich, *The Modern School Movement: Anarchism and Education in the United States* (Edinburgh and Oakland: AK Press, 2005)

Catherine Burke and Ken Jones (eds), *Education, Childhood and Anarchism: Talking Colin Ward* (London: Routledge, 2014)

Robert H. Haworth (ed.), *Anarchist Pedagogies: Collective Actions, Theories, and Critical Reflections on Education* (Oakland: PM Press, 2012)

Daniel Murphy, *Tolstoy and Education* (Dublin: Irish Academic Press, 1992)

Strike! and London Learning Cooperative, *Radical Pedagogy, Strike!* 19 (Autumn 2017)

Judith Suissa, *Anarchism and Education: A Philosophical Perspective* (Oakland: PM Press, 2010)

Colonization

Maia Ramnath, *Decolonizing Anarchism* (Oakland and Edinburgh: AK Press/Institute for Anarchist Studies, 2011)

Harsha Walia, *Undoing Border Imperialism* (Oakland and Edinburgh: AK Press/Institute for Anarchist Studies, 2013)

Roger White, *Post Colonial Anarchism: Essays on Race, Repression and Culture in Communities of Color 1999–2004* (Oakland: Jailbreak Press, n.d.)

Prisons and Policing

Peter Kropotkin, *In French and Russian Prisons* (Montreal: Black Rose, 1991)

Kristian Williams, *Our Enemies in Blue* (Oakland and Edinburgh: AK Press, 2015)

Work

CrimethInc., *Work: Capitalism. Economics. Resistance* (Salem, OR: CrimethInc. ex-Workers' Collective, n.d.)

David Graeber, 'On the Phenomenon of Bullshit Jobs', *Strike!* 3 (Summer 2013)

Housing

Squatting Europe Kollective, *The Squatters' Movement in Europe: Commons and Autonomy as Alternatives to Capitalism*, ed. Claudio Cattanco and Miguel A. Martínez (London: Pluto, 2014)

Colin Ward, *Housing: An Anarchist Approach* (London: Freedom Press, 1976), online at https://libcom.org/library/colin-ward-housing-anarchist-approach

Colin Ward, *Cotters and Squatters* (Nottingham: Five Leaves, 2002)

Movements

Chris Dixon, *Another Politics: Talking Across Today's Transformative Movements* (Berkeley: University of California Press, 2014)

Laura Portwood-Stacer, *Lifestyle Politics and Radical Activism* (London and New York: Bloomsbury, 2013)

Richard J. White, Simon Springer and Marcelo Lopes de Souza (eds), *The Practice of Freedom* (London and New York: Rowman & Littlefield International, 2016)

Anarchist Geographies

Federico Ferretti, Gerónimo Barrera de la Torre, Anthony Ince and Francisco Toro, *Historical Geographies of Anarchism: Early Critical Geographers and Present-day Scientific Challenges* (London: Routledge, 2018)

Marcelo Lopes de Souza, Richard J. White and Simon Springer (eds), *Theories of Resistance: Anarchism, Geography and the Spirit of Revolt* (London and New York: Rowman & Littlefield International, 2016)

CHAPTER 3: PRACTICES

Anarchism and the First World War

Matthew S. Adams and Ruth Kinna (eds), *Anarchism, 1914–18: Internationalism, Anti-Militarism and War* (Manchester: Manchester University Press, 2017)

Organization

Alexander Skirda, *Facing the Enemy: A History of Anarchist Organization from Proudhon to May 1968*, trans. Paul Sharkey (Edinburgh and Oakland: AK Press, 2002).

Black Bloc

Francis Dupuis-Déri, *Who's Afraid of the Black Blocs? Anarchy in Action around the World*, trans. Lazer Lederhendler (Oakland: PM Press, 2014)

Intersectionality

Kimberlé Crenshaw, Instructors' Guide: Free Resources on Intersectionality, Critical Race Theory Across Disciplines, online at http://www.racialequitytools.org/resourcefiles/Kimberle-Crenshaw-Instructors_-Guide-1.pdf

Francis Dupuis-Déri, 'Is the State Part of the Matrix of Domination and Intersectionality? An Anarchist Inquiry', *Anarchist Studies*, 24 (1), 2016, online at https://www.lwbooks.co.uk/anarchist-studies/24-1/is-the-state-part-of-the-matrix-of-domination-and-intersectionality-anarchist

Dysophia 4, *Anarchist Debates on Privilege* (2013), online at http://dysophia.org.uk/dysophia/

Davita Silfen Glasberg, Abbey S. Willis and Deric Shannon, *The State of State Theory: State Projects, Repression, and Multi-Sites of Power* (Lanham: Lexington Books, 2018)

Jamie Heckert and Richard Cleminson (eds), *Anarchism and Sexuality: Ethics, Relationships and Power* (London: Routledge, 2011).

Pioneer Health Centre

Wellcome Library Blog, 'The Pioneer Health Centre and Positive Health', online at http://blog.wellcomelibrary.org/2015/04/the-pioneer-health-centre-and-positive-health/

Mujeres Libres

Martha A. Ackelsberg, *Free Women of Spain: Anarchism and the Struggle for the Emancipation of Women* (Oakland and Edinburgh: AK Press, 2004)

Utopianism and Intentional Community

Laurence Davis and Ruth Kinna (eds), *Anarchism and Utopianism* (Manchester: Manchester University Press, 2014)

Dennis Hardy, *Alternative Communities in Nineteenth Century England* (London: Longman, 1979)

Andrew Rigby, *Communes in Britain* (London: Routledge and Kegan Paul, 1974)

Theodore Roszak, *Where the Wasteland Ends: Politics and Transcendence in Postindustrial Society* (New York: Doubleday, 1972)

Lucy Sargisson and Lyman Tower Sargent, *Living in Utopia: New Zealand's Intentional Communities* (London: Routledge, 2004)

Nigel Todd, *Roses and Revolutionists: The Story of the Clousden Hill Free Communist and Co-operative Colony 1894–1902* (Nottingham: Five Leaves, 2015)

Zadforever, Revenge Against the Commons, April 2018, online at https://zadforever.blog/2018/04/24/the-revenge-against-the-commons/

CHAPTER 5: PROSPECTS

Carne Ross, *The Leaderless Revolution: How Ordinary People Will Take Power and Change Politics in the 21st Century* (London: Simon & Schuster, 2011)

Rojava

Michael Knapp, Anja Flach and Ercan Ayboğa, *Revolution in Rojava: Democratic Autonomy and Women's Liberation in Syrian Kurdistan*, trans. Janet Biehl (London: Pluto, 2016)

Internationalist Commune of Rojava, *Make Rojava Green Again* (London: Dog Section Press, 2018).

Index

Baja California, Mexico, 52
Baker, Sir Herbert, 3
Bakunin, Michael: biographical
    summary, 274–6
– and burn out, 243
– and conspiracy, 47, 49
– critique of Marx, 14–15, 17–18, 26–7
– and education, 98, 104
– on human behaviour, 84
– and the International, 18–20
– on religion and authority, 68–71, 73–5
– revolutionary activities, 49–50
– on Rousseau, 63
– on theory and experience, 76, 251
– *Federalism, Socialism and Anti-Theologism*
    (1867), 275
– *God and the State* (1882), 276
– *The Paris Commune and the Idea of the
    State*, 26, 35
– *Reaction in Germany* (1842), 275
– *Statism and Anarchy* (1873), 276
Barcelona, 40, 98, 120, 279–80, 345, 347
Bauer, A. J., 236–7
Bedborough, George, 302
Beeby, Elizabeth, 307
Belinsky, Vissarion, 275
Belmas, Julia, 324, 325
Berkman, Alexander, 85, 130, 151, 153, 282,
    283, 306–7
Berneri, Camillio, 340
Berneri, Giovanna, 340
Berneri, Marie-Louise, 204, 208, 321, 340–1
Bevington, Louisa: biographical
    summary, 339–40
– *Common Sense Country* (1895), 205–6,
    207
– *Anarchist Manifesto* (1895), 206
Bey, Hakim (*aka* Peter Lamborn Wilson),
    138–40, 223, 318
biographies and life stories, in anarchist
    literature, 49–50
Bismarck, Otto von, 21
Black, Bob, 138–9, 173, 318
Black Cross Network, 316
Black Fist (anarchist collective), 316
Black Flag (journal), 354
Black Panther Party, 327–8, 335, 355–6

Black Rose collective, 245, 353
Blast (journal), 307
Blomfeld, Sir Reginald, 3
Blood of the Flower statement, 245–6
Boétie, Étienne de la, *The Politics of
    Obedience*, 262–3
Bolce, Harold, 210–11
Bolshevik revolution, 116, 127, 129,
    130, 287
Bonanno, Alredo, 135, 166, 268, 319, 330
Bookchin, Murray: biographical
    summary, 320
– and class struggle, 136
– critique of, 238–9
– and democracy, 227
– rejection of consensus
    decision making, 232–3
– social anarchism, 142–3, 144, 237
– social ecology, 228–32, 246
Boston Anarchist Club, constitution,
    185–6
Bresci, Gaetano, 293
Brontë, Charlotte, *Jane Eyre*, 59
Brown, Tom, 126, 320–1, 353
Brownstone Utopia (community), 274
Buber, Martin, 206, 207

C

Cabet, Étienne, 47
Cafiero, Carlo, 43, 100, 101, 117, 276–7,
    291, 299
Cánovas del Castillo, Antonio, 347–8
Carnot, President, 118, 120, 321–2
Carpenter, Edward, 311, 313, 317
Caserio, Sante Geronimo, 120, 321–2
Ceylon Social Reform Society, 307
Chicago *see* Haymarket Affair,
    Chicago (1886)
China Assassination Corps, 314
Chomsky, Noam, 226, 249–51, 341
Christie, Stuart, 257, 350
Churchill, Winston, 243
City Lights Bookstore, 309
class, and anarchist activism, 150–6
Class War (UK group), 156
class-struggle anarchism, 136–8, 150

Cleyre, Voltairine de: on anarchist
optimism, 271
– biographical summary, 277–8
– critique of colonization, 77, 80–3, 84
– on cultural contexts of anarchism, 53
– notoriety of, 173
– on suffragette direct action, 168–71
Cluchette, John, 328
Cohn-Bendit, Daniel, 245, 351
collectivization, land, 195–9
colonization, 77, 78–83
Coming Insurrection, The (anarchist tract, 2007), 134–5
Common Ground (collective, New Orleans), 249, 259–61, 351
Commonweal (newspaper), 332
communalism, democratic, 228–32
Communards, 22, 23, 38
communism, and anarchism, 43, 192–5, 199–203
Communist Manifesto (1848), 47, 150
community associations, 165
Comstock Laws, 181, 343
conquest, 75–7
consensus decision-making, 227, 232–7
constitutions: anarchist, 177–81
– communist, 192–5
convergence, anarchization through, 254–61, 266–8
Coomaraswamy, Ananda, 78, 307–8
counter-cultural movements, 131
Courbet, Gustave, 23, 277
CrimethInc., 140
crow, scott, 248–9, 259, 351
Cuba, 148
Czolgosz, Leon, 282, 295

D

Dada, 265
De Ligt, Bart, 322–3
Debord, Guy, 230, 341–2
Deepwater Horizon disaster, 266
DeLeon, Daniel, 295
democracy, anarchist misgivings over, 224–8

democratic communalism, 228–32, 246
Der Sozialist (journal), 329–30
dialogues, used in anarchist propaganda, 254–7
Díaz, Porfirio, 290
direct action, 166, 168–72
Direct Action (Vancouver), 324, 325
Dirlik, Arif, 52
disjuncture, anarchization through, 261–8
disobedience, 265
domination: concept of, 58–60
– and conquest, 75–83
– and hierarchy, 68–75
– and law, 60–8
Dreyfus Affair, 292, 352
Droit Social, Le (newspaper), 331
Drumgo, Fleeta, 328
Dupuis-Déri, Francis, 132, 134
– *Anarchy Explained to My Father*, 256–7

E

École Rénovée, L,' 279
education: anarchist goals of, 83–7, 96–9, 112–13
– propaganda, 99–103
– schooling, 86, 87–94, 98
– skill-sharing, 103–12
egoism, 67, 145, 202, 330
Ehrlich, Carol, 245, 352
El Derecho a la Vida (newspaper), 36
Elizabeth, Empress of Austria, 118
Ellis, Havelock, *Sexual Inversion* (1896), 302
Eltzbacher, Paul, 42, 43
Ely, Richard, 19, 45
Emancipation of the Serfs (Russia, 1861), 29, 286
En-dehors, L' (journal), 254, 258, 259, 317
Engel, George, 22, 23, 24, 37, 278–9
Engels, Friedrich, 47
Engländer, Sigmund: biographical summary, 308–9
– on domination and the law, 61–8
English Anarchist Circle, 302
Ère Nouvelle, L' (journal), 317
Escapologists' Manifesto, 140, 141

Haymarket Affair, Chicago (1886), 22–40, 279, 280, 281, 288, 295, 296–7, 301, 303
Hegel, Georg Wilhelm Friedrich, 70
Heiminsha ('Commoners' Society), 328, 334
Heine, Heinrich, 308
Helcher, Herman, 278
Henry, Émile, 118–19, 292, 326
Herzen, Alexander, 275
Hewetson, John, 315
He-Yin Zhen, 170–2, 325
Heywood, Ezra, 284–5
– *Uncivil Liberty*, 33
High Treason Incident (Japan, 1910), 41, 108, 120, 328–9, 337
Hill, Gord, 100, 326–7
Hill, Joe, 41, 285–6
hooks, bell, 162–3, 257, 327
'Human Cost' (performance art), 265–6
Humbolt, Alexander von, 107
Hurricane Katrina, 249, 259–61, 356

I

illegalism, 123, 132
Imperial War Graves Commission, 3–6
India, English colonization of, 78–9
India Society, 307
individualist-anarchists, 121–5, 127, 181–2, 199–203
Industrial Workers of the World (IWW or Wobblies), 137–8, 285, 297
insurrectionary anarchism, 134–6
International Alliance of Social Democracy, 276
International Anti-Militarist Bureau/ Union, 322, 333
International Labor Defence, 297
International League for the Rational Education of Children, 279
International London Anarchist Congress, 117
International of Anarchist Federations (IAF-IFA), 136, 137
International Workers' Association (IWA), 138
International Workingmen's Association (IWMA *or* First International), 13–14, 18–21, 26, 291

internationalization, anarchist, 210–14
intersectionality, 157–64
Invisible Committee, 134, 264
Ishikawa, Sanshiro, 108, 311
Ishill, Joseph, 303
Isou, Isidore, 342
Ito Noe, 334

J

Jackson, George, 133, 327–8
Jacobs, Harriet, 29
Japan: Anarchist League of Japan, 311
– *Heiminsha* ('Commoners' Society), 311, 328, 334
– High Treason Incident (Japan, 1910), 41, 108, 120, 328–9 *see also* Ishikawa Sanshiro; Kotoku Shushi; Miyashita Takichi; Osugi Sakae; Uchiyama Gudo
Journal of Eugenics, 344
Jubilee Street anarchist club, 300
Jura Federation of the International, 19, 286, 299, 323
Justice (newspaper), 338

K

Kaczynski, Ted (Unabomber), 316
Kanak rebellion (1878), 34, 294
Kate Sharpley Library, 354
Kenyon, Sir Frederic, 2–5
Kinckel, Gottfried, 308
King, Martin Luther, 115, 119
Knights of Labor, 296, 297, 303
knowledge hierarchies, 96
Kotoku, Shushi, 120, 311, 337
Kropotkin, Peter: on anarchist movements, 52
– on Bakunin, 27
– biographical summary, 286–7
– on class struggle, 34–5
– and communist school of anarchism, 43
– and co-operation, 259
– economic plan of, 208–14
– and education, 88
– in the First World War, 127, 129, 292

PELICAN BOOKS

PELICAN BOOKS

PELICAN BOOKS